Benjamins Translation Library (BTL)

ISSN 0929-7316

The Benjamins Translation Library (BTL) aims to stimulate research and training in Translation & Interpreting Studies – taken very broadly to encompass the many different forms and manifestations of translational phenomena, among them cultural translation, localization, adaptation, literary translation, specialized translation, audiovisual translation, audio-description, transcreation, transediting, conference interpreting, and interpreting in community settings in the spoken and signed modalities.

For an overview of all books published in this series, please see
www.benjamins.com/catalog/btl

EST Subseries

The European Society for Translation Studies (EST) Subseries is a publication channel within the Library to optimize EST's function as a forum for the translation and interpreting research community. It promotes new trends in research, gives more visibility to young scholars' work, publicizes new research methods, makes available documents from EST, and reissues classical works in translation studies which do not exist in English or which are now out of print.

General Editor

Yves Gambier
University of Turku

Associate Editor

Franz Pöchhacker
University of Vienna

Honorary Editor

Gideon Toury
Tel Aviv University

Advisory Board

Rosemary Arrojo
Binghamton University

Michael Cronin
Dublin City University

Dirk Delabastita
FUNDP (University of Namur)

Daniel Gile
Université Paris 3 - Sorbonne Nouvelle

Amparo Hurtado Albir
Universitat Autònoma de Barcelona

Zuzana Jettmarová
Charles University of Prague

Alet Kruger
UNISA, South Africa

John Milton
University of São Paulo

Anthony Pym
Universitat Rovira i Virgili

Rosa Rabadán
University of León

Sherry Simon
Concordia University

Şehnaz Tahir Gürçaglar
Bogaziçi University

Maria Tymoczko
University of Massachusetts Amherst

Lawrence Venuti
Temple University

Michaela Wolf
University of Graz

Volume 123

Memes of Translation. The spread of ideas in translation theory. Revised edition
by Andrew Chesterman

Memes of Translation

The spread of ideas in translation theory

Revised edition

Andrew Chesterman
University of Helsinki

John Benjamins Publishing Company
Amsterdam / Philadelphia

The paper used in this publication meets the minimum requirements of the American National Standard for Information Sciences – Permanence of Paper for Printed Library Materials, ANSI z39.48-1984.

DOI 10.1075/btl.123

Cataloging-in-Publication Data available from Library of Congress:
LCCN 2015045490 (PRINT) / 2015048313 (E-BOOK)

ISBN 978 90 272 5868 7 (HB)
ISBN 978 90 272 5869 4 (PB)
ISBN 978 90 272 6738 2 (E-BOOK)

© 2016 – John Benjamins B.V.
No part of this book may be reproduced in any form, by print, photoprint, microfilm, or any other means, without written permission from the publisher.

John Benjamins Publishing Company · https://benjamins.com

Table of contents

Preface   IX

CHAPTER 1
Survival machines for memes   1
1.1 Introducing memes   1
1.2 Five translation supermemes   3
    1.2.1 Source-target   3
    1.2.2 Equivalence   4
    1.2.3 Untranslatability   6
    1.2.4 Free-vs-literal   8
    1.2.5 All-writing-is-translating   9
1.3 The locus of memes   10
1.4 A Popperian meme   12
1.5 Update   13

CHAPTER 2
The evolution of translation memes   17
2.1 Words   18
2.2 The Word of God   19
2.3 Rhetoric   21
2.4 Logos   24
2.5 Linguistic science   27
2.6 Communication   31
2.7 Target   34
2.8 Cognition   38
2.9 Theory in the current meme pool   40
2.10 Update   44

CHAPTER 3
From memes to norms   49
3.1 Normative vs. prescriptive   50
3.2 Norm theory   52
3.3 Norms of language   54

3.4 What counts as a translation? 56
3.5 Translation norms 61
    3.5.1 Toury's norms 61
    3.5.2 Expectancy norms 62
    3.5.3 Professional norms 65
3.6 General translation laws and normative laws 68
    3.6.1 Translation laws 68
    3.6.2 Normative laws 71
    3.6.3 Explanations 72
3.7 Norms as constraints 75
3.8 On expectancy norms for English 79
3.9 Update 82

CHAPTER 4
Translation strategies　　　　　　　　　　　　　　　　　　　　　85
4.1 General characteristics of strategies 85
4.2 A classification 89
    4.2.1 Syntactic strategies 91
    4.2.2 Semantic strategies 98
    4.2.3 Pragmatic strategies 104
4.3 Motivation 109
    4.3.1 The significance threshold 110
    4.3.2 Compensation 112
4.4 Update 112

CHAPTER 5
Translation as theory　　　　　　　　　　　　　　　　　　　　　115
5.1 Tentative Theory, Error Elimination and translational competence 115
5.2 Retrospective assessment 121
5.3 Prospective assessment 125
5.4 Lateral assessment 130
5.5 Introspective assessment 133
5.6 Pedagogical assessment 135
5.7 Mind the gap! 138
5.8 Update 141

CHAPTER 6
The development of translational competence   145
6.1   Stages of expertise   145
6.2   The significance of memes   148
6.3   Suggestions for teaching   150
6.4   Ontogenetic = phylogenetic?   156
6.5   Bootstraps   163
6.6   Update   164

CHAPTER 7
On translation ethics   167
7.1   Background issues   167
7.2   Norms, actions and values   170
7.3   Clarity   173
7.4   Truth   176
7.5   Trust   178
7.6   Understanding   181
7.7   The Translator's Charter   184
7.8   Emancipatory translation   186
7.9   Update   191

Epilogue	195
Appendix	197
References	201
Author index	219
Subject index	223

Preface

> I see humanity as a family that has hardly met. I see the meeting of people, bodies, thoughts, emotions or actions as the start of most change. Each link created by a meeting is like a filament, which, if they were all visible, would make the world look as though it is covered with gossamer. Every individual is connected to others, loosely or closely, by a unique combination of filaments, which stretch across the frontiers of space and time. Every individual assembles past loyalties, present needs and visions of the future in a web of different contours, with the help of heterogeneous elements borrowed from other individuals; and this constant give-and-take has been the main stimulus of humanity's energy. Once people see themselves as influencing one another, they cannot be merely victims: anyone, however modest, then becomes a person capable of making a difference, minute though it might be, to the shape of reality. New attitudes are not promulgated by law, but spread, almost like an infection, from one person to another.
> (Zeldin [1994] 1995: 465–466)

In Classical Greece the source of truth, knowledge, revelation, was the oracle. A person officially designated to go and consult an oracle was known as a *theoros* (θεωρός; Liddell and Scott 1940: s.v.). Interestingly enough, the same term was also used of someone who was sent to attend a festival in some official capacity. Yet another sense of the word is that of 'magistrate', and more generally 'spectator', or 'one who travels to see' people and places (ibid.). The *theoros*, then, was interested in truth, knowledge, but also in pleasure. The word contains a sense of rational judgement (as a magistrate's title), but the core meaning is simply someone who sees, who sees with a purpose.

From this noun came the verb *theorein* (θεωρεῖν) 'to see, gaze upon'. This seeing was distinct from older verbs of seeing, in that it emphasized the function of the seeing rather than the seeing itself. It meant 'to be a spectator', i.e. a spectator *of something*; it stressed the conscious, deliberate activity of seeing rather than some kind of purely passive perception (Snell 1975: 15).

And by this path came the noun *theoria*, (θεωρία) 'theory'. It carried both the outward sense of 'a looking at, a viewing' and the inner sense of 'contemplation, speculation' (OED, s.v. *theory*).

There is a delightful anecdote in Herodotus ([1920] Book I, §29–30) about the wise man Solon, who had come to work as a legislator for the Athenians, and then evidently felt that he needed a break. So he left home and set out on a voyage "to see the world", as Godley translates it. The original Greek literally states that he went out into the world "for the sake of *theoria*" – i.e. in order to see and contemplate.

It is in this sense that the term "theory" is used in this book. Theories themselves come in many shapes and sizes: some are a good deal more scholarly/scientific or more formalized than others, some are empirical, others metaphorical; some are at a high level of generality, others are more specific.

The book has three main aims. The first is metatheoretical: it offers a view of theory, in fact quite a few theories. It explores some of the main ways in which translation has been seen and contemplated, and suggests a conceptual framework within which a number of disparate views of translation can be linked.

The second aim is theoretical. On this level, I set out to develop a particular theoretical view of translation, one that has been greatly influenced by the philosophy of Karl Popper. I propose, in effect, a Popperian theory of translation. I also draw on norm theory and to some extent on action theory, in an attempt to weave various strands into a coherent whole. My fundamental building-blocks are the concepts of norm, strategy and value, plus Popper's concepts of tentative theory, error elimination , and the evolution of objective knowledge.

My underlying metaphor for translation comes from the notion of memes: a meme is simply an idea that spreads (memes are explained in more detail in Chapter 1). The metaphor comes from sociobiology: ideas spread, replicate themselves, like genes do. My motive in using this metaphor as an umbrella-idea to cover many aspects of this book is to provide an alternative to the traditional transfer metaphor of translation. The meme metaphor highlights an aspect of the translation phenomenon that I want to foreground: the way that ideas spread and change as they are translated, just as biological evolution involves mutations. In this light, a translator is not someone whose task is to conserve something but to propagate something, to spread and even develop it: translators are agents of change. Translators, in fact, make a difference... The metaphor thus gives less priority to the notions of "preserving identity" or "sameness" which underlie the more traditional image of "carrying something across", a something that somehow remains unchanged. I offer the meme metaphor as a helpful way to look at translation. If it works as a way of stimulating new insights, fine; if not, we can forget about it. The applications of Popper's ideas do not depend on the meme metaphor; nor do my arguments about norms, strategies and values.

The third aim is more practical. Many practising professional translators are suspicious of theory, or may be of the opinion that there is no such thing as a theory of translation anyway. Translator trainees, too, often feel that what they need is simply more practice, not high-flown talk about abstract theory. In response to such claims, I argue that a translator must have a theory of translation: to translate without a theory is to translate blind. I also argue that theoretical concepts can be essential tools for thought and decision-making during the translation process. My third aim is thus to demonstrate that translation theory can be useful – to translators themselves, to trainees and to their teachers.

The book thus attempts to cover a fairly wide field, but certainly not the whole of Translation Studies. In particular, I do not focus on the technical side of translation: computer aids, terminological databases and the like; nor on interpreting. Nor am I interested in giving prescriptive advice: my attitude to norms is descriptive, not prescriptive.

The overall movement of the book goes from theory to practice. Chapter 1 introduces the concept of the meme, borrowed from sociobiology into cultural evolution studies. By way of illustration, it discusses five "supermemes" of translation theory: the source-target metaphor, the equivalence idea, the myth of untranslatability, the free-vs-literal argument, and the idea that all writing is a kind of translating. Memes are then argued to exist primarily in Popper's World 3, and a Popperian meme is introduced that will be a recurrent theme in the book.

Chapter 2 outlines the evolution of (Western) translation theory, in terms of eight major stages, each building on and reacting to its antecedents and overlapping with them. These stages are not transitory but cumulative, so that the present picture we have of the phenomenon called translation – the total pool of ideas about translation, as it were – is composed of strata from all the previous stages. The chapter ends with a review of some conflicting ideas about translation theory in the current "meme pool".

Chapter 3 argues that some ideas about translation eventually become norms, and that norm theory provides powerful tools for thinking about both translation theory and translation practice.

Chapter 4 shifts the focus from product to process. Given that there are translation norms, how do translators seek to conform to them? This question is discussed in terms of the notion of translation strategies, which depend on and are oriented towards translation norms.

How do we assess attempts to conform to norms? Chapter 5 offers a Popperian approach to translation assessment, based on the view that any translation is itself a theory: a theory of the source text. As such, it undergoes the same sort of assessment, criticism, error elimination and corroboration as any other theory.

Chapter 6 is practical, pedagogical. It discusses what implications a Popperian translation theory has for translator training. What relation might there be between the evolution of translation theory and the maturing of an individual translator?

Chapters 1–3 thus explore how translation norms arise, and Chapters 4–6 discuss various effects they have on translation practice. Chapter 7 then focuses on the ethical values underlying the norms that govern translational action.

Update

This revised edition includes Update sections at the end of each chapter, where I outline some of the later developments in research concerning the theme of the chapter, and in my own thinking, since the book was first published in 1997. I have also made some minor textual improvements and corrections and added some later references to the text.

Acknowledgements

Several friends and colleagues were kind enough to comment on parts or preliminary versions of the original text, and were thus of invaluable assistance in the error elimination process. Thank you: Ritva Leppihalme, Mary Hatakka, Nely Keinänen, Seija Paddon, Ria Bülow-Møller. Thank you too, anonymous reviewers, for some critical comments on earlier versions and for drawing my attention to some errors and to works I had overlooked. I have also benefited from other feedback on the first edition. And special thanks to whoever it was who anonymously left in my pigeon-hole the Morgenstern poem and its translation, discovered in a concert programme, as "a small contribution to translation theory". Finally, a big "merci" to Yves Gambier for his encouragement and suggestions for this revised edition.

Any remaining weaknesses or errors are of course my own responsibility.

AC, Helsinki, January 1997
Revised edition: Helsinki, December 2015

CHAPTER 1

Survival machines for memes

1.1 Introducing memes

Translations are survival machines for memes.

Memes? The concept comes from sociobiology, where it was introduced by Dawkins in *The Selfish Gene* (1976). He explains how he wanted a term which would be parallel to "gene" to describe the evolution of cultural phenomena, which (he argues) are subject to the same kinds of Darwinian laws of natural selection as genes proper:

> [A meme is] a unit of cultural transmission, or a unit of *imitation*. 'Mimeme' comes from a suitable Greek root, but I want a monosyllable that sounds a bit like 'gene'. I hope my classical friends will forgive me if I abbreviate mimeme to *meme*. If it is any consolation, it could alternatively be thought of as being related to 'memory' or to the French word *même*. It should be pronounced to rhyme with 'cream'.
>
> Examples of memes are tunes, ideas, catch-phrases, clothes fashions, ways of making pots or building arches. Just as genes propagate themselves in the gene pool by leaping from body to body via sperm or eggs, so memes propagate themselves in the meme pool by leaping from brain to brain via a process which, in the broad sense, can be called imitation. If a scientist hears, or reads about, a good idea, he passes it on to his colleagues and students. He mentions it in his articles and lectures. If the idea catches on, it can be said to propagate itself, spreading from brain to brain. (1976: 206; p. 192 in the 1989 edition)

Like genes, memes are replicators. Examples that Dawkins discusses are the idea-of-God meme and the Darwinian-theory meme. These ideas do not necessarily exist in identical form in different human brains, but there is enough similarity between, say, different people's ideas of Darwin's theory for them to have a common denominator, and it is this common denominator which is the meme. "An 'idea-meme'," writes Dawkins ([1976] 1989: 196), "might be defined as an entity that is capable of being transmitted from one brain to another." The fashion for jeans, we might say, has spread like genes.

On this view, ideas that turn out to be *good* ideas survive; i.e. those that are conducive to the survival of their carriers: people. By analogy with biology, these are known as mutualist memes, being of mutual benefit to themselves and their carriers. Bad ideas (at least in theory, and in the long run) do not last; they are parasitic memes, because they eventually kill their host. Of course, it may take some considerable time before bad ideas are generally recognized to be potentially threatening in this sense. If a meme is to survive, it must beat its rival memes, i.e. it must win new adherents, gain ever wider acceptance. In science, for instance, the spread of an idea-meme can be plotted via a citation index: we can see how a given meme starts to spread slowly, reaches a peak of reference-frequency, and perhaps thereafter fades again.

Dawkins argues that memes represent a new and different kind of evolution, although this evolution follows the same general Darwinian laws of selection, conservation and propagation as genetic evolution. Plotkin (1993:769), summarizing earlier work on cultural evolution, indicates the parallel quite explicitly:

> [C]ultural units, which we can call memes after Dawkins (1976), occur in various forms; selectional processes then result in these units being differentially propagated by copying and transmission systems which move the units about in space and may conserve some of them in time. The differential survival of these units resulting from the action of such selection and transmission processes leads to changes in the frequencies of these units in the cultural pool over time; the culture shows descent with modification. In other words, cultural change is wrought by cultural evolution.

Memetic evolution can even counter genetic evolution: culturally transmitted ideas and practices can become more powerful than purely genetic pressures – an obvious example is contraception: cultural values and practices override biological ones. (For critical discussions of the parallels between genetic and memetic evolution, see Hull 1982, and the references in the Update section below.)

Like "gene", "meme" is a concept that can be defined and used at varying levels of generality. However, I find it useful to use the term *supermeme* for memes at a particularly high level of generality.

Memes often occur in complexes, memomes, in mutual dependence with other memes. The idea-of-God meme, for instance, might thrive in complex cooperation with the patriarchal-authorities-know-best meme. It is often insightful to think of a theory (a theory of translation, for instance) as a memome, a meme-complex.

Ideas and conventions that survive many generations, and are successfully transmitted from one culture to another, thus prove themselves to be interesting and relevant to a wide circle of human beings. They become "received ideas", commonplaces, topoi. They may even be felt to be good for human survival, in some way; at the very least, if they survive we can reasonably assume that they must serve *some* purpose which is seen at least by some people to be useful. At any given time, there will therefore exist a *meme pool* of such ideas, just as there exists a gene pool of so-far-surviving genes. In fact, we could even define a culture in precisely these terms, as a population of memes (Hailman 1982:232).

Anecdotal evidence of the influence of memes is suggested by an article in *The Economist* (February 9, 1994, p. 99) discussing candidates for modern wonders of the world. After listing the jumbo jet, the microprocessor, the telephone, the contraceptive pill, the oil rig, the H-bomb and the moon landing site, the writer proposes an eighth wonder that has also had immeasurable influence on modern life: Heisenberg's uncertainty principle (roughly: that we cannot simultaneously be certain about both the location and the momentum of a particle). This is an excellent example of a meme, and of the effect that mutualist memes can have.

Dawkins argues that human (and plant and animal) bodies are in fact survival machines for genes: they are the means whereby the genes ensure their own continuing replication, their own immortality. Human beings are also survival machines for memes, but they are not the only ones (although they are always at least indirectly involved in meme transmission). Meme transmission within a culture takes place through imitation and of course also through language. But for a meme to be transmitted verbally across language boundaries, if both sender and receiver lack the relevant multilingual competence there needs to be a translation. Indeed, the need for translation is a neat criterion for the existence of a cultural boundary (Pym 1992a:26). We can thus see translations as survival machines for memes crossing cultural boundaries.

1.2 Five translation supermemes

Some memes encapsulate concepts and ideas about translation itself, and about the theory of translation. Let us call them translation memes (cf. Chesterman 1996a). These memes are one of the central themes of this book: the most important types will be theoretical concepts, norms, strategies and values. Chapter 2 will look at the evolution of translation memes, but first I shall introduce five supermemes of translation. They are ideas of such pervasive influence that they come up again and again in the history of the subject, albeit sometimes in slightly different guises. Some appear to be distinctly more beneficial than others.

1.2.1 Source-target

The source-target supermeme is the idea that translation is directional, going *from* somewhere *to* somewhere. The widespread acceptance of this supermeme has, in modern translation studies, given us the notions of Source Text (ST) and Target Text (TT).

The dominant metaphor underlying this supermeme is that of movement along a path: cognitive linguistics would talk of a "path schema", with the translation itself being the "trajector" moving along this path. Translations are thus seen as "moving" from A to B. Belonging to this same meme-complex there is also the accompanying idea that translations are "containers" for something else; as they are formed, translations "carry across" something from A to B.

This supermeme clearly captures something of value about translation, but there is one important aspect which it misses: although they are directional, translations do *not* in fact move. If an object moves from A to B, when it arrives at B it is no longer at A. But translation does not eliminate the presence of the source text at A. True, some source texts may never have a source readership apart from the translator, in that they are produced solely as input for a translation, remaining unpublished in the source language. Such a source text may therefore be redundant after the act of translation; it may only exist as a note in the translator's file, or a deleted computer document (for instance, the Finnish original of an information brochure for foreign students in Finland, to be published only in English). But this is not to say that texts automatically cease to exist at their point of departure after being translated: normally, source texts do not then cease to exist.

On the contrary: a translation of a novel, an advertisement, a contract, or whatever, has merely extended the readership of (the memes carried by) these texts, it has spread their memes. But the memes themselves do not *move:* they are not absent from the source culture when they appear in the target culture. They do not move, they spread, they replicate. In place of the metaphor of movement, therefore, I would suggest one of propagation, diffusion, extension, even evolution: a genetic metaphor. Evolution thus suggests some notion of progress: translation adds value to a source text, by adding readers of its ideas, adding further interpretations, and so on.

1.2.2 Equivalence

The equivalence supermeme is the big bugbear of translation theory, more argued about than any other single idea: a translation is, or must be, equivalent to the source, in some sense at least. This idea too is based on the path metaphor, in fact on the trope of "metaphor" itself. After all, the very term "translation" in English and related languages has the same root as "metaphor" – carrying across. If your view of translation is that you carry something across, you do not expect that this something will change its identity as you carry it. A metaphor states that two different entities can be seen as identical in some respect: X = Y. Source text and target text are "the same". Exactly what this "sameness" consists of is, of course, open to endless debate.

One frequent ploy is to break up equivalence into various subtypes, for instance a binary opposition between two main types. Nida (1964) distinguishes between formal and dynamic equivalence, for instance, the former focusing on the message itself (aiming at the same form and meaning) and the latter on its reception (aiming at the same effect). The two types are not mutually exclusive, however; formal equivalence may exist (in theory) at the lower grammatical levels of morpheme, word, phrase, perhaps up to sentence breaks, while dynamic equivalence more naturally has to do primarily with the text as a whole (see Jakobsen 1994a). Other scholars prefer different labels but make the same basic distinction between two main kinds of translation: semantic vs. communicative (Newmark 1981), overt vs. covert (House 1981), documentary vs. instrumental (Nord 1991), imitative vs. functional (Jakobsen 1994a).

Other classifications have been more complex: equivalence has been split up into functional, stylistic, semantic, formal or grammatical, statistical and textual subtypes, and then hierarchies are posited which give some subtypes higher priority than others, under different conditions. (See e.g. Koller 1979; Retsker 1993.) Such priorities obviously depend on text-type, communicative situation etc. In literary translation, for instance, it is commonly assumed that there should be a "sameness" of image or conceptualization, i.e. a kind of stylistic-semantic equivalence (see e.g. Tabakowska 1993:72 and elsewhere).

Against this preoccupation with "sameness" alternative concepts have been proposed, positing a weaker degree of equivalence such as matching (Holmes 1988) or family resemblance (Wittgenstein 1953: §66f.; see e.g. Toury 1980:18), or similarity (e.g. Chesterman 1996b): Hervey and Higgins (1992:24) take a translation to be "equivalent" if it is "not dissimilar in relevant respects". These reflect the pragmatic reality that, in fact, (total) equivalence is a red herring, in that it is normally unattainable, and hence not a useful concept in translation theory. Pragmatically speaking, it can be argued that the only examples of absolute equivalence are those in which an ST item X is *invariably* translated into a given TL as Y, *and vice versa*. In terms of information theory, the information would thus remain invariant under reversible encoding operations. Typical examples would be words denoting numbers (with the exception of contexts in which they have culture-bound connotations, such as "magic" or "unlucky"), technical terms (oxygen, molecule), and the like (cf. Retsker 1993; however, technical terms can also be slippery – see Kußmaul 1995:98). From this point of view, the only true test of equivalence would therefore be invariable back-translation. This, of course, is unlikely to occur except in the case of a small set of lexical items such as a finite terminological field, or simple isolated syntactic structures, set phrases and the like *(auf dem Tisch <=> on the table)*. The larger the syntatic unit, the less probable the possibility of absolute equivalence will be.

Some scholars have argued that the idea of equivalence is an illusion and should be abandoned (e.g. Snell-Hornby 1988). Others appear to define translation in terms of equivalence and equivalence in terms of translation, so that any translation is equivalent by definition. A non-equivalent translation, on this view, is a contradiction (cf. Toury 1980:70). If translation theory studies translations, and all translations are by definition equivalent, it might seem that we can dispense with the term altogether, and focus instead on the wide variety of relations that can exist between a translation and its source. Of course, we could call these relations 'kinds of equivalence', but then we are no longer talking about strict sameness. (But see the Update section at the end of this chapter.)

1.2.3 Untranslatability

This supermeme is closely linked to the previous one: if translation is defined in terms of equivalence, and since absolute equivalence is practically unattainable, translation must surely be impossible. Alternatively: it is assumed that equivalence is, by definition, perfect; but perfection, in practice, is unattainable. This is the problem at the centre of Mounin's discussion (Mounin 1963). This supermeme constitutes the basic "objection prejudicielle" against translation (Ladmiral 1994:85f.). Another classical discussion of this idea is the famous essay by Ortega y Gasset (1937), who argues that translation is necessarily "a Utopian task" (although he goes on to say that in this respect, translation is like many other human activities and aspirations, including communication in one's mother tongue).

This view has been held particularly with respect to literary translation: a typical example is Friedrich (1965), whose starting-point is what he takes to be the "reality" of untranslatability from one language to another. This fundamental untranslatability is simply assumed by Friedrich as given, although the rest of the essay of course belies this belief, in that it discusses literary translation as something that does nevertheless take place.

Another classical variant of this supermeme is the traditional argument that poetry is untranslatable. "Poetry by definition is untranslatable" claims Jakobson ([1959] 1989:59–60) – despite the fact that poetry is of course translated. Such views are obviously linked to the equivalence supermeme: no "translation" that is not totally equivalent *is* a translation.

There are interesting religious and philosophical roots underlying this supermeme. One is the Biblical legend of the Tower of Babel (taken up again by Derrida 1985), the myth explaining why human beings find it impossible to communicate with each other properly across languages. Another is the long shadow of

Aristotelian binarism: categories (such as "translatable") are discrete: things are either absolutely translatable or not, and therefore mostly not. Yet another has been the idea promoted by ecclesiastical authorities of more than one religion that the divine Word should not be tampered with, not translated into vernacular languages, or not translated at all. And such views of course link up with attitudes of cultural isolationism; the fear of the Other; the belief that the world is composed of unconnected and impermeable billiard balls; the denial of the Oneness and inter-relatedness of everything.

The diametrically opposing view is expressed e.g. by Benjamin ([1923] 1963:185): languages share a kinship that is marked by a convergence, so that "[l]anguages are not strangers to one another, but are, a priori and apart from all historical relationships, interrelated in what they want to express", as Zohn's translation puts it (Schulte and Biguenet 1992:74).

An opposing view is also crystallized in Katz's (1978) Effability Principle, according to which any proposition can be expressed by some sentence in any language (although this principle is thus explicitly restricted to propositional meaning). Keenan (1978) rejects Katz's principle, and thus agrees with the untranslatability thesis at least in its weak form: nothing is translatable *exactly*. Keenan argues that this is because human languages are by their very nature "imprecise", fuzzy: they have to be, in order that we can talk about unlimited phenomena, in unlimited situations, to unlimited numbers of addressees, and so on. The built-in vagueness of language is thus functional: if languages were well-defined systems like mathematics, we would be less efficient communicators.

From the linguistic angle, the untranslatability idea looks like a restriction of language to *langue* only, to language as system; it seems to deny the role played by *parole*, by what people can do in their actual use of language. Translation is, after all, a form of language use; and from this point of view nothing is untranslatable: that is, everything can be translated somehow, to some extent, in some way – even puns can be explained. No communication is perfect, so why should translation be? Semiotically speaking, we could say that communication succeeds to the extent that the message decoded and interpreted by the receiver overlaps in some relevant way with that sent by the sender. Whereas the equivalence supermeme focuses on the overlap, the untranslatability supermeme focuses on the non-overlapping part of the message: each supermeme then assumes that the part it sees is actually the whole picture.

Moreover, it seems particularly shortsighted to maintain a belief in untranslatability in the face of the actual fact of translation. Looked at empirically, however, certain texts do tend to be more easily translated than others. Texts tend to be easier to translate when source and target cultures are in close cultural contact or share a similar cultural history, when source and target languages are related, when the source text is already oriented towards the target readership (tourist brochures...), etc. (See e.g. Toury 1980: 24–25, summarizing previous work by Even-Zohar.)

1.2.4 Free-vs-literal

Given that translation is nevertheless done, despite the impossibility of perfect equivalence, the terms in which it has been discussed have long been dominated by a single supermeme: the binary opposition between free and literal translation. Occasionally attempts are made to introduce a third term (e.g. Dryden [1680] 1975), but the overall polarity has long remained between these two extremes.

"Literal" is an unfortunate term: for some it means "word-for-word and therefore ungrammatical, like a linguist's gloss"; for others it means "the closest possible grammatical translation, probably not sounding very natural". In both cases, the stress is on closeness to the original form.

A neat view of the relation between literal and free is given by Barkhudarov (1993). He correlates the literal/free parameter with the translator's choice of unit of translation: the smaller the unit of translation, the more literal the result, and the larger the unit, the freer the result (where the units are morpheme, word, phrase, clause, sentence). The appropriate unit of translation depends (among other things) on the kind of text: a translation that is "too literal" is based on too small units, and one that it "too free" on too large units.

In the modern age, at the literal extreme we find Nabokov's equation of literalness and absolute accuracy ([1955] 1992: 141), at least as regards literary translation:

> The person who desires to turn a literary masterpiece into another language, has only one duty to perform, and this is to reproduce with absolute exactitude the whole text, and nothing but the text. The term "literal translation" is tautological since anything but that is not truly a translation but an imitation, an adaptation or a parody.   ([1955] 1992: 134)

In close agreement, and not only for literary texts, is Newmark's claim that literal translation should always be preferred where it is possible: "provided that equivalent-effect is secured, the literal word-for-word translation is not only the best, it is the only valid method of translation" (1981: 39).

An example of the other extreme is Robinson (1991), who argues that translators have the right to translate just how they feel, exploiting a wide range of relations between source and target. Indeed, he writes that ultimately the only valid criterion for a translation is that source and target text should "stand in some kind of recognizable relation to each other" (153). This is a long way from the traditional equivalence requirement, some kind of "sameness".

The dominance of this supermeme is indeed closely bound up with notions of equivalence. An advocacy of literal translation goes hand in hand with an adherence to formal equivalence, while free translation tends to prioritize functional equivalence. The required degree of literalness or freedom depends partly on the text-type etc.

The disadvantage of this supermeme is that it takes one particular type of translation – literal translation – and sets it up as one end of a single dimension. This rather prejudges the whole issue, and prevents us from looking at other dimensions.

1.2.5   All-writing-is-translating

Semiotically speaking, all writing, including translating, is the mapping of signifieds onto signifiers: we put meaning into words (cf. Jakobson 1959). This supermeme thus stresses not the impossibility of translation but its possibility, its familiarity. Translating is no more than a form of writing that happens to be re-writing. Learning to speak means learning to translate meanings into words (cf. Paz 1971). Furthermore, translation is also like the comprehension of everyday speech, as Schleiermacher ([1813] 1963: 38) points out: we often have to rephrase another person's words in our own minds, in order to understand.

It is frequently said that we also translate across time within the same language, as when we read Chaucer in a modern English translation. And even without such a translation, when reading Chaucer in the original we are still somehow interpreting him into our own language. This hermeneutic view of translation has been stressed e.g. by G. Steiner (1975) and Paepcke (1986).

The idea that all writing is translating also emerges strongly in postmodern approaches to intertextuality, from Benjamin to Derrida and beyond: the basic argument here is that no texts are original, they are all derivative from other texts, parasitical upon them; writers do not create their own texts but borrow and combine elements from others, linking up in the global textual web. Our words are not ours: they have been used before, and our own use is inevitably tainted by their previous usage, in other people's mouths. There are no "originals"; all we *can* do is translate. (For a discussion, see Gentzler 1993, especially Chapter 6.)

Associated with this idea is a particular attitude to meaning. Whereas the equivalence supermeme would assume that meanings are somewhere "out there", already existing in objective reality, this supermeme would oppose such a notion. Instead, it takes the view that meaning is something that is negotiated during the communication or interpretation process itself, it grows out of this process and is shaped by it, in the same way as it has been shaped by all previous communication. It is not "given-for-all-time" but "made", both historically and instantaneously. Where the former supermeme stresses accuracy, therefore (in the sense of conforming to an objective "truth"), this supermeme would stress appropriateness (that is, appropriateness to a particular communicative situation). Against both these homogenizing notions of meaning, however, it is easy to argue that some meanings are more objective and stable than others, and that the relative priorities of accuracy and appropriateness are contingent on many conditions.

The all-writing-is-translating supermeme thus stands in opposition to the untranslatability one: it represents the belief that not only is translation possible but that it is in principle not so very different from other kinds of language use. Technically speaking, this is a mutualist supermeme, benefiting both itself and the host organism.

1.3   The locus of memes

Where do memes exist? To answer this question I turn to the philosophy of Karl Popper. Let us look first at his concept of the three Worlds.

This has been one of Popper's most influential contributions to the philosophy of science (see especially Popper 1972: 106f.). World 1 consists of physical objects, such as chairs, trees, spiders. World 2 is the subjective world of states of consciousness, mental states, "behavioural dispositions to act" (106). And World 3 is "the world of *objective contents of thought*, especially of scientific and poetic thoughts and of works of art" (106; italics original). World 3 is the world of ideas, not as they exist in an individual's mind (World 2) but as they exist in the public domain, in books, libraries, databases; as they exist "objectively". World 3 contains theories, problems, hypotheses, arguments. A book, as a physical object, exists in World 1, but a book's contents exist in World 3: a book can be burned, but its *contents* are not thus destroyed.

Popper's three worlds obviously interact with each other. A theory starts life in World 2, in someone's head; when expressed in words or figures it enters World 3, and a book containing it can prop open a door in World 1. As physical objects, spider's webs exist in World 1, but such webs are produced by the innate "behavioural disposition to act" in the spider's World 2, and our shared *idea* of such webs exists in World 3. World 2 phenomena obviously affect World 1 objects, and vice versa. More interestingly, World 3 also interacts with both the other worlds. World 3 phenomena are, first of all, the products of the interaction between Worlds 1 and 2; but – and this is the main point at issue here – World 3 phenomena also affect World 2 (and thereby World 1). Ideas, for instance, affect the way we think and behave. Theories can affect the way we view the world and act within and upon it.

The way World 3 impinges upon Worlds 1 and 2 is not deterministic, however. Because the interaction between the three worlds is in constant flux, feedback from one world to another is inherent. Because of the existence of this flexible feedback and the constant adjustments it gives rise to, Popper needs a concept of influence or control which is somewhere between full determinism and complete randomness. He calls this non-deterministic control, exercised in particular by World 3 over World 2, *plastic control* (e.g. 1972:239f.). Critical arguments are a means of plastic control over behaviour; our theories exert a plastic control over ourselves.

In Popper's own words:

> [T]he control of ourselves and of our actions by our theories is a *plastic* control. We are not *forced* to submit ourselves to the control of our theories, for we can discuss them critically, and we can reject them freely if we think they fall short of our regulative standards. So the control is far from one-sided. Not only do our theories control us, but we can control our theories (and even our standards): there is a kind of *feed-back* here. (1972:240–241; italics original)

So in which of these Worlds do we find memes? The answer is: in all three. As unexpressed thoughts, memes exist in World 2. But they presumably also exist in World 1, as neural patterns of synapses in the brain. A biologist puts it this way:

> Any cultural trait that is taken over by a given individual from another individual must accordingly be thought of as the transfer of a particular pattern of synaptic hotspots within the associative networks of one brain to the associative networks of another brain. (Delius 1989:44)

Elsewhere in the article from which the above quotation comes, Delius glosses memes as "constellations of activated and non-activated synapses within neural memory networks" (45), and talks about them competing "for synaptic space" (67). Tantalizingly, such ideas also seem compatible with Edelman's theory of neuronal group selection (see Edelman 1992): the human brain appears to be even more astonishing than one might think.

Most interestingly and relevantly for our purposes, however, memes also exist in World 3. Indeed, as ideas, theories, arguments and the like, memes are very typical inhabitants of World 3. As such, they of course affect our Worlds 1 and 2, so that the survival of the inhabitants of World 1 (such as ourselves) depends to some extent on what memes prevail in World 3 and on the nature of the influence (plastic control) they have.

Memes may even be felt to exert more influence than we feel comfortable with. In his exploration of the notion of consciousness (i.e. something in World 2), Dennett (1991: 202) gives graphic expression to this uncomfortableness: "I don't know about you," he says, "but I'm not initially attracted by the idea of my brain as a sort of dung heap in which the larvae of other people's ideas renew themselves, before sending out copies of themselves in an informational Diaspora." Dennett's view of meme influence is evidently more deterministic than Popper's plastic control.

From this point of view, translation memes, i.e. theories and ideas about translation in general, inevitably affect the way translators think and translate. Not necessarily explicitly, of course, for an amateur translator may operate only with vague, implicit ideas about what an acceptable translation is, perhaps a personal intuitive theory of some kind. The relation between theory and practice will be one of my key themes in what follows.

1.4 A Popperian meme

Before looking at the evolution of translation memes one further item needs to be added to our introductory framework. This is Popper's schema which he uses to describe the process of scientific methodology, and in fact to describe the acquisition of all rational knowledge. It is as follows:

$$P1 \rightarrow TT \rightarrow EE \rightarrow P2$$

All knowledge acquisition, says Popper, starts with a Problem, P1. Confronted with this, we propose a Tentative Theory (TT) or tentative hypothesis, a trial solution, which is of course unlikely to be perfect, given the fallibility of human nature. A theory, at its simplest, is seen here as a problem-solving hypothesis, a proposed answer to a question. One of Popper's more radical claims is that it is totally immaterial how we actually arrive at this tentative theory: by sheer chance, imagination, rational deduction, a flash of insight in a dream – whatever.

The tentative theory is then subjected to a process of Error Elimination (EE), and it is the rigour of this methodological stage which distinguishes science proper from pseudoscience or non-scientific knowledge. (No claim is being made here about the relative *values* of scientific vs. non-scientific knowledge: they are simply different kinds of knowledge.) At this stage, the Tentative Theory is exposed to tests and criticism of all kinds, it is compared with alternative theories, checked for internal consistency, checked against the data and against new data, checked for the testable hypotheses it generates, and so on, in a determined effort to prove it wrong, i.e. to falsify it. A theory that cannot be falsified (potentially, at least) may or may not be a good theory, but it is not, for Popper, a scientific one. A theory that has been exposed to rigorous testing and criticism, that has survived more or less intact so far, is a well-*corroborated* theory; but being intrinsically a hypothesis, a theory in Popper's sense can never be finally confirmed or proved right, although it may be supported by further evidence. What matters is not whether a theory can be *verified* or not – for no verification can ever be final – but whether it can in principle be *falsified* or not.

The result of the Error Elimination process is a new Problem, P2; and so it continues. Theories do not automatically lead to "the truth", but they do aim to get increasingly closer to verisimilitude.

A caveat is required here. As might be expected, Popper's theory of scientific theorizing has itself not gone without criticism. He has been criticized, for instance, for underestimating the process whereby hypotheses are painstakingly arrived at, and for being too anarchistic on this point (see e.g. Niiniluoto 1978); for overestimating the strength and significance of the falsifiability criterion and underestimating the way that the acceptance, survival and rejection of scientific theories may also depend on social and ideological factors – theories may become gradually "frustrated", not dramatically falsified (see especially Kuhn 1970); and on other counts as well. My goal here, however, is not to present a critique of Popper's philosophy of science as such, nor to examine how it has been received and developed since, nor to evaluate its originality or Popper's debt to other thinkers such as Peirce. (Readers are referred to Popper's own intellectual autobiography – Popper 1992 – and the references therein.) I simply find inspiration in a number of Popper's ideas, and seek to apply these to some of the problems posed by translation theory, and especially the problem of setting up a translation theory in the first place (Chesterman 1994a).

The next chapter will use Popper's schema as a means of structuring the way in which ideas about translation have developed. It will thus represent an outline Tentative Theory of this historical process.

1.5 Update

By surprising coincidence, in the same year that this book was first published another translation scholar, Hans Vermeer, published an article in *Target* speculating on the relevance of the *meme* concept to translation (Vermeer 1997). Neither of us was aware of the other's interest in this subject at the time. Vermeer relates memes to the notion of culturemes, which he had made use of in some of his own work. Vermeer's article raised many questions about memes, some of which

I have offered answers to, although many more still remain open. Vermeer also touches on the topic in a later issue of *Target* (Vermeer 1998), in the context of a brief discussion of intentionality, but does not develop the idea further there.

The meme metaphor has also been found useful by Franz Pöchhacker, in his introduction to Interpreting Studies (2004). However, the notion cannot be said to have entered the mainstream of Translation Studies. This may be partly due to critical responses to the meme concept in general. Some of these were collected in Rose and Rose (2001), and I summarized and commented on several of them in Chesterman (2005a). One of the most interesting crititicisms concerns the ontological status of memes: are memes only metaphors, or do they really exist in some way? If they do exist, is this form of existence significantly similar to the way genes exist, or significantly different? Opinions differ... Even if they are taken to be no more than a metaphorical way of conceptualizing how common ideas spread, I still find this a stimulating way of thinking, and not just about translation. True, any purely memetic account of the evolution of ideas still remains to be embedded in a rich historical and social context – a task which this book does not much deal with.

In some schools of behavioural science and cultural studies memetics seems to be flourishing. I refer interested readers to this website listing online publications on memetics: http://www.lycaeum.org//~sputnik/Memetics/, and to Susan Blackmore's site at http://www.susanblackmore.co.uk/memetics/. Key volumes on memetics that have appeared since 1997 include Aunger (2000) and Blackmore (1999); see also Dennett's philosophical books and papers defending Darwinism, both biological and cultural (e.g. 2004, Chapter 6). Two relevant French references are Changeux (2003) and Cavalli-Sforza (2005).

I have more recently noted with interest that a Darwinist approach to translation is evident in the "eco-translatology" theory, which seems related to a memetic approach. Eco-translatology is founded on the idea that translation can be analysed in terms of selection and adaptation, like biological evolution. Translation practice is seen as an ecosystem, interacting with its environment. The theory has been mainly promoted so far by Chinese scholars (see e.g. Hu 2003), and is claimed to be partly inspired by ancient Chinese wisdom. At the time of writing, it is not yet so widely known in the West, although there have been five international symposia on this approach to date.

The *equivalence supermeme* has continued to flourish, despite the criticisms directed against it (see e.g. Snell-Hornby 1988), and despite the importance of the skopos idea (see 2.6). Even though it does not seem helpful to define equivalence in terms of identity, except for special limited cases, it is still widely held to be an essential concept which can distinguish translation from other acts of communication. In my own work (e.g. 1998: Chapter 1) I have argued that Translation

Studies can best interpret equivalence as relevant similarity, and discussed the different kinds of similarity typically focused on by Translation Studies and Contrastive Studies: divergent (roughly, where a likeness is created, e.g. by imitating) and convergent similarity (roughly, where a likeness is perceived between two separate entities).

Anthony Pym (e.g. 1995) has consistently defended the relevance of the equivalence idea to translation practice and Translation Studies. He argues that equivalence is a matter of belief: the translator believes – and implicitly claims – that the finished target text is equivalent (in some relevant way), and the client and/or reader normally accepts this belief and thus assumes equivalence. More recently (2007, 2010), he has proposed a distinction between two basic kinds of equivalence: natural equivalence and directional equivalence, which can also be thought of as the above-mentioned two types of similarity. The two types also characterize the foci of different kinds of translation theory. *Natural* equivalence between words and structures etc. in a given pair of languages already exists (e.g. in bilingual dictionaries; cf. "correspondence" in lexicography) before a given act of translating, and this relation is reversible; the translator just has to know the natural equivalent, or find it. *Water* in English is *Wasser* in German, and vice versa. (Cf. convergent similarity.) *Directional* equivalence, on the other hand, is created by the translator in a given context, and is not reversible. A directional translation might be very free indeed, and different translators of a given item, looking for a target item based on directional equivalence, would most likely come up with different solutions, which might all be valid. (Cf. divergent similarity.)

Arguments and proposals concerning the equivalence supermeme certainly continue to invigorate Translation Studies. And not only Translation Studies: Patrick Cattrysse includes a critical analysis of the translation equivalence debate in his book on Adaptation Studies (2014: Chapter 13.2.4). He calls for more conceptual and terminological clarity. For instance, he argues that Pym's terms "directional" and "natural" are not polar opposites, and that the reversibility criterion is more complex than it may appear.

CHAPTER 2

The evolution of translation memes

People have been translating for thousands of years: it is one of the many useful things we can do with language. And people have also been thinking about translation for almost as long. Ideas about translation – about how to do it, how not to do it, when it seems impossible, and so on – have sprung up like mushrooms. Presumably, some of these ideas, these translation memes, have failed to win any general acceptance and have thus faded without trace. Others have remained current for quite some time before giving way to others. And still others appear to be practically indestructible: cf. the supermemes in the previous chapter.

This chapter suggests a way of surveying the evolution of translation memes. Recall Popper's schema introduced above. Each attempt to solve a problem (i.e. each Tentative Theory) eventually gives rise to a further problem (P2), in an endless process, approaching ever closer to "truthlikeness". Each theory evolves out of, and reacts to, a preceding one; each new theory seeks to correct or refine some aspect of an earlier one, or even offer an alternative starting point altogether, in different socio-cultural conditions. My focus here is on the ideas themselves, and I shall not discuss their socio-cultural causes in any detail.

With this general picture of theory development in mind, let us now take a bird's-eye look at the growth of translation theory. My intention here is not to offer a detailed history of the field, nor do I claim to introduce new insights: much fuller and deeper treatments are available elsewhere (see e.g. Kelly 1979; Berman 1984; Rener 1989; Bassnett 1991; Copeland 1991; Vermeer 1992; Ballard 1992; Venuti 1995a). My outline here is largely restricted to the European tradition. The idea of this chapter is to introduce some of the main strands of translation-theoretical thinking, and to argue that these strands still play a role in current work and practice. It may well be that if we are to build a comprehensive theory of translation, we shall have to incorporate all of these strands in one way or another, because each of them highlights one particular aspect of the phenomenon we call translation. The theoretical situation today is fragmented: one reason for taking such a general view here is the need to find a perspective from which the different strands can be related.

I shall distinguish eight major stages in this evolution (following Chesterman 1995). Each stage can be seen as a particular meme or meme-complex, concerned with a particular question (P1) or set of questions. At each stage a number of theoretical concepts and insights emerge, some of which survive into the meme pool of subsequent stages. The peaks of these stages are roughly chronological, but there is a good deal of overlap, so that the stages are cumulative rather than strictly successive: the stages primarily represent clusters of ideas rather than historical periods.

For clarity of exposition, to sum up each stage in the evolution of translation memes I suggest a dominant metaphor, which seems to encapsulate the set of ideas asociated with that stage. D'hulst (1992) makes the valuable point that such metaphors have an enormous influence on the way scholars and practitioners conceive of translation. However, if we look through the spectacles provided by a single metaphor alone, we run the risk of missing insights that would be facilitated by some other metaphor. A modern theory of translation needs to draw on many such metaphors.

My eight meme-complexes and their associated metaphors thus offer a way of structuring the current meme pool of ideas about translation: it contains traces of them all.

2.1 Words

Etymologically, as noted above, English "translate" means 'carry across'. It would appear that among the very first questions raised about translation, perhaps three thousand or so years ago, was "*what* is carried across?" And the answer was something like: we carry across the meanings inside words. For words are repositories of meaning. And words are the building blocks out of which language is constructed. Words are the first units of translation.

Rener (1989) shows how the first theoretical ideas about translation in the west became closely tied up with the classical Greek view of language. Language was seen as a structure, a whole consisting of arranged parts. The prevailing metaphor was an architectural one: as a building is made of smaller units called bricks etc., so language structure is made of smaller units called words.

Words are signs. A formal sign was taken to represent a meaning. For Plato, the meanings represented by word-signs were not only constant but absolute, elements of the true reality: Platonic Ideas. Far removed from the messy world of the everyday, "meanings" were manifestations of the Ideal: perfect, eternal. (For more detailed expositions, see Kelly 1979 and Robinson 1991.) For Aristotle too, signs mirrored reality. Translation was possible, because reality remained constant: the meaning of a word did not change when it was expressed via another form.

It has taken a long time for this general conception of meaning to be toppled off its pedestal. It is therefore not surprising that it has also dominated (at least western) thinking about translation theory. The idea of absolute and invariant meanings has been a very long-lasting translation meme. Perhaps its survival had something to do with the need to cling to something permanent amid the flux of translation.

In practice, what the translator was thought to do was this: like a stone mason, he de-constructed the original structure and then used the same bricks to build a new structure elsewhere. The bricks were now not the words themselves, but the word-meanings they contained or represented. Because the translator used the same bricks, the same word-meanings, equivalence was guaranteed. The metaphor I propose for Stage 1 is thus "translation is rebuilding."

Offshoots of this meme are to be found in many contemporary concepts, theories and applications of meaning, such as denotation (vs. connotation); lexical semantics, especially componential analysis; lexicography and terminology studies.

Furthermore, it is the reaction to this meme that triggers off the whole debate about translatability: *can* words of different languages actually "mean the same"? As long as meanings were conceived of as absolute, objectively existing "out there", it was easy to answer "yes". But this assurance gradually became worn away: *all* words? all words in all contexts? all words all the time?

2.2 The Word of God

From a focus on individual words (P1) there obviously had to emerge a focus on the structures in which words were arranged, for words alone, unstructured, do not make a language. It is this focus on formal structure which was associated with much of the early thinking on the translation of religious texts. Many of the foremost translators and theorists of this stage (in the West) were themselves involved in such translations, primarily of the Bible. And it was the specific nature of this particular text-type that gave rise to the next major theoretical issue (a first P2, as it were).

Because: if you believe that the scriptures are indeed the Word of God, and if you believe that you have a mission to spread this Word, you quickly find yourself in a quandary. The Word is holy; how then can it be changed? For translation does not only substitute one word-meaning for another but also reconstructs the structural form in which these word-meanings are embedded. Yet in holy texts, it was felt, even the form was holy. To meddle with the original form of the scriptures was to risk blasphemy, heresy; a translator might even risk his life (several centuries later, the translator Dolet was indeed burnt at the stake for "mistranslating" Plato in such a way as to suggest something heretical about the posthumous existence of the soul).

There were two ways out of this quandary, two Tentative Theories or ideas that had to work in tandem. One was to extend the idea of the meaning (Latin *significatio*) of a text in such a way that the meaning was not just carried by individual words but by the text as a whole; then, by analogy with the invariance of word-meaning, this extended meaning could also be claimed to remain constant in spite of the change of form (Latin *sonum*) it underwent in translation. God's Word remained God's Word, regardless of the language it was expressed in. (Incidentally, God could also inspire the translators of the Word just as he had inspired its original writers; this made it easier to translate with a clear conscience.) As with word-meanings, equivalence was presupposed: it was accepted that the divine truth contained in Holy Scripture was absolute and would therefore be preserved across languages.

But this solution depended on a second theoretical idea, on another translation meme that has also been endowed with impressive longevity. This was the idea of (maximally) literal translation, "word-for-word" but preserving target-language grammaticality. In other words, it was accepted that the translator would have to make some formal (structural) changes during the process of translation, but these were to be kept to a minimum. Jerome was quoted by the French bishop Huetius ([1683] 1992:92) as saying that even the very word order in sacred scriptures is a mystery.

This translation meme was motivated in the first place by fear: the fear of heresy and its consequences. It was also motivated by a respect for the authority of the source text. These are strong motivations, and we find frequent expressions of this attitude in what translators have written about their own work. In the early 16th century, Erasmus wrote that he preferred "to sin through excessive scrupulousness rather than through excessive license" ([1506] 1992:60) – i.e. to translate too literally rather than too freely. Pym (1994) argues that in 12th-century Toledo, literalism functioned as a protection, allowing translators to translate works that would otherwise have been disapproved of or censored. Indeed, this is the translation meme that starts the argument about free vs. literal translation, which so dominates the traditional literature on translation.

It is important to appreciate that this particular meme seems to have started life in the context of biblical translation, to which it was particularly appropriate, of course. From there, it spread to certain other contexts in which the form of the original text was somehow felt to be particularly significant: philosophy, scientific and technical texts. In the late 17th century, for instance, we find Huetius arguing that such texts should be translated with close attention to the form of the original, without undue embellishment ([1683] 1992: 86f.), because only in this way could the translator guarantee to preserve truthfulness.

There are a number of contemporary manifestations of this meme. One is Nida's concept of minimal transfer (e.g. 1964), which he defines as a transfer that incorporates all and only the formal changes that are necessary to render the target text grammatical. This concept is closely linked to that of Nida's formal equivalence: (maximal) sameness of form rather than of effect.

Another example is the notion of semantic translation (vs. communicative translation) developed by Newmark (1981): a semantic translation is one that follows the form of the source text as closely as possible.

A third example is to be found in the general approach advocated by Vinay and Darbelnet ([1958] 1969). They outline a series of "translation procedures" ranging from "direct" (including "literal translation") to "indirect" (including various formal, semantic and pragmatic changes). The gist of their argument is that one should translate as directly as possible, only having recourse to more indirect procedures when the result of a direct procedure is plainly inexact or ungrammatical. In their opinion, then, the whole argument about free vs. literal translation is a red herring: one simply translates as literally as possible, for unmotivated changes ("freedom") lead to inexact, less-than-optimal, translations. (See Chapter 4 below for more on translation strategies.)

Reverence for the source text, and the consequent insistence on literal translation, is also evident in the ideas of some modern literary translators. Nabokov is a good example, as mentioned in the previous chapter.

This reverence is also evident in what seems to be the dominant metaphor for this stage: "translation is copying". Translators themselves have no authority, they are totally subservient to the source text; they are humble copiers; deviation from the original is a sin.

2.3 Rhetoric

The subsequent problem that arose was, of course, that not all texts are holy scriptures or the like. Should other texts too be translated in the same literal way?

One of the first scholars to make the link between translation method and text-type was Jerome, who himself translated both religious texts and literary classics. He argued that non-sacred texts should be translated more freely. This does indeed seem to correspond to what translators of sacred and less sacred works usually did.

Schwarzwald-Rodrigue (1993), for instance, shows that translations of Biblical and (less sacred) Mishnaic texts into Ladino (a Judeo-Spanish language) consistently follow these different attitudes to the status of the source text: the Mishnaic texts are translated less literally.

As the kind of texts that were translated shifted from biblical to secular, especially in the Renaissance period, so the dominant translation meme also shifted. Translation became more like interpretation, commentary, adaptation, even explanation. Translators gave priority to the needs and tastes of their readers rather than the strict form of the source. To some extent, this move away from ST dominance must have been a natural reaction to "over-literal" translations that had been heavily marked by source-language (SL) interference and thus sacrificed target-language (TL) acceptability. The argument was often couched in terms of the opposition between servile adherence to the letter versus noble faithfulness to the spirit of the original (e.g. Dacier [1711] 1992: 12–13).

This memetic shift was also a reaction against the servile status of the translator. In the 16th century, Dolet argued bluntly that translators should not become slaves to the original, by merely rendering word for word ([1540] 1992: 27). And later, in the 18th century, d'Alembert used similar images of servitude to criticize over-literal translators who submitted themselves to the yoke of the original, becoming mere copiers rather than genuine rivals ([1758] 1992: 111).

A rival is a much more forceful agent than a passive copier. The idea of the translator as the rival of the original writer goes back to Quintilian, with his advocation that translators should engage in a struggle with the original, to emulate and even surpass it rather than copy it (see e.g. Lefevere 1992: 50, 87). At this stage, the dominant metaphor for translating is imitating, not copying. One imitates a process, a creative process, rather than a passive product; imitating requires its own creative force, even a virtuoso sense of "I can do this better than you can". Translators began to assume more authority, more responsibility for the authorship of their translations.

I call this stage that of rhetoric, for the first signs of it occur in that other classical tradition of language study: not grammar but rhetoric. (For a detailed study of the influence of the rhetoric tradition on translation theory, see Rener 1989.) In Roman education, translating from Greek (like paraphrasing within Latin) was an important rhetorical exercise in its own right, a form of language practice. But the benefit of such practice was not only felt by the individual orator; it was frequently argued that such translation also benefited the target language as a whole.

This meme of target-language enrichment is something very different from the thinking of the previous stage. It represents the first of many pendulum swings between source dominance and target dominance. Translation is now seen not as source-oriented copying but target-oriented rhetoric, its main concern being audience reception. There is more of a pride in the target language and its potential: source texts are there to be exploited for the benefit of the receiving culture.

The meme is a prolific one, and no more than some representative examples of its manifestation will be given here. One early instance is the traditional argument that we should translate non-sacred texts sense for sense, not word for word, found e.g. in Cicero. During the Middle Ages, vernacular translations of poetry and prose were often very free indeed, and raised the perennial question of how free a translation can get before it becomes something other than a translation, such as an adaptation (a point that we shall return to in a later chapter). (See Copeland 1991.) Even biblical translation came under the influence of the new meme: Luther took great care to make his German translation fit naturally into the vernacular, in order that its function should be more effectively served. Clarity, intelligibility, readability, fluency – these were the things that mattered. (See Venuti 1995a for a critical discussion of the origins and history of the fluency ideal; Venuti himself argues that the ideal has canonized a bourgeois cultural dominance, and that it should be resisted. I take up this ethical issue in Chapter 7, below.)

This rhetorical tradition reached its height during the Renaissance, with a paramount emphasis on what we might call the entertainment value of a text. Combined with a strong target-reader orientation, this inevitably led eventually to translations of inordinate freedom, perhaps *belles* but frequently *infidèles*. In the 17th century we thus have Cowley defending his Pindar translations with the justification that "I have ... taken, left out, and added what I please ..." ([1656] 1975:66), because, in keeping with the fashion of the time, his priority was the style of the original, not its content. Compare Dryden, making Virgil speak like a late 17th-century English gentleman ([1680] 1975); or Pope's Homer in powdered wigs. A more extreme example is offered by de la Motte, whose cavalier translation of the *Iliad* reduced the work by about half by simply cutting out the "uninteresting episodes" and passages that shocked or bored contemporary taste, so that the final translation could be actually presented as being better than Homer's original ([1714] 1992:28–30). The manifestation of this meme in Dutch 18th-century translation, stressing a prospective rather than retrospective (source-oriented) orientation, is described by Korpel (1993). The meme continues into the 19th century, with Fitzgerald plundering and reshaping the *Rubaiyat* at will, and even into the 20th, with Robinson's (1991) virtual rejection of any authority other than that of the translator him- or herself. In fact, Robinson's whole book *The Translator's Turn* is an extended argument in favour of this view of translation (see especially p. 134f.).

One of the most interesting manifestations of the Rhetoric meme is to be found in the ideas of certain postmodern scholars of translation. A striking image here is translation as cannibalism, absorbing the value of an original text and thus nourishing the target language and culture (see e.g. Vieira 1994).

2.4 Logos

Just as the Rhetoric stage was in part a reaction against the previous literalism, so too it provoked its own inevitable reaction in turn. Already in 1680 Dryden was warning against the excesses of both free imitation and over-literalism, and advocating a middle path. A hundred years later, Tytler similarly sought to balance natural target-language style with a respect for the content of the original ([1790] 1978:16f.).

However, it was not until the German Romantic movement that a genuinely new meme entered the pool, with respect to literary translation. An early expression of the new attitude comes in Schleiermacher's argument against imitation in his essay "Ueber die verschiedenen Methoden des Uebersezens" (based on a lecture given in 1813; reprinted in Störig 1963:38–70). Imitation, like copying, is ultimately impossible, he argues, and mere paraphrase destroys the spirit of the original. In place of these, rather than carrying the translation to the reader, the translation of literature should aim at a style that is deliberately marked, strange, foreign, so that the reader feels the translation to be unfamiliar and is thus moved back towards the original; the experience should be as if a foreign spirit were blown towards the reader. In other words, the pendulum swings back towards the original again. (But see Pym's critical analysis of Schleiermacher's binarism in Pym 1997, Chapter 1.)

Note how this attitude reflects a particular view of equivalence. The Word-of-God stage had to presuppose total equivalence, and the Rhetoric stage, where it respected equivalence at all, prioritized stylistic equivalence above semantic and formal. But now equivalence of effect (pragmatic equivalence) is essentially denied, inasmuch as target readers are deliberately exposed to a textual strangeness that did not necessarily form part of the source readers' reading experience. Formal equivalence, however, is now given more weight: what this stage tended to mean in practice was a closer adherence to the textual structure of the original.

Although equivalence of effect was thus implicitly denied, the actual effect of translations was a central concern. It was linked to a functional view of language as a whole: language was seen as a creative force, something that gave shape and form to the world and to human experience. Language was *logos*, the creative Word. To use language was thus to imitate the act of divine creation.

To make sense of this memetic shift, two background factors must be borne in mind. One was the revival of hermeneutics, offering an alternative philosophy of language, stressing its function not as an instrument of communication but as a vehicle of expression, self-expression and creation. (This is discussed at length in Kelly 1979; for the classical and medieval roots, see also Copeland 1991.)

The other factor was the geopolitical situation of Germany itself, where these ideas first began to spread in Europe. At this period, Germany was only starting to grow into a single nation-state, and for the leading intellectuals of the time the major force of the unification process was the German language. A shared language would create and unite a nation. This idea is an obvious development of the previous meme that translations enrich the target language. As the language of a nation is its spirit, a nation too can be enriched by enriching its language.

This view of language gave translators enormous status and responsibility, for it is translators that have the power to give a nation the memes that it lacks. By bringing new forms and ideas into the target culture, translators do indeed help to shape that culture; they are instrumental in the creation and development of a national culture. And it is this role that suggests an appropriate metaphor for this stage of translation theory development: translating is creating. A translator is an artist who shapes language.

Translating was the bringing of *Erklärung*, enlightenment: the changes it brought about in the target culture were therefore beneficial, metamorphoses towards a higher stratum of development. It is this image that underlies Goethe's ([1819] 1963) understanding of translation, as an organic change of form; a given text translated at different periods would embody different stages in this metamorphosis, according to the evolutionary stages of the source and target cultures and to the target culture's degree of familiarity with the source text. A plain prose translation would be followed by a "parodistic" one fully adapted to the target language and culture, and then later still by an "interlinear" one, closer to the original. (This idea is a source of the retranslation hypothesis: see Update below.)

The meme-complex that constitutes this Logos stage also has later manifestations that are still current in today's meme pool. One line of inheritance can be traced through Walter Benjamin's classic essay on "Die Aufgabe des Übersetzers" ([1923] 1963), the task of the translator. Here we find the same image of the translator as the bringer of light, the light of the pure language that underlies all languages; the same necessity of spurning total target-language naturalness in order to preserve a visible echo of the original. For Benjamin, a true translation should be transparent, not blocking the light of the original but allowing the underlying pure language (*die reine Sprache*) to shine through. It is the translator's task to break through the barriers of his own language, in order that it can renew itself via contact with this "pure language".

Benjamin's ideas were followed up by the American translation workshop tradition that grew partly out of the New Criticism movement (see Gentzler 1993). Here too, translation appears as a semi-mystical process embedded in creative writing. Translation can reveal the true meaning of a literary work, the universal essence of language; it is the interpretation tool *par excellence*. For Ezra Pound, a translator should be able to find meaning that even the original author was not aware of (Gentzler 1993: 19–29). Frederick Will spoke of the feeling in the translation workshops that they were "working toward the single language which lies between, or among […] all the national languages" (1973: 158, cited in Gentzler 1993: 35) – Benjamin's image exactly. Gentzler sees this whole tradition as revolving around the concept of energy in language (1993: 40); it is admittedly difficult to be explicit about such abstractions, yet this energy looks very much like logos in another guise. Similarly, Berman (1984), Venuti (1992, 1995a) and May (1994) argue against the trend to "domesticate" (naturalize) literary translations; they propose a return to the deliberately "foreignizing" practices of the German Romantic Hölderlin.

Venuti takes up the notion of "abusive fidelity" from P. Lewis (1985) and Derrida (1985), a fidelity that deliberately rejects the fluency ideal in favour of a translation that resists the normal usage of the target language, challenging the target-language norms by playing with signifiers. Lewis argues that this kind of "strong translation" is the most appropriate way of translating texts such as Derrida's writings, which themselves break source-language norms of usage. In so doing, the translator draws attention to the translation itself as text. Venuti argues that such a translation procedure is ethically motivated, in that it resists the "ethnocentric violence" inevitably committed by fluent translations. The foreignizing strategy he advocates also involves the exploiting of anachronistic corners in the target language. Bad translation negates the Otherness of the foreign by transmitting it as familiar; good translation preserves this Otherness, by whatever means possible. May (1994) argues that translators of Russian literature into English have tended to neglect or under-use certain aspects of the narrative style of the original, such as the use of Free Indirect Speech or an intrusive narrator, in favour of a more fluid style more in keeping with target-language ideals of clarity, explicitness and accessibility. Such a translation method is said to devalue the intrinsic opacity of language, favouring information transfer at the expense of aesthetic play.

It seems paradoxical that these scholars are currently arguing for a translation method similar to the one advocated by 18th and early 19th-century German intellectuals, but with the opposite intention; this is perhaps partly because of the different historical positions of the target languages concerned. Schleiermacher wanted to *boost* the status of German, he had clear nationalistic aims; but Venuti wishes to *reduce* the hegemony of major languages such as English and force them to accept the Otherness of texts from other cultures. It is also paradoxical that if English, for instance, is indeed stretched and expanded in this way, accommodating and accepting more and more Otherness, its hegemony may well *increase* as a result, like the way Hinduism survived and spread by tolerating and adapting all kinds of other beliefs.

Another later manifestation of the Logos meme is to be found in the work of Heidegger ([1957] 1963), who also entertained quasi-mystical ideas of translation as a mode of access to true Being, a way of escaping the constraints of *a* language by returning to "originary" Language. We are on similar ground in Foucault (e.g. 1971), with his stress on the way discourse moulds its users, the autonomy of language, and the value of translation as a way of reaching the Other; and of course also in Derrida (1985), playing with the slippage between languages.

In fact, Derrida and other deconstructionists at times come surprisingly close to the kind of memetic view of translation (i.e., translations as survival machines for memes) that was introduced in the previous chapter. One point that comes up repeatedly in deconstructionist texts on translation is the questioning of the status of the original: suppose the original text is not primary, but secondary, dependent on the translation? Memetically, this is of course true: a text will not gain readship, will not "live", outside the language of its birth unless it is granted a translation. The cross-cultural, international survival of a text indeed depends upon its translation. In keeping with the anti-positivist thinking associated with the Logos meme-complex, Derrida denies that translation can "transfer" some objectively existing "meaning", denies the existence of any such meaning in the first place, and denies any kind of equivalence; rather, he sees the process more as a perpetual modification of the original, what we might call a kind of memetic mutation. Translations give life, life both beyond that of the original text itself and beyond that of the original author. Translations propagate memes through both space and time. (See also A. Benjamin 1989; Koskinen 1994a, b; Arrojo 1996.)

The general status of meaning within the Logos meme is thus very different from what it had been earlier. Meanings are no longer seen as primarily conventional, objective, stable, existing "out there"; rather, they are ever-shifting, ever-slippery, never original, always relative. Where the Rhetoric meme stressed adaptation to the target culture and hence the desired familiarity of the translation, the Logos meme stresses its Otherness.

On this view, the death of the author serves to usher in the age of the translator. Oittinen (1995) celebrates the "translator's carnival", a space-time during which established statuses are overturned and the translator wears the crown.

2.5 Linguistic science

It is obvious that the ideas discussed in the foregoing section pertain primarily to literary translation: they can have little relevance to the wide range of other kinds of translation covering everything from legal and technical documents to tourist brochures and advertisements. It is indeed unfortunate that the theory of translation often continues to be equated, entirely without justification, with theories of literary translation only – see the anthology edited by Schulte and Biguenet (1992), for instance.

This limited scope naturally provoked historical reactions, too. When it led to the artificially archaistic translations favoured by some of the Victorian translators, calls began to be made for a different approach. Matthew Arnold ([1924] 1992) advocated a more scholarly approach, translations that would be appreciated by scholars who also had access to the original source texts; but he too was thinking of literary translation only, specifically of the Greek classics.

A more irritated response to the Logos stage is expressed in the early 20th century by Willamowitz-Moellendorff, who criticizes the German Romantic approach to translation (and the hybrid texts it produced), which was bound to a certain period in German history and culture and was unable to provide a basis for a more general theory of translation ([1925] 1963). In place of such naive amateurs, he exclaims, what we need are professional philologists, linguists.

Interestingly enough, a scientific, linguistic view of translation is also foreshadowed (and rejected) in Schleiermacher's essay on translation, referred to above, where Schleiermacher writes scornfully of those who merely paraphrase the original, who succeed only in laboriously rendering the content but irrevocably killing the spirit of the original. And it is Schleiermacher who introduces what we can take as the dominant metaphor of this linguistic focus: the paraphasing translator treats the elements of the two languages as if they were mathematical signs, which simply by means of addition and subtraction can be reduced to the same value (1963: 46). In other words, on this view to translate is to decode and then recode: translating is transcoding.

It is surely significant that the famous letter from Weaver to Wiener, at the dawn of the great project in machine translation, couches translation in exactly the same terms. Weaver writes (1955: 18): "One naturally wonders if the problem of translation could conceivably be treated as a problem in cryptography. When I look at an article in Russian, I say: This is really written in English, but it has been coded in some strange symbols. I will now proceed to decode."

The linguistic reaction thus meant a return to the positivistic tradition after the romantic excursion. Modern linguistic influences in translation theory are associated with the general pursuit of objectivity and explicitness, with more priority given to the equivalence supermeme, and with a concern for a true scientific method. It is during this stage that in the German-speaking world the term *Übersetzungswissenschaft* begins to be current, symbolizing the wish of translation scholars that their subject should be granted genuine scientific status.

The prototypical manifestation of what I will call the Linguistics meme in translation theory is seen in early machine translation, for which strict equivalence is a *sine qua non*. Instead of waffling about mystical energy, practitioners of machine translation are concerned with the practical rules of language use. They have to believe that these rules exist, and that they are as stable as those of gravity; if there were no rules, "everyone would speak his own version of the language, and no one would understand anyone else" (Toma [1976] 1989: 168). Further, it must also be possible to formulate explicit algorithms for transferring signs of one language into signs of another. (Only up to a point, say the critics; but I shall not enter further into machine translation here, except to point out that the most recent machine translation systems, such as Google Translate, are not rule-based but statistical and corpus-based.)

With respect to human translation, Catford's *A Linguistic Theory of Translation* (1965) marks another central version of this meme. I refer in particular to his notion of unconditioned (= regardless of context) and conditioned (= in context) equivalence probabilities which specify how likely it is that a given source item X will be translated as a target item Y: invaluable information for the translating computer, of course. Catford's analysis of shifts has also been influential in classifying the various kinds of formal difference that can be observed between a source item and its translation: differences of structure, grammatical class etc. More complex analyses of shifts are discussed by Malone (1988) and Leuven-Zwart (1989–1990). (See also Chapter 4, below.)

Within this same meme we can also place the work on contrastive stylistics by Vinay and Darbelnet ([1958] 1969), contrasting English and French. Although they claim to be "following the mind" as it moves from one language to another, Vinay and Darbelnet are in fact primarily concerned with developing an extensive taxonomy of differences, both formal, semantic and stylistic, between their two languages. Some of these differences are, however, formulated as dynamic transfer procedures, and we shall return to them in Chapter 4.

Contrastive analysis as a whole is of great relevance to this meme (see for instance Hartmann 1980, 1981; Chesterman 1998). To do a contrastive analysis you need a third term, a *tertium comparationis*, i.e. something that remains invariant across the comparison (or at least something whose variance is relevantly constrained). In translation theory the name given to this invariance has been equivalence, and this becomes a central concern at this stage in the overall development of the theory. What remains invariant in translation, if anything? Throughout this stage this illusive invariance is pursued from the purely formal, through the semantic, stylistic and textual to the pragmatic. (The last two were favoured domains of the influential Leipzig school: see e.g. Neubert and Shreve 1992.) It gradually becomes clear that at none of these levels can we expect to be able to define a total identity, absolute equivalence. Not only is total formal equivalence a chimera, but no two meanings are ever absolutely the same, and no two styles or situations or even functions either.

Where the Logos-stage translators believed in a universal pure language, machine translation scholars have often posited some kind of mathematical neutral plane, perhaps stated in the universal language of logic, and other linguists have talked of a universal deep structure. In the theory of human translation, Nida (e.g. 1964) posited a "kernel level" which served a similar purpose: analysing a source text down to its simpler kernels made for easier transfer to the target language, because at this level languages were claimed to differ less than at the surface level.

Nida's view of equivalence illustrates the tendency of translation theorists to extrapolate from particular text-types. (Both the Linguistics stage and the following Communication stage tend to be represented by translation-theoretical ideas that are not so readily applicable to literary translation, for instance.) Nida's concern is biblical translation, but he rejects the formal equivalence assumed by the Word-of-God stage because this so often leads to stylistic awkwardness or downright unintelligibility. In its emphasis on the naturalness of the target text, on readability, on ease of decoding, on translation as exegesis, Nida's work reflects the ideas of the Rhetoric stage; but his insistence on sameness of effect (dynamic equivalence) is a clear symptom of this Linguistics stage. It is as if the sameness simply *must* be somewhere: since it cannot be located at the formal level, and since the function of a sacred text is assumed to be constant across different readers (i.e. to convert to, or confirm in, the faith), equivalence must lie precisely in the effect of such a text. This position tends to be not so much argued, with evidence, as assumed: it seems a statement of belief. (Recall Pym's view: see 1.5 above.)

The linguistic problem of translational equivalence has been a major concern also in the East European and Russian traditions of translation studies. One example of how this supermeme continues to survive is Shveitser (1993). This is a critical discussion of "equivalence" and "adequacy" (both terms are confusingly used in a number of different senses in the literature). He points out that equivalence is a notion within *parole*, not *langue*; that equivalence of higher units (such as whole texts) should take precedence over that of lower units (such as sentences); that equivalence between sender's intention and target-text effect is paramount. Moreover, it appears that *if* equivalence holds on various levels of form, semantics and function, then two texts are "fully equivalent" (51). This "full equivalence" is then said to be "an idealized construct", although "[t]his does not mean that full equivalence does not exist in reality at all" (51): it may only exist under "relatively simple communicative conditions".

2.6 Communication

In this stage the dominant metaphor for translation is sending a message to someone: I will call this the Communication meme. In reaction to previous over-emphases on either source or target, work coming within the scope of this meme-complex seeks a balance between the two: the translator is in the middle, a mediator between original writer and ultimate reader, owing loyalty to both sides. The stage represents a broadening of focus to cover the whole sociological process of translation, including a range of non-linguistic factors.

Some aspects of this approach can be seen already in Nida (e.g. 1964; Nida and Taber 1969), with his focus on the overall communicative situation of the translator and his use of notions from communication and information theory, such as channel, noise, redundancy, information load and the like.

The meme is taken further e.g. by Wilss (1977, 1982). Wilss shares the hermeneutic view of translation as a universal process of interpretation; as such it is only partly formalizable. Wilss' general theory, however, is not philosophical but linguistic, and linguistics is seen first and foremost as a communication discipline. His translation theory is an empirical one, encompassing both the translation process and the final product: translated texts are to be evaluated primarily in terms of communicative efficacy.

For Reiß and Vermeer (e.g. 1984) the communicative efficacy of a translation is primarily determined by the degree to which it fulfils its *skopos*, its aim or goal. They give the skopos concept a major theoretical status: translation is a form of action, and all action is governed by its purpose. They stress that it is the skopos of the translation that matters, not that of the original: these two skopoi may be the same (or may be assumed to be so), but this is not necessarily the case. The skopos of a text, its intended function or effect, is thus distinguished from its actual effect on its recipients. Furthermore, this view allows the concept of translation to be extended to various forms of adaptation and the like, with target texts that overtly have different functions from the original (e.g. literary adaptations for children, linguistic-gloss translations, summary translations). "Equivalence" is no longer at a premium.

Holz-Mänttäri (1984) widens the focus still further, also placing translation within a general theory of social action: the translator here stands at the centre of a communicative chain running from the initial commissioner (requester) of the translation to the ultimate receivers. The translator is regarded as an independent expert, a cultural mediator who has the authority to carry responsibility for the target text. (We are a long way now from the image of the humble copier.) Translatorial skills are not purely linguistic, either; they include the ability to find necessary background information, evaluate the relation between text and illustrations, estimate the degree of cultural adaptation needed, and so on. Translation is a cross-cultural event, as Snell-Hornby (1988) also stresses: translation theory cannot rely on linguistics, even contrastive linguistics, alone.

A central image for Holz-Mänttäri is that of the translator as text-designer. The text-to-be-designed is in the target language, of course, and one of the factors affecting the design is the source text. But many other factors are also relevant, such as time, money, readership, writer's intention, commissioner's intention, text-type, and so on. The relative weights attached to these various input factors will vary according to the particular translation task; some tasks assign a high priority to the source text itself, for instance (legal texts…), whereas in other tasks it may have a lower priority (advertisements…).

A sociological approach is also taken by Pym (1992a, b), who proposes a broad socio-politico-economic framework for the physical and semiotic transfer of texts. Additional issues here include those of what gets translated when, and who decides, and why. Pym too stresses the ethical accountability of translators.

Nord (1991) further illustrates this mode of research on translation theory. Her model of translation-oriented text analysis includes both extratextual factors (sender identity and intention, recipient identity, medium, place and time of communication, motive of communication, text function) as well as textual ones.

A philosophical framework which seems conducive to the continuing relevance of this Communication meme in translation theory is that developed by Malmkjær (1993), which draws on Davidson's response (see e.g. 1986; and below, Section 3.3) to Quine. Quine (1960) had argued against the possibility of translation in the sense of a determinate relation of equivalence between source and target utterances: translation is necessarily indeterminate, because no two people necessarily interpret a given utterance in the same way, even within the same language community, let alone across language boundaries. Quine's view thus implies that all communication is indeterminate: talk of absolute translational equivalence becomes meaningless (compare Keenan's argument against the Effability Principle, 1.2.3).

Against this view, Malmkjær builds a model of translation based on the convergence, in translational communication, of writer's and reader's beliefs about what the other knows and believes: translation is successful to the extent that the reader interprets the target text in the way the translator believed he would, and to the extent that the translator has interpreted the source text in the way its writer had intended. Note: a *convergence* or similarity of beliefs, not an identity; communication is something relative, not absolute. The model is a complex one: in simplified summary, factors influencing the translator's decisions are based on the translator's knowledge of the requester's aims, original readers, prospective target readers, original writer, use of the target text, context of source and target; and also on the influence of the source text itself (a realistic acknowledgement of the possibility of interference). Translational success is relative to the degree of convergence between the relevant factors. The crucial factors that differentiate translation from other kinds of communication are (a) the influence of the source-text language on the target-text language, and (b) the translator's knowledge of the aims of the requester (commissioner) of the translation.

It seems to me that this kind is argument is conclusive with respect to the empirical reality of translation and indeed other communication. It runs parallel to other work that also comes within this general approach: work in discourse analysis (see e.g. Hatim and Mason 1990). For instance, Gutt (1991) has argued that the fundamental principle governing translation is none other than relevance, the same relevance that governs any kind of discourse; a successful translation resembles the original in a way which is relevant to the aim of the writer/requester and the needs and cognitive environment of the reader. A similar point is made by Hönig and Kußmaul (1982: 58f.), who propose the guiding principle of "sufficient degree of precision" – relevance in another guise. Such views place translation theory firmly within the domain of pragmatics.

Gutt and others have moreover pointed out the fundamental fallacy in the assumption of "same effect" or "same function", that hangover from the equivalence debate. (In literary translation, the hangover appears as "same literary or artistic effect", as e.g. in Levý 1969.) Since any language-user interprets any utterance partly in terms of his or her previous experience of the language and of life, no two readers ever come to a given text with exactly the same set of cognitive assumptions; if this is true even within the same language, how much more true must it be for readers of a different language and/or culture altogether. We might consequently call the belief in the possibility of exactly the "same effect" the *homogeneous readership fallacy*. It represents a kind of linguistic idealism, but rests on no tenable theoretical foundations beyond the trivial truth that all readers are members of the human race.

The Communication meme is well represented in Zlateva (1993), a collection of Russian and Bulgarian papers. It is entitled "Translation as social action", and the idea of translation as a natural social and cultural activity runs right through the book. This has perhaps been a fruitful result of the Marxist insight that formal structures are (at least partly) determined by economic and social structures. (See Update section below for more recent work in the sociology of translation.)

2.7 Target

The Communication stage has been marked by a gradual weakening of the status of the source text. Eventually, indeed, the idea arises that we could turn translation theory upside down and start not with the source but the target. That is, we could start by looking at the texts that the target culture itself designates as translations (on whatever criteria). We could examine their status as independent texts in the target culture, comparing them with non-translated texts in this culture. We might then, with hindsight as it were, look back to the source texts they derive from, and examine the decisions made by their translators; but the starting point will be the *fait accompli* of the translated text itself. It is perhaps significant that the texts thus examined have often been literary ones – yet again, the meme tends to be bound to a particular type of translation.

Like the Rhetoric stage, this cluster of ideas thus gives priority to the target (the pendulum swings again). But whereas the Rhetoric meme highlighted imitation of the source text as a way of enriching the target culture, the Target meme encompasses a broader range of translation functions and relegates the source to secondary status. (Predictably, this perception in turn will eventually give rise to further reactions, proposals to reinstate the source text etc.)

This meme appears in the 1970s in the work of Even-Zohar (see e.g. his papers reprinted in 1990), and was influentially developed in translation theory by Toury, Holmes, Lefevere and others. This stage of translation thinking is surveyed e.g. by Gentzler (1993), who also explores its roots in Russian formalism and in Levý's work on literary translation (1969). See also the papers in Leuven-Zwart and Naaijkens (1991) and the appropriately named journal *Target*. The term Translation Studies is often used to describe this general research approach (after an influential paper by Holmes, originally 1972, republished in his 1988 collection).

One key aspect of this meme is its insistence on a descriptive approach rather than a prescriptive one. Whereas much previous thinking had focused on what a translation *should* look like – e.g. as determined by some kind of equivalence, by readership taste, by revelation of an underlying pure language, by optimal communicativeness – the Target meme on the contrary focuses on what translations actually *are* like, with no preconceptions about possible optimal versions. This means that this research has a strong empirical bias. It also provides access to research both on the actual end-products, i.e. the translations themselves, and on the processes that lead to these products. In other words, it is interested not only in what translations are but in what translators do, in a given culture at a given time and also more generally. (In this respect, too, it reinforces current interest in what I discuss under the following meme, below.)

A further consequence of this approach is its understanding of what actually constitutes a translation. In keeping with its general target orientation, the concept of a translation is understood in whatever terms a given target culture happens to understand it at a given time. That is to say, a translation is any text that a given culture accepts as a translation, even a "bad" translation. A "sameness" concept of equivalence is thus by no means the only kind of relation that can exist between source and target texts. Indeed, the aim of Toury's "discovery procedure" in translation research (1995: 36) is to find out what concept of equivalence a given translator actually had, with respect to a given translation task: the nature of this concept is what we set out to discover, it is not an already established fact from which we start.

Some have thought this approach to equivalence to be somewhat cavalier (see e.g. Snell-Hornby 1988: 25), but it does have the advantages of being realistic, pragmatic, and including a much wider range of texts under the translation umbrella. (This point will be elaborated in the following chapter.) It also allows for understandings and definitions of translation to change over time (as, indeed, I am illustrating myself through this exploration of a sequence of translation memes).

Another central theoretical concept here is that of the polysystem. In its most general sense, the whole of a culture is seen as a network of systems. Some of these are semiotic, and some of these again are linguistic. And some of the linguistic systems are literary: these comprise the totality of texts accepted as "literary" in a given culture at a given time. Translated texts also form a subsystem of their own. The primary research interest here has been on literary translation, with research that sometimes borders on comparative literature; one theme has been the ways in which the subsystem of translated texts overlaps with that of literary texts. To enter the target culture as a literary text, a translation must not only enter the subsystem of translated texts but also that of literary texts. A given text may change its position in the polysystem over time. Non-literary source texts may become part of the literary target polysystem (letters, diaries perhaps), and other texts may shift out of it. Systems and polysystems, in other words, are not static but dynamic, ever shifting and developing as the culture itself changes. (For more detailed discussion of these points, see Toury 1995, 2012; and Even-Zohar 1990.)

Some translations themselves may serve to shift the literary subsystem of the target culture: a classic example is the Authorized Version of the Bible in English (1611). Such texts become "primary" texts, introducing new norms and displacing the more conservative, "secondary" ones. In this way this meme also incorporates the target-enrichment idea of the Rhetoric meme, and even something of the cultural-creation idea of the Logos meme.

A major object of research here is thus the concept of the norm. Toury and others have explored and extended norm theory in some detail, and examined the way in which norms of various kinds influence the translator's decisions, and also influence the reactions of the target readership. Heylen (1993), for instance, studies in detail the development of theatrical translation norms in France over a 200-year period, norms that prioritized adherence to target-culture usage rather than fidelity to the source text and its poetics: French translations of Hamlet tended to be strongly acculturated, and themselves influenced other translations in the French theatrical polysystem. To a large extent, too, it is norms that determine the kinds of texts that tend to get translated in the first place. We shall return to norms in the following chapter.

In keeping with the dynamic concept of the polysystem, scholars working within this general approach have been interested in the literary interaction between cultures at different historical periods, and the way in which translations have played a part in this. As an activity, translating is lined up alongside other forms of rewriting such as anthologizing and historiography. Issues of ideology and power are raised, and the notion of manipulation has become current, particularly after the publication of an influential collection of papers entitled *The Manipulation of Literature. Studies in Literary Translation* (Hermans 1985). This suggests the dominant metaphor for this meme: translation is manipulation. Whatever the equivalence advocates might argue in theory, in actual fact "all translation implies a degree of manipulation of the source text for a certain purpose" (Hermans 1985: 9; see also Fawcett 1995). And translated texts, in turn, manipulate the target culture, including the target culture's perception of the source culture. Compare the effects of dubbing versus subtitling, for example: dubbing tends to be the preferred policy in nationalistic cultures which resist the foreign, whereas subtitling is more used in cultures that are readier to accept the foreign (see e.g. Danan 1991). Central and peripheral cultures, moreover, see and affect each other differently. (Recall, in this respect, the Logos meme, too.)

Some translation research within this general approach has been strongly ideological, and hence less purely descriptive. Cheyfitz (1991) argues that translation is always a form of foreign policy, always an act of violence, and often serves those in power at the expense of the underdogs. With respect to the history of translation between English and Native American languages, he shows how translations into English were designed to "civilize" the Native American culture, moulding it into the European norm, neglecting or suppressing what made the Indian cultures different, such as their lack of interest in material property and the value they gave to kinship. For Cheyfitz, this history constitutes a "poetics of imperialism": "the translation of the Indians into proper English" (1991: 10). A similar overall argument is advanced by Niranjana (1992): translation (i.e. traditional, fluent translation) inevitably involves repression of the Other, a cultural colonialization; translations are ways of "containing" the Other, of domesticating it, and hence of denying the validity of its Otherness. Robyns (1994) identifies various ways in which cultures react to the potential intrusion of the Other: whether Otherness is acknowledged at all, and whether it is permitted to intrude without being transformed into the domestic. Robyns' metaphor for translation is one of migration, the migration of discourse – here too we find the notion of spreading ideas (rather than transferring a meaning) highlighted by our meme metaphor. For later work on translation and ideology, see e.g. Calzada Pérez (2003) and Baker (2006).

One fascinating case study of the manipulative influence of translation is that of Inoue (1991) on the making of the postwar Japanese constitution. Inoue shows how the English and Japanese texts of this constitution have different illocutionary forces, how the Japanese version deliberately introduced certain features that would make the text more compatible with traditional Japanese values, and how some concepts were left vague so as to allow different interpretations by each side. The English and Japanese versions, which arose as mutual translations more or less in parallel, reflect a tolerable marriage between Western and Confucian conceptual systems, one that was ultimately acceptable to both sides precisely because of the leeway of interpretation provided by inherently flexible terms. On one hand, the result was the successful selling of MacArthur's constitution to the Japanese; on the other, it was the successful subtle moulding of American ideals to accord with the traditional values of Japanese society.

Translators thus have manipulative power. But translators are not entirely free agents, of course: their own work, and indeed attitudes, are also subject to constraints, they themselves are manipulated. Lefevere (1992), for instance, explores a number of constraints that influence not only decisions about what is to be translated but also the translation process itself: these include ideology, the power of patronage (the requester or commissioner of the translation), target-language poetics norms, the universe of discourse (subject matter), and of course the natures of the source and target languages themselves (see further below, 3.7). One of his innovative concepts is that of the "refracted text", one that has been adapted, rewritten or translated with an ideological or artistic slant overtly different from that of the original. The work of some feminist translators is a good illustration of this (see e.g. von Flotow 1991).

In addition to the main issues outlined above, descriptive research here has also looked at the phenomenon of secondary or indirect translation (translation via a third, mediating language), and even pseudo-translations (texts that are, or have been, claimed to be translations but in fact are not). Both these topics are explored e.g. by Toury (1995, 2012). There has also been a growing interest in such issues as translation copyright (Venuti 1995b), and the paratexts of translations (i.e. subsidiary material surrounding a text, such as title pages, editorial prefaces, blurbs on the cover etc.: see e.g. Kovala 1996).

All in all, the descriptive approach takes a highly pragmatic view of (mostly literary) translation, looking at it in a broad socio-cultural and ideological context, rather like the way in which literary pragmatics has been exploring literary phenomena (see e.g. Sell 1990). A major project in this context is the Göttingen research group, which has undertaken an in-depth study of literary translation into German (see Schultze 1987; and subsequent volumes).

In simple terms, then, Translation Studies of this kind deals with cultural data and investigates how such data can affect people's lives (Bassnett and Lefevere 1990: 12). (See Update section for further comments.)

2.8 Cognition

I mentioned above that one of the interests of the Target meme is what translators actually do, what decisions they make and why. "Every descriptive study of translated texts involves the description of translational *solutions* along with their *relationships* to their counterparts in the source texts, with an intention of reconstructing the *considerations* (or the decision processes) which yield them", argued Toury (1980: 89; emphasis original).

Expanding on this idea of the translator's "considerations", Toury later proposed that one of the goals of Translation Studies should be to discover "translation laws": the laws that govern translatorial behaviour (see e.g. Toury 1991). In Toury's sense these laws would be behavioural rather than cognitive (and I return to them in the following chapter), but they do illustrate a growing interest in the translating process. Whereas the Target-culture meme stressed translation as something that people do, the Cognition meme stresses that people do it in their heads. The overall metaphor I propose for this meme is, therefore: translation is thinking.

Typical issues here are: what goes on in the translator's head? What do I, as a translator, experience as I translate? What is a translator's self-awareness like? Indeed, does it help to be self-aware? How does the translator's decision-making process work?

Current research within this approach is influenced by ideas in cognitive linguistics and cognition science, and is perhaps also inspired by the same fascination with the whole phenomenon of consciousness that has led to developments in brain research. (See, for instance, Dennett 1991.) More indirectly, we can also discern the long shadow of Chomskyan mentalistic linguistics, with its fundamental hypothesis of language being a window on the mind, with linguistics as a branch of psychology. The ultimate goal of the questions raised by this meme is no less than an understanding of the mind itself.

The meme has a surprisingly long ancestry. In 1685 we find the Earl of Roscommon writing as follows, in a verse essay of "good advice" to translators (in Lefevere (ed.) 1992: 43):

> The first great work (a Task perform'd by few)
> Is that your self may to your self be True:
> No Masque, no Tricks, no Favor, no Reserve;
> Dissect your Mind, examine ev'ry Nerve.

In other words, a translator should, above all, be self-aware.

There are a number of manifestations of this meme in later work. The idea of translation as a decision-making process appears in the works of several scholars. Levý (1967), for instance, develops the application of game theory to this process: each decision is affected by the sum of all previous decisions; at each decision-point, the costs and benefits of each option can be weighed up and the best decision taken according to the Minimax principle: minimum effort, maximum effect. Similarly, Jumpelt (1961) called for a translation theory that would focus on the factors that affect the translator's choices: the primary focus of such a theory would not be linguistic but psychological. There are also pedagogical applications of the notion of translating as problem solving, for instance Hervey and Higgins (1992), and Kiraly (1995).

Some of Wilss' work also relates to this approach, especially his later work (e.g. 1988). Classifications of translation procedures are psychological rather than linguistic, one important criterion being degree of habituation. The concepts of intuition and creativity also receive more attention.

Gutt's theory of translation and relevance (1991) looks at first sight like a pragmatic one, but his basic theoretical domain is in fact cognitive: the mental state of the translator. He says explicitly (20) that the domain of relevance theory, and by implication also the proper place of translation theory, is "mental faculties rather than texts or processes of text production". His own study seeks to account for translation "in terms of the communicative competence assumed to be part of our minds" (20).

Perhaps the most typical manifestations of this meme, however, are think-aloud protocol (TAP) studies. Based on verbal reports by practising translators, recorded as they are actually translating, these studies have provided tentative but tantalizing insights into "what goes on in the translator's head" (as Krings put it in the title of his book (1986), which helped to pioneer this line of research). Interesting results of this research include information about the way translators proceed by alternating and spiralling between automatic processing and conscious problem-solving; the kinds of problem-solving strategies translators tend to use; the positive effect of the translator's own subjective involvement in the text and its topic; the influence of the translator's perception of his or her own role; and the cognitive processing differences between professionals and trainees or amateurs. (See, for instance, Gerloff 1986; Faerch and Kasper 1987; Tirkkonen-Condit 1990, 1991; Kußmaul 1991; Jääskeläinen 1993; Fraser 1993; Kiraly 1995. See also Update, below.)

An important spur to this kind of empirical research has been the criticism of more speculative models of the translation process such as Nida's three-stage one (analysis, transfer, restructuring). Lörscher (1989), in particular, pleaded powerfully for a more empirical approach to the study of the translator's decision-making process, and his own later work exemplified this (e.g. 1991).

Another influence has been the computer. Tommola (1986), for instance, reported on experiments in which the translator's keyboard was linked to a computer in such a way as to record each key-depression over time. The data can then be analysed for evidence of deletions, restructurings, pauses, etc. (See Update section.)

One of the most startling claims that have been made in this context is that of Gentzler (1993: 195), when he suggests that the study of translation may not only reveal insights about human consciousness but even about unconsciousness; that translation studies allow us some access to what is "out of sight". Quite how such claims might be empirically justified is not clear to me, but the prospect is certainly an intriguing one.

2.9 Theory in the current meme pool

The current pool of translation memes is a highly heterogeneous one, containing traces of all the preceding memes or meme-complexes (and perhaps others too). These traces have roots in different historical periods: some seem to derive from what I have called the Linguistics stage, with its stress on formal equivalence and its underlying positivistic philosophy; others (which tend to equate translation theory with the theory of literary translation only) originate in the Logos stage, marked by a hermeneutic approach and an occasionally almost mystical belief in the powers of a pure language; and others again have a grounding in communication theory or cultural studies, or aspire to psychological realism. Moreover, some memes in the pool appear to be in the ascendant while others are fading.

However, one fundamental reason for the heterogeneity seems to be a lack of agreement about what (if anything) a theory of translation should look like, and it is this aspect of the current meme pool that I now turn to (cf. also Chesterman 2007).

The diversity of views on this point might, of course, be taken as a positive sign of feverish intellectual activity; but it also recalls the old Indian tale of the blind men and the elephant: each touches a different part of the animal – the tail, the foot, the ear etc. – and believes that this particular part represents the whole. Consider the following quotations:

> Translation theory is a misnomer, a blanket term, a possible translation, therefore a translation label, for *Übersetzungswissenschaft*. In fact translation theory is neither a theory nor a science, but the body of knowledge that we have and have still to have about the process of translating. (Newmark 1981: 19)

> Had translation depended for its survival on theory, it would have died out long before Cicero. (Kelly 1979: 219)

> Traditional translation theory has been intensively investigated.
> (Snell-Hornby 1988: 8)

> [T]he time is ripe (perhaps overripe) for a theory of translation to emerge.
> (Bell 1991: 4)

> Translation theory goes hand in hand with translation methodology at every stage, so that it acts as a body of reference both for the translation process procedure and for translation criticism. [...] It is an applied and interrelated discipline... [...] As I see it, any talk of a single translation theory [...] is a waste of time. (Newmark 1981: 37)

> Translation theory, like most Western sciences of language and other human behavior, is traditionally an immaterial business: an ideal model of the finished product to be striven for by the translator; an ideal map or flow chart of procedures (to be) followed by the human translator and – ultimately – programmed into the computer. (Robinson 1991: ix)

> [M]ost of the theoretical presentations [about translation] that we have had until now, although they have called themselves theories, are not really theories in the strict sense. (Holmes 1978: 57)

> [T]he only endeavour approaching this "strict sense" [i.e. that of Holmes, in the preceding quotation here] could well turn out to be Quine's theory of indeterminacy in translation, widely thought to be a theory not of translation but of untranslatability. (Pym 1992a: 181)

> A Theoretical Account of Translation – Without a Translation Theory.
> (Gutt 1990: 135)

The contradictions here are striking: we have no theory of translation; we have a lot of theory of translation; translation theory is practical, applied; translation theory is idealistic; translation theory is a theory of untranslatability; a theoretical account of translation does not need a translation theory. At bottom, these disagreements reveal very different views about what actually constitutes a "theory".

Popper's schema can be of use here, in disentangling this conceptual mess. Recall that, on Popper's view, a theory is a tentative answer to a question, a hypothetical solution to a problem. The nature of any theory will therefore be crucially determined by the nature of the question it is designed to answer.

Through this chapter I have suggested metaphors to encapsulate the main theme of a particular translation meme. These metaphors have been of some expository use, but in some sense they also themselves represent theories, inasmuch as they are "views" of translation. Many of the traditional ideas about translation also had to do with the question of what translation (or translating) *is*, or what it is *like*, and the answers (i.e. tentative theories) were often in the form of metaphors or similes (see e.g. Koller 1972: 40f.). Some of the most common of these early answers were:

- translating is like giving a musical performance of an original
- a translation is a reproduction of a work of art, a copy
- translating is giving something a change of dress
- a translation is a struggle, a conflict between two languages
- to translate is to betray the original

A more recent one that we have already met is:

- translating is transferring information, decoding and recoding; a translator is like a computer.

Such metaphorical theories can be valuable conceptual tools; they may provide enlightenment, insight, understanding; yet they are not empirical theories in the scientific sense (on Popper's criterion) because they cannot be falsified, being basically interpretations.

Translation theory has of course also posed many other, more specific questions, in addition to the basic one of what translation *is*. Many variants of Popper's initial problem, P1, have been investigated and answers proposed. Some of the general questions that have received attention are:

- What is the best way to translate?
- What is untranslatable?
- What is equivalence?
- How does translation affect culture?
- How could we programme a machine to translate?

- How should translations be assessed?
- How can translation best be taught?
- What counts as a translation?
- What are the general laws of translation behaviour?
- What goes on in the translator's head?

Let us now return to the conflicting views on theory that were cited above, and see whether they can be reconciled in the light of Popper's view of how theory develops, as a progression from the initial problem (P1) to Tentative Theory (TT) to Error Elimination (EE). I will suggest glosses for them, adding some comments in brackets, in the same order, without repeating the quotes themselves.

> *Newmark*: Translation theory is the accumulation of all the TTs that have so far survived the EE process. (To the extent that this set of tentative theories is in principle falsifiable, this body of knowledge is empirical and hence scientific.)
>
> *Kelly*: Pre-Ciceronian theory was metaphorical, not empirical.
>
> *Snell-Hornby*: There are a great many P1s, and corresponding TTs, and we know a great deal about them.
>
> *Bell*: We have no final, all-embracing truths about translation (true, but trivially so). And/or: there is no one answer, or closed set of axiom-like answers, that can be satisfactorily given to all the questions we want to ask about translation, i.e. no translation Theory Of Everything (true, but trivially so, again).
>
> *Newmark*: TT goes hand in hand with EE. There is no translation Theory Of Everything.
>
> *Robinson*: "Ideal translations" serve as a regulative idea in theory formulation. Some tentative theories answer questions about how to programme computers to translate.
>
> *Holmes*: Most TTs about translation are not formalized; the various mini-theories (TTs) do not relate systematically into a well-defined set.
>
> *Pym*: It is widely thought that the most rigorously corroborated TT so far has enabled us to distinguish a fundamental P (about translatability) from its negation (and thus to define this P more precisely). (Pym summarizes Quine's point as being that translators may "legitimately disagree" about how something should be translated: there can be no one translation that is necessarily predetermined to be correct. In other words: for any given P1 "how to translate X?" there will be more than one possible TT.)
>
> *Gutt*: The P1 "what is a translation theory?" can be seen as a specific instance of a more general P2. (Gutt argues that the problems of translation theory can be subsumed under those dealt with by Relevance Theory.)

I think this kind of analysis reveals something of the current state of the art in translation theory. In terms of Popper's schema, differences of opinion seem to stem from three main sources. First, scholars vary in what they take as their initial problem, P1. Second, they vary in their criteria for an acceptable answer to a P1. And third, they vary in respect to their point of focus on Popper's schema: some focus on the problem itself, others on TT and others on EE. It is largely because of all these differences that "translation theory" as a whole still remains somewhat incoherent.

The main strength of the theoretical knowledge that we have is the wide range of questions dealt with (P1s). One main weakness is the lack of empirical EE, so that TTs often remain on a metaphorical level. Another is the lack of an overall framework which would relate lower-level TTs in some consistent manner without denying their relevance. To argue as Gutt does that translation is subject to the same principles that govern any other form of communication is (trivially) true; nevertheless, translation theorists are interested precisely in what makes translation *different* from other forms of communication. An awareness that P1 is a subtype of P2 is conceptually helpful, but it does not necessarily sweep P1 away.

2.10 Update

At the end of this chapter in the original edition, I made a few predictions about where Translation Studies seemed to be heading at that time. I thought there would be more empirical and experimental research, and more interest in socio-cultural issues, ideology and ethics. I looked forward to more work proposing and testing explanations of various kinds, both reasons (internal to the translator) and causes (external). If all of the eight meme-complexes presented continued to be influential in guiding research, I thought there would be a need for some kind of overall theoretical framework that would relate them.

Although those particular predictions have turned out to be reasonably good, not much progress has been made in the search for a unified general theory of translation. Indeed, one of the outcomes of the Forum debate in *Target* that was initiated by Rosemary Arrojo and myself (Chesterman and Arrojo 2000) was the widely felt view that our understanding of translation is best enhanced by using a multitude of different theories and approaches; not everyone is looking for an overall theory. And not everyone feels at home in an empirical framework like the descriptive-explanatory framework that underlies the approach taken by this book. Some scholars are more inspired by a hermeneutic view, and others by the needs of translator training and the development of translation aids. (See *Target* issues 12.1 to 14.1, 2000–2002.)

However, it still seems that there is a general consensus on the current goals of translation research, regardless of the methodologies chosen. In general terms, we are all trying to better *understand* the object of our research. More specifically, research has the following general aims:

a. to describe what translation is and what translators do;
b. to explain why translations are the way they are and why translators do what they do, and to make predictions about translatorial behaviour;
c. to assess the effects and consequences of translations.

Working toward these goals means investing in textual analysis, sociological and cultural analysis, historical analysis, cognitive research on translators' decision-making, ethical and ideological analysis, and so on: Translation Studies is a huge field. Some research also brings in a quality variable: what translation procedures etc. tend to have the best effects (on which readers)? (And what is meant by "best"?)

One of the criticisms I received on my eight stages of the evolution of translation memes was that I had not paid enough attention to the social background of the ideas I was discussing; my Popperian view of the theoretical development was oversimplified. Translation theories do not emerge only from the context of previous theories, but also from socio-cultural contexts (as Kuhn argued against Popper: see Fuller [2003] 2006). Pym (2011) is one scholar who has since helped to fill this gap, pointing out for instance how skopos theory served an institutional need to raise the academic status of translator training in Germany and distinguish it from traditional language teaching, and how Descriptive Translation Studies evolved mainly in small cultures where translation was highly valued, stimulated by meetings of key scholars at particular conferences. Other views of the development of translation theory that have appeared during the last decade or so include Snell-Hornby (2006) and Munday (2012); and see also several general handbooks such as *Handbuch Translation* (Snell-Hornby et al. 2004), the *Routledge Handbook of Translation Studies* (Millán and Bartrina 2012), and the Benjamins *Handbook of Translation Studies* (Gambier and Doorslaer, four volumes 2010–2013).

With respect to the *Linguistics meme* (cf. 2.5), one major new development has been corpus studies and the search for so-called universals of translation. Borrowed from linguistics, the corpus studies methodology has inspired a good deal of empirical and statistical work on translations. Pym (2011) suggests that the popularity of this approach, which originated in the UK, had to do with the influx of foreign students to British universities and their translation departments, bringing with them enticing possibilities of contrastive research between

English and other languages. One of the pioneers was Mona Baker, whose seminal paper (1993) popularized the term "universals", borrowed from linguistics. The term "universal" itself was perhaps somewhat misleading, because scholars were looking for probabilistic tendencies. Other terms were also used, such as Toury's "laws" of interference and standardization (1995).

Looking for translation universals meant setting up large computer corpora of translations and comparable non-translations, and/or translations plus their source texts, and doing statistical analyses on the relative frequencies of items of different kinds, with the aim of discovering linguistic patterns that make translations different from other texts. Various hypotheses concerning general translation tendencies have been proposed and tested, and this work is continuing, with corpora being set up in different languages and unversities. Comparing translations with their source texts, many studies have examined claims e.g. about translators' tendencies to explicitate, to normalize style and dialect, and to translate more closely when a given (literary) text has already been translated before into the same language (the so-called retranslation hypothesis). Comparing translations with non-translated texts in the same target language, studies suggest e.g. that translations tend to use simpler language yet also untypical collocations, and to under-represent items that are special to the target language (this latter claim is known as the unique items hypothesis: see e.g. Tirkkonen-Condit 2004). This search for so-called universals has not gone uncriticized. Critics have pointed out, for instance, that the corpora used in these studies are not representative of *all* translations – e.g. they do not include obviously bad translations – and that we do not even have an agreed definition of what constitutes a translation in the first place. Others have argued, rather differently, that these tendencies are just signs of poor quality. For further discussion and references, see especially Mauranen and Kujamäki (2004), and relevant entries in the handbooks mentioned above.

The search for possible universals has also been relevant to a very different issue in translation research. This is the feeling, among some scholars, that translation theory is too dominated by western ideas: we should take more account of concepts and research coming from other parts of the world: only in this way, the argument goes, can we gain an understanding of what translation means and has meant *universally*. This debate is illustrated in the discussion on universalism in issues 7(1) and 7(3) of the journal *Translation Studies*, starting with Chesterman (2014).

What I called the *Communication meme* in translation research has expanded enormously over the past two decades, in what we have experienced as a "sociological turn". Here, the central focus is no longer on texts as such but on people: translators of course, but also editors, revisers, clients and readers of different kinds, translation company managers, and so on. Scholars have borrowed from sociology both theories (such as Bourdieu, Actor Network Theory) and methods (such as questionnaires, interviews). This new turn has investigated the sociology of translations as products (translation flows between cultures, market and economic issues, etc.); the sociology of translators themselves (e.g. their power – or lack of it – as agents, the role of their professional associations); and the sociology of the translation process (e.g. revision procedures, and translation policies in organizations and institutions). One trend of this kind of research has been an interest in different kinds of processes, illustrating a distinction originally made by Toury, between the translation act and the translation event. The translation act is defined as taking place at the cognitive level; as such, it is not directly observable, but we can make inferences on the basis of what we observe. The translation event, on the other hand, is defined as taking place at the behavioural level, e.g. from the first commissioning of a work (or selection of a translator) to the final delivery, payment, and even reader reactions. (See Toury 1995: 249, and his expanded discussion in 2012: 67). For examples of work on the sociology of translation, see e.g. Pym at al. (2006), and Wolf and Fukari (2007), and for a programmatic outline see Chesterman (2009). The journal *Translation Studies* has a special focus on sociological approaches.

The empirical *descriptive view* introduced under the Target meme has continued to expand, for instance in the direction of the sociological studies mentioned above, and also in historical studies (see e.g. vol. 20, no. 1, 2014, of *The Translator*, a special issue on translation and history). A key work in the methodology of translation history is Pym (1998). Increasing attention – both descriptive and applied – has also been given to audiovisual translation, in its various forms. For a brief survey, see e.g. Gambier (2012). Some of the enormous influence of Toury's work in Descriptive Translation Studies can be seen in Pym et al. (2008).

Research on translation and *cognition* has also flourished, with the use of new technical tools such as the Translog keystroke logging program developed at the Copenhagen Business School, which has later also incorporated data from eye-tracking (see Jakobsen 2011 for an introduction to this kind of research, and Carl et al. 2016 for some of the newest work). The interest in the cognitive processes that are inferred to underlie translation has also brought translation research closer to the study of interpreting (e.g. Ferreira and Schwieter 2015). There have been a number of special journal issues on this theme. Examples are: *Describing Cognitive Processes in Translation: Acts and Events* (vol. 8 no. 2 of *Translation and Interpreting Studies*, 2013); *Interdisciplinarity in Translation and Interpreting Process Research* (special issue of *Target*, 2013, vol. 25 no. 1); *Minding translation* (special issue of *MonTI*, 2014, no. 1, available online at http://dti.ua.es/

es/documentos/monti/monti-especial-1-portada-indice.pdf). See also the papers on process research published in the journal *Translation & Interpreting* (vol. 7, no. 1, 2015), with a useful survey of the state of the art in this area.

CHAPTER 3

From memes to norms

What happens to translation memes when they survive for some time in the meme pool? If a meme comes to dominate (for any reason: practical, political, cultural, aesthetic…), and competing memes fade, one course of development is that such a meme becomes regarded as a norm – whether imposed by an authority or simply accepted as such. For instance, at certain periods of history the translation traditions introduced in the preceding chapter became *de facto* norms. Perhaps the most extreme example is the Word-of-God meme: when and where this dominated, translations carried out within the framework of other, competing memes would simply have been declared wrong, or "not translations" at all; the translator might even have been penalized: recall the fate of Dolet, who lost his life for translating too freely, for breaking the prevalent norm.

At their strongest, these norms seem like memes that have been set in concrete, rigidly determining both the theory and the practice of translation. We might indeed define norms, preliminarily and pre-theoretically, as memes which are accepted (for whatever reasons – even threats) by a community as being conducive to behaviour perceived as useful: behaviour that favours the survival of the individuals concerned, for instance. They thus become dominant by gradual emergence or via antagonistic struggle, or both, and highly influential on thought and behaviour (cf. Zalan 1990).

This chapter offers an account of translation norms. It is based partly on norm theory and partly on work that has been done by other scholars on translation norms. The aim is not to offer explanations of *why* certain memes seem to have become norms: see some of the general historical and political factors mentioned in the preceding chapter, and the references cited there. Rather, the aim is to present an analysis of the concept of a translation norm, and to suggest a way of classifying the main kinds of norms that seem to be relevant to translation theory.

In order to avoid misunderstandings, we must start with some conceptual clarifications, especially regarding the term "normative".

3.1 Normative vs. prescriptive

It has become customary in Translation Studies to make a clear distinction between prescriptive and descriptive approaches to the subject. This is a point associated particularly with the Target-culture meme-complex, as mentioned in the previous chapter. The distinction is well motivated. Research on what translations and translators actually *are* (or have been) is by definition descriptive. Applied research, or translator training, naturally focuses on what translators *should* do, on what translations *should* be like, prescriptively; but this is not the task of translation theory itself.

The problem arises, however, when the term "normative" is thrown into this distinction. For some scholars, "normative" seems to be identical with, and no more than, "prescriptive". To take just one example: Bell (1991: 10) writes:

> Translation theory finds itself today seriously out of step with the mainstream of intellectual endeavour in the human sciences and in particular in the study of human communication; to our mutual impoverishment. The fundamental cause of this state of affairs is, we firmly believe, the *normative* approach – the setting up of a series of maxims consisting of do's and don'ts... (Emphasis added)

For other scholars, "normative" seems to be both prescriptive and descriptive, at the same time. Komissarov (1993: 64) begins a paper on translation norms by asking to what extent translation theory should be normative, "to what extent should it strive to formulate some principles, rules and recommendations?" Principles and rules can be formulated descriptively, as one can describe the principles of orienteering or the rules of chess, for instance; but recommendations are something different: prescriptive.

Both these examples illustrate unfortunate usages: the first because it appears to deny the term "normative" any legitimate scientific sense – the kind of perfectly standard sense it has in norm theory, for instance; and the second because it confuses a descriptive sense with a prescriptive one.

The point is, of course, that "normative" is an ambiguous term. The Collins English Dictionary offers the following definitions:

> 1. implying, creating or prescribing a norm or standard, as in language: *normative grammar.*
> 2. of, relating to, or based on norms.

The first of these senses is prescriptive, the second descriptive. In its perfectly ordinary descriptive sense, then, "normative" means simply "having to do with norms". Descriptively, we can try to state what the norms seem to be within a given field of behaviour. True, this often means no more than making inferences from the evidence provided by people's actual practice. Strictly speaking, descriptive statements of norms are thus causal hypotheses: I submit that people tend to stand on the right on escalators (in countries where they do) because they accept the existence of a norm to this effect. Whether or not an individual person *follows* these norms, what attitude one might have towards them, what consequences one might personally draw from their existence – these are quite different questions. True, a descriptive statement of a norm may sometimes be intended prescriptively, as in indirect speech acts ("Excuse me, but people normally stand on the right here in Helsinki, you know…"), and also interpreted prescriptively; but the two senses can still be kept apart.

Even more unfortunately (at least for norm theory), the term "norm" itself also tends to be misunderstood. For some, norms appear to become bogeys set up by nasty theoreticians to humiliate hard-working translators. Here is Robinson's view, for instance (1991:xi; emphasis original, underlining added):

> It is instructive to note, for example, what has happened when translation theorists have insisted that translation is fundamentally a cognitive process governed systematically by abstract structures or normative rules: they have, almost by definition, situated themselves methodologically at an Archimedes point above or beyond the complexity of translation practice and then convinced themselves that practical translation typically fails because it cannot lift itself up out of the muck and mire of specific cases. Translators traduce, in this view, because they translate intuitively. They translate now this way, now that, however feels right in each isolated situation, without organizing their intuitive decisions into a coherent system of norms – or else, worse, they intuitively organize their decisions into the *wrong* system of norms (word-for-word instead of sense-for-sense, say). "We could help them!" these theorists cry. "We have considered the matter at a more comprehensive general level and could guide them to the right decision in *every* situation."

This looks like parody; but I think it is not. It genuinely represents the view that any attempt to state norms is an encroachment on the free intuition of the translator, a view based on an exclusively prescriptive concept of norms. Such a view has no bearing on the arguments and analysis proposed in this book. In the preceding chapter, for instance, I have outlined some of the ways in which often prescriptive ideas about translation have developed, but my own overall approach has been descriptive, albeit argumentative in places.

Henceforth, throughout this book, I shall use the terms "normative" and "norm" in a purely descriptive sense. I am thus taking translation theory to be (among other things) a normative discipline, so that its object is the description, understanding and explanation of translation norms. We shall return to other aspects of this point below. But before we come to norms of translation, we need to set the scene with a look at norm theory itself.

3.2   Norm theory

This is not the place for a detailed excursion into norm theory, but there are a number of norm-theoretical points that should be clarified before we proceed. Like translation theory, norm theory too has been split between prescriptive approaches ("imperative theories") and descriptive ones ("practice theories"). I shall take the latter view, strongly endorsed by Bartsch (1987): that is, norms are here understood not to be "orders or prescriptions which are issued by a superior to a subordinate" (Bartsch 1987:76), but rather descriptive of particular practices within a given community.

Bartsch defines norms as the "social reality of correctness notions" (xiv). On this view, people in a given community inevitably share certain ideas about the "correctness" of a particular act of behaviour (or indeed a particular entity or artefact): there is a degree of agreement as to whether the act is "correct" in some sense. To take my example again: in some cultures people tend to keep to the right when standing on escalators: this is "the norm", this is "correct behaviour", and is agreed to be such. One does not break this norm with impunity: standing on the left (if there is a crowd) can justifiably arouse comments, "excuse me's", even criticism ("You should be on the other side, this side is supposed to be kept free").

As "social reality", norms exist intersubjectively. Individuals have individual knowledge of norms, but norms are only recognized by virtue of their social existence. Norms reside in the social consciousness, but they must be (at least potentially) accessible to individual consciousness, for, as Itkonen (1983:73) puts it, "norms not known to exist do not exist".

More technically, a norm may be defined as follows (adapted from Bartsch 1987:76):

> Let S = a given society, C = a given set of conditions, X = any individual belonging to S, A = a given act.
> Then: there exists a norm governing A if and only if all the following conditions hold:
> 1. Most members of S regularly do A under C.
> 2. If X does not do A, members of S may criticize X and other members of S will regard such criticism as justified.
> 3. Members of S use such expressions as "X ought to do A under C" or "it is the rule that under C, people in S do A" or "the right thing to do under C is A" in order to justify their own or others' actions or criticisms.

Note that all these conditions must hold in order for us to postulate the existence of a norm. Condition (1) alone merely states a common practice, condition (2) adds the point that the practice is accepted as being valid and desirable, and condition (3) the point that norms are accessible to intersubjective consciousness: we know them and can talk about them.

Norms thus stand midway between judicial laws and conventions. Mandatory laws are absolute, objective; they are established by an authority and enforced by an authority; law-breakers (when caught) are penalized by an authority. True, all these authorities act in the name of society, but it is their nature *qua* authorities that makes a law a law. Conventions, on the other hand, represent practices that are "weaker" than norms: breaking a convention is merely "unconventional", and does not provoke generally justified criticism (see, on this distinction, D. Lewis 1969). Conventions, in other words, are not binding: they are arbitrary regularities of behaviour, arbitrary in the sense that they do not necessarily have any external motivation. At their weakest, conventions are merely fashions: they embody statistical preferences only.

We have so far been considering norms in a rather general, behavioural sense, as guiding actions such as standing on an escalator: these are in fact social norms. But there are other types too: in particular, there are ethical norms and technical norms (see Bartsch 1987: 170f.). Ethical norms have also been studied descriptively. Indeed, entire ethical theories have been based on objective descriptions of the ethical norms existing in a given society at a given time; these can be compared with the norms of other times and places, attempts can be made to set up "universal norms", and the like. (One classic example is Jodl 1918; see Chesterman 1993.)

Technical norms may be further subdivided into process norms and product norms. Process (or production) norms regulate processes, specifying correct or good methods for doing something. Product norms define what counts as a "correct" product.

I shall argue below that translation theory needs all these types of norms: social, ethical and technical.

What about the function of norms? Ultimately, norms have an evolutionary function: they make life easier (for the majority at least). They do this, ideally, by regulating behaviour in such a way that it is optimally beneficial to all parties, by creating and maintaining social order, by facilitating material and social interaction, even by facilitating cognitive processing. In brief, norms save both time and effort. They "reduce the complexity of perceiving and evaluating states of affairs and behaviour and thus make effective action possible" (Bartsch 1987: 173).

More specifically, we can say that norms have this contributory effect by virtue of their function as expectations: reasonable expectations make it easier to predict the future and hence act rationally. Bartsch puts it this way (1987: 173):

> Successful ways of perceiving and acting become persistent and thus 'frozen patterns' of orientation. They are more than social habits as they acquire a normative force in the population. As norm kernels [i.e. the actual contents of norms], the regularities in these patterns provide the individuals in [a population] P with an orientation towards reality (facts, possible states of affairs) and action; this orientation is coordinated for the members of P. It consists basically of expectations about socially relevant things and events, of expectations about the behaviour and intentions of others, and of expectations about others' expectations about one's own behaviour and intentions.

We shall also return to this crucial notion of expectation below.

Thus far we have been looking at norms as positive phenomena, serving a useful purpose. The concept of regime discussed by Pym (e.g. 1992a: 140–141) stresses this positive aspect: a regime is defined as a set of principles, norms and regulations based on participants' expectations, the purpose of which is to facilitate international relations in a particular field. Yet norms may also be felt more negatively as constraints, as restrictions to be challenged or overruled. I shall take up this more critical point of view at various points in subsequent chapters.

One further preliminary point needs to be made about norms at this stage, and that concerns their validation. How do we know that a norm is valid? There are two basic views on this. One (the imperative theory) argues that norms are validated by a norm authority, from above, and are sometimes even imposed by such an authority. The other (the practice theory: cf. the conditions for norms specified above) argues that norms are validated by their very existence: in other words, if a norm is acknowledged to exist, it is automatically acknowledged to be valid. There are no non-valid norms, although there might of course be "ex-norms" that are no longer valid and hence no longer current norms. On this view, then, one could fairly say "N used to be a norm but most people don't follow it nowadays", but it would be contradictory to say "N *is* a norm but most people don't follow it". By contrast, note, it would not be contradictory to say "L is a law but most people don't obey it". It would not be contradictory, of course, to say "there are two clashing norms here, N and M, in two different subsections of the population; some people follow N and others M".

I think translation norms have both kinds of validation, both by authority and by practice, as we shall see in due course.

3.3 Norms of language

Before turning to translation norms, however, it will be useful to recall certain key concepts regarding norms of language as a whole. At the most general level, norms of language fall into three main types. In the first place, there are product norms describing the notions of "correct" phonology, morphology, syntax, semantics, lexis etc. in a given speech community. Recall that "correct" means no more than "accepted as being correct by (most of) the members of this community". These norms are, in the view of many linguists at least, the object of study of linguistics (see Itkonen 1983).

But these product norms, these expectancies of the speech community, are in turn based on two higher-order norms, in fact process norms. One of these is the communication norm. Informally stated, this norm requires us (as speakers) to communicate in such a way that others recognize our intention, and (as hearers) to interpret in accordance with the speaker's intention. To do this is to behave rationally: to behave in such a way that an action is adequate to its goal, the goal here being the achievement of understanding.

This communication norm is given a more explicit philosophical treatment by Davidson (1986). In Davidson's account, when we set out to communicate with a hearer we already have some idea about how the other party is likely in general to interpret whatever we say: this expectation is the speaker's "prior theory". (Writing this book in English, I implicitly expect you to understand the general norms of standard English.) But on a given speech occasion, we may wish the hearer to interpret slightly differently: this is the speaker's "passing theory", the one I want you, the hearer, to use now. (In this book I want you, for instance, to understand "normative" in an exclusively descriptive sense.) The hearer also has a prior theory (general expectations pertaining to the interpreting of certain kinds of utterances) and a passing theory (the one the hearer actually uses to interpret a given utterance). Communication is successful to the extent that hearer's and speaker's passing theories converge: to the extent that you actually do interpret me the way I intend you to interpret me.

The communication norm is obviously a pragmatic one, and has much to do with Gricean notions of co-operation and relevance (Grice 1975), and other social norms governing interaction between people. Grice has been criticized for extrapolating Anglo-American or Western European norms into universals (see e.g. Wierzbicka 1991), and his maxims must evidently be interpreted with respect to particular cultures, but I do not think this detracts from their universal applicability. For example, with respect to his maxim of manner (be clear, etc.), the normative degree of indirectness or ambiguity may vary from culture to culture. The actual interpretation of the communication norm, for instance in terms of how much information should be given, or even with what degree of truthfulness, must surely be culture-bound.

The second higher-order norm of language is an ethical one: Bartsch calls it the norm of honesty, or sincerity, and formulates it thus: "Conform to the norms of communication (interaction) as long as you must assume that the hearer (partner) cannot directly recognize the breaching of the norms!" (1987: 61). In other words, if you do breach norms, e.g. in ironic usage, do so in such a way that your hearer recognizes that you are breaching them. Compare Grice's maxims of quality (do not say things you believe to be false, or for which you lack adequate evidence) and manner (be clear, unambiguous, etc.). Obviously, *not* to follow this norm would be to distort the communication. This might, of course, indeed be the intention, as in propaganda, lying, disinformation and the like.

Two further points need to be made on norms of language. The first one returns to the distinction made above between norms and conventions. From the phylogenetic point of view, norms of language are conventions, to the extent that any language structure or usage is "arbitrary": these norms *originate* in conventions (conventions being one example of memes, as I suggested earlier). But ontogenetically, that is, from the point of view of any individual entering a speech community and indeed any individual already in such a community, norms of language are experienced not as mere conventions but as being prescriptive (Bartsch 1987: 110). If I wish to communicate rationally in English, there is a limit to the amount of deviance which my English-speaking hearers will accept; and it is precisely the norms of language that set the boundaries to this permissible deviance.

The second point concerns the fuzziness of norms. Snell-Hornby, for instance (1988: 49f.), follows Coseriu (1970) in placing norms midway between abstract *langue* and concrete texts. The *langue* or language system exerts a more-or-less absolute prescriptive force but actual texts are fairly idiosyncratic realizations. Coseriu also saw norms as being prescriptive, but Snell-Hornby feels them to be "not entirely" prescriptive: for her they seem to be akin to conventions, prototypes. She stresses that linguistic norms are not rigid lines of demarcation between permitted and non-permitted usage: norms have fuzzy boundaries, and some seem stronger than others. Stylistic norms, for instance, can sometimes be broken with more impunity than grammatical norms. In my discussion of norms I would like to maintain the distinction between norms and conventions (as defined above). However, I take the point about the inherent fuzziness of norms, ranging from "obligatory" to "preferred", and will assume it as self-evident in what follows.

3.4 What counts as a translation?

One further preliminary point still needs to be discussed: what counts as a translation? What, in fact, shall we be postulating translation norms *about*? The point

I wish to stress here is a very simple one, and has also been made forcefully by others (such as Toury 1985; 1995: 23–39). In brief, a translation is any text that is accepted in the target culture as being a translation. i.e. as falling within the accepted range of deviance defined by the target-culture product norm "translation". (The word "translation" is English, of course, so I am assuming here that there are words in other languages that can be translated as "translation". However, I am not assuming that all the various words that can be translated into English as "translation" are strict synonyms. There is wide and documented variation between languages on how the general idea of translation is conceptualized and lexicalized. See e.g. Chesterman 2006.)

This culture-bound definition has implications. First, as Toury stresses, a translation is a translation in the target culture, not the source culture, and so the norms defining its acceptable range are primarily target-culture norms. However, other parties are also involved in the attribution of translation status: the client (in whichever culture) may set explicit norms governing what counts as a translation and what does not count, such as the conditions imposed on legal translators; and other attributors are of course translators themselves. Indeed, the translator of X is actually the first to propose Y *as a translation* of X. Translation norms thus do not exist exclusively in the target culture: some may have their origin in the source culture, and some in the intercultural state inhabited by the translator (as Pym stresses, 1992: 163f.). It is the target culture which nevertheless *confirms* translation status.

Second, the target culture designates certain texts as translations largely on the implicit say-so of their translators: the relation between the target culture and its translators is therefore fundamentally one of trust – a culture must trust those who translate into it, and also out of it. It may assign such "translation status", of course, according to the authoritative decisions of only certain members of the target culture, such as bilinguals or other experts. A translator who claimed that text T was a translation and was later discovered to have lied would lose this trust. Further, just as a target culture grants or accepts translation status, so it may also withdraw such status at a later date, for some reason or other. Classical examples are "pseudotranslations", texts which were originally accepted as translations but later turned out to be fakes: Macpherson's Ossian, for example, or Chatterton's "medieval" poems. It follows, then, that there is nothing which is theoretically absolute or permanent about translation status. In principle, even a text quite sincerely claimed and accepted as a translation could be criticized and even rejected as such by the same culture, perhaps centuries later, as expectations change.

Third, it is by no means the case that a translation has to be "perfect", or to conform to one particular type only, in order to be accepted as a translation. Even normal linguistic usage shows this: a "bad translation" is still a *translation*, still a member of the category "translation", albeit not a desirable one. There is an important theoretical difference, then, between saying that a text (or a segment or item in a text) is "a bad translation" and saying that it is "not a translation at all". One corollary of this, of course, is that translation theory should not neglect "bad translations".

In particular, it is not the case that a translation must meet the demands of some kind of "absolute equivalence" or "adequacy" before it can be granted translation status. Indeed, the literature is full of examples of translations which are far from being "equivalent" to their source texts in any customary sense. Much-quoted examples are the experimental symbolist translations of phonetic form alone, such as those of the Zukovskys from Catullus or Jandl from English (see Toury 1980: 44), or the volume-length spoof entitled *Mots d'heures: gousses, rames* which purports to be the D'Antin manuscript. This latter is a collection of phonetic translations into French of "Mother Goose Rhymes" by van Rooten (1967). An example:

> Un petit d'un petit
> S'etonne aux Halles
> Un petit d'un petit
> Ah! degres te fallent
> Indolent qui ne sort cesse
> Indolent qui ne se mene
> Qu'importe un petit d'un petit
> Tout Gai de Reguennes.

Compare the English:

> Humpty Dumpty sat on a wall,
> Humpty Dumpty had a great fall.
> All the king's horses and all the king's men
> Couldn't put Humpty together again.

The most extreme example I have so far come across, of what counts as a translation, is the following Finnish translation, in a concert programme, of a German poem by Morgenstern (1969). Note that it is overtly claimed by the translator to be a translation and is accepted by the target readership to be one, albeit a most eccentric one. But even eccentric translations are *translations*. The title of the poem may be glossed (from both the German and the Finnish) as "Night-song of a/the fish". The original German is as follows:

Fisches Nachtgesang

—
⌣ ⌣
— — —
⌣ ⌣ ⌣ ⌣
— — —
⌣ ⌣ ⌣ ⌣
— — —
⌣ ⌣ ⌣ ⌣
— — —
⌣ ⌣
—

The Finnish translation runs:

Kalan yölaulu

—
⌢ ⌢
— — —
⌢ ⌢ ⌢ ⌢
— — —
⌢ ⌢ ⌢ ⌢
— — —
⌢ ⌢ ⌢ ⌢
— — —
⌢ ⌢
—

Suom. Reijo Ollinen

What is going on here, and why is this a translation? The title has been translated conventionally, but in order to get the point of the translation of the poem itself the reader must know that the Finnish verb *kääntää*, which means 'to translate', also has the literal meaning 'to turn'. The translator, Reijo Ollinen, has in effect "turned" (some of) the elements of the poem upside down. Yet the point is actually made more subtle because the Finnish rubric *Suom. Reijo Ollinen* ('Trans. Reijo Ollinen') does not use this verb but another, *suomentaa*, meaning literally "to put into Finnish". The wit and validification of the translation thus turn on the reader's awareness of an ambiguous word that is not actually present in the text at all.

Further analysis of this playful translation might point out that the Finnish verb *kääntää* also has the slang sense 'to steal', so that the translator can be thought of as having 'stolen' the original poem (recall that Hermes, god of translators, was also the god of thieves...). And perhaps the Finnish fish looks sadder than the German one, but I will leave it at that. The point of the example is simply to illustrate how far the boundaries of "what-is-a-translation" may extend.

Are there any boundaries at all, in fact? Can *anything* be a translation? Surely not. Toury (1995:33f.) suggests three conditions or "postulates" which must be met if we are to reasonably assume that a given text is a translation: (a) there exists or has existed a source text, i.e. another product, normally in another language; (b) the assumed translation has been derived from this source text via a transfer process; and (c) there is an intertextual relationship between the two texts. The most problematic condition is the last one: what kinds of intertextual relationships count as translational ones? Answers to this question have varied enormously across cultures and periods. At the most general level, we can perhaps say that the required relation must be one of *relevant similarity*; but this then raises the question of what we mean by 'relevant', and indeed what we mean by 'similarity' (see Chesterman 1996b, 1998). In a discussion of the limits of interpretation, Nouss (1994) follows Eco in underlining the role of the community consensus, or Gadamer's interpretative tradition, in establishing a minimum range of acceptable interpretation. Semiosis is theoretically infinite, but in practice it is limited by what the community concerned will accept – in other words, by norms.

A key point in Toury's argument here, with which I would agree, is that discovering the precise nature of the realized intertextual relationship is a valid goal in one kind of translation research (cf. his "discovery procedure"), not a definition from which this research starts. That is, one reason for studying translations is to discover the concept of "equivalence" or "relevant similarity" held by a particular translator or a particular culture at a given time, for a given kind of text, etc. The minimum requirement is simply that a text is claimed to be a translation, and that it is accepted by the client and/or the readers as a translation in the target culture: it is accepted as conforming to the prevalent translation norms. On this view, then, the boundaries of the concept "translation" are ultimately not set by something intrinsic to the concept itself, but by the ways in which members of a culture use the concept.

This view of translation thus makes a clear distinction between category judgements (is this or is it not a translation?) and evaluative judgements (is this a good/acceptable etc. translation?). Category judgements need not be seen as black-and-white, of course: there can be prototypical instances, less typical ones, eccentric ones, peripheral ones etc. But there is no necessary correlation between prototypicality and quality, as the examples above have suggested. We shall return to questions of quality in Chapter 5, and see also the Update below.

3.5 Translation norms

3.5.1 Toury's norms

Some norms function as "solutions to problems posed by certain interaction situations" (Ullmann-Margalit 1977:9, cited by Bartsch 1987:104). Translation norms are of this type, for they exist to regulate the process whereby communication can take place in a situation where it would otherwise be impossible. The applicability of norm theory to translation studies has been pioneered by Toury, and I shall outline his ideas first. (See also Hermans 1991.)

Toury's original interest in the late 1970s (see e.g. 1980, and also 1995, 2012) was in literary translation, and his initial framework of norms was set up with that in mind. This framework starts with *preliminary norms*: these have to do with translation policy in a given culture, concerning for instance what works of literature are deemed by publishers and others to be worth translating, and whether or not these can be translated through an intermediate language ("secondary translation", also known as indirect translation). These are questions of social, cultural and economic policy, perhaps also political policy, and fall outside the main focus of this book. The norms that interest me here are those that come into play after a client has commissioned a translation, those that guide the translator's work itself.

These norms, which "direct actual decisions made during the translation process" (1980:54), Toury calls *operational norms*. Here he includes all the norms that affect the "matrix" of the text, its segmentation and verbal formulation (cf. Toury 1995:58f.). They are "textual norms", either generally linguistic/stylistic or specifically literary (determining appropriate genres etc.). In norm-theoretical terms, Toury's operational norms are primarily product norms, regulating the form of a translation as a final product. As such, of course, they also affect the decision-making process, although Toury gives less emphasis to process norms. He does, however, postulate one additional type of norm which he calls the *initial norm*. This has to do with "the translator's basic choice between two polar alternatives" (1980:54), subjecting himself "either to the original text, with its textual relations and the norms expressed by it and contained in it, or to the linguistic and literary norms active in TL [the target language] and in the target literary polysystem, or a certain section of it" (1980:54). The choice of the source language as initial norm leads to a translation that is "adequate", and the choice of target language norms to one that is "acceptable". (This use of the term "adequate" has been adopted by some scholars but is avoided by others on account of its ambiguity; still others use "adequate" to mean what Toury means by "acceptable". I shall henceforth avoid the term.)

3.5.2 Expectancy norms

The following analysis of translation norms concerns the area covered by Toury's operational and initial norms, but from a different angle. I start by positing two kinds of translation norms, corresponding quite conventionally to product norms and process norms. I will take the product ones first. Because, as argued above, these product norms are ultimately constituted by the expectations of the target language readership, I shall call these *expectancy norms.*

Expectancy norms are established by the expectations of readers of a translation (of a given type) concerning what a translation (of this type) *should* be like. These expectations are partly governed by the prevalent translation tradition in the target culture, and partly by the form of parallel texts (of a similar text-type) in the target language (cf. Hermans 1991), i.e. by the prevalent scenes and frames in the target culture. They can also be influenced by economic or ideological factors, power relations within and between cultures and the like. They cover a wide range of phenomena. Readers (who may or may not include the client) may have expectations about text-type and discourse conventions, about style and register, about the appropriate degree of grammaticality, about the statistical distribution of text features of all kinds, about collocations, lexical choice, and so on. Hermans (1991: 166) puts it this way:

> [T]he "correct" translation ... is the one that fits the correctness notions prevailing in a particular system, i.e. that adopts the solutions regarded as correct for a given communicative situation, as a result of which it is accepted as correct. In other words: when translators do what is expected of them, they will be seen to have done well.

Agreed. However, note that "correct" here does not need to imply the existence of a single correct translation; rather, as "correctness notions", norms can be met in a variety of ways. There is usually more than one way in which translators can do what is expected of them. We might therefore prefer to speak of translations being more or less "appropriate" or "acceptable" or the like. In this way we can define a range of possible translations, within which several may be "appropriate", even if some are felt to be better than others.

Expectancy norms thus also allow us to make evaluative judgements about translations. Some translations may conform to expectancy norms more closely than others. In theory, we can distinguish, within the total set of translations in a culture, a fuzzy subset of texts which are felt to conform very closely, prototypically as it were, to the relevant expectancy norms: such translations tend to assume the status of "norm-models" which in fact embody the norms in question. Other translations, felt to be outside this subset, are still accepted as being translations, albeit not norm-embodying ones. (This distinction will be relevant to the pedagogical aspect of translation studies: see Chapter 6.)

For some translations, "covert" ones (House 1981), readers in a given culture at a given time may expect them to be indistinguishable from native, non-translated texts: a covert translation that is recognized to be "different" from non-translated, similar (parallel) target-language texts can thus be judged unsatisfactory in some way. (At least, this would be the default judgement on such a translation; there may, of course, be additional factors that would override this judgement – see Chapter 5.) Examples of such covert translations might include business letters, advertisements, technical manuals etc.: translations of such texts typically do not form a category separate from non-translated target texts of the same type, within the target polysystem.

For other, "overt" translations (in a given culture, at a given time), the target-language expectancies might be different: translations of this type might be felt to occupy a different category or sub-category in the target polysystem, one specifically reserved for translations. Literary translations are one example: when I read Tolstoy in English, I cannot overlook the fact that I know he did not write in English originally; I expect "local colour", Russian forms of address, etc. Another example is interlinear glosses in linguistics texts, which are not even supposed to be fluent or natural but to illustrate the structure of the original. A third would be certain kinds of legal texts, such as those dealing with company law in country A but translated into the language of country B. In short, overt translations tend to be the norm for any text that is particularly closely bound in one way or another to the source culture.

Whether a translation is expected to be overt or covert will also depend partly on the cultural tradition in the target language, including the translation tradition itself. In some cultures, for instance, successfully covert translations may even be treated with suspicion, because readers have come to expect that translations are always overt (i.e. "unnatural") in some way. A translation that is really natural may even raise doubts about its accuracy, suspicions that the translator must have been too free.

Expectancy norms are primarily validated in terms of their very existence in the target language community: people do have these expectations about certain kinds of texts, and therefore the norms embodied in these expectations are *de facto* valid. But in some situations these norms are also validated by a norm authority of some kind, such as a teacher, an examiner, a literary critic reviewing a translation, a reviser, a publisher's reader or editor, and so on. Within any society, there is usually a subset of members ("experts") who are believed by the rest of the society to have the competence to validate such norms. This authority-validation may do no more than confirm a norm that is already acknowledged to exist in the society at large: in this sense, the norm authorities genuinely "represent" the rest of the society and are presumably trusted by the other members to do so.

There may be situations where there seems to be a clash between the norms sanctioned by these norm authorities and the norms accepted and current in the society at large. For instance, the general public may have rather low expectations about the readability of bureaucratic texts (whether translated or not), simply because they have become accustomed to such a quality. But these expectations actually relate to what typical translations of this kind *are* like, not what they *should* be like. Moreover, norm authorities might claim that the readability level of such badly written texts do not meet some higher requirement of clarity; further, such criticism might be agreed with by other members of the society when brought to their attention, and pressure might even be brought to bear on writers and/or translators to conform to these higher requirements.

What about translations that deliberately seem to go against expectancy norms? Some literary translators might claim that their intention is precisely to break these norms – recall the discussion of the Logos meme in the previous chapter. And translations of advertisements sometimes appear deliberately to flout the expectancy norms of the target culture. In such cases, the expectancy norms are broken because of some higher priority: loyalty to some aspect of the form of the source text, for instance, or a particular ideological conviction about the best way to represent the source culture, or the desire to produce a more persuasive text.

For instance: there is an advert often seen here in Helsinki in December, going around town on the side of a tram, by a Finnish company offering cruises on the Baltic Sea. It reads: *Meri Christmas*. Note: this is an advert aimed primarily at Finns; they are thus expected to know what the English word *Christmas* means; they obviously know what *meri* means ('sea'); and they are expected to know the English expression *Merry Christmas*. The wit and the effect of the advertisement thus depend on the English-language proficiency of a Finnish audience, who are not being addressed exclusively in the mother tongue. The bilingual appeal of the ad suggests also that it is directed particularly at educated Finns; and the fact that it appears on a Helsinki tram indicates that the primary target audience is an urban one. The ad can thus exploit the fashionable glamour of being, and going, "international".

The effect of such norm-breaking only works *because* it goes against the expectations of the readers: here, that Finnish speakers should be addressed by other

Finns in Finnish. Norm-breaking usages, including norm-breaking translations, can thus indicate the existence of the norms that are being thus broken. However, if, in time, people come to *expect* that norms actually should be broken in certain kinds of texts or translations – e.g. that certain kinds of adverts for Finnish consumers will be more effective if they use some English words – this expectancy may itself become a norm: an expectancy norm for that kind of text.

Expectancy norms, then, are not static or permanent, nor are they monolithic. They are highly sensitive to text-type – not all text-types are necessarily expected to conform consistently to fluent standard usage – and they are open to modification and change. In this respect, translation theory could benefit by some of the work done in critical linguistics on language awareness: I shall come back to this later (7.8).

3.5.3 Professional norms

The second major category of translation norms is that of process norms: these regulate the translation process itself. From the translator's point of view, these norms are subordinate to the expectancy norms, because they are themselves determined by the expectancy norms: any process norm is determined by the nature of the end-product which it is designed to lead to.

Where lies the source of these process norms for translation? Recall the point made above, about the existence of norm authorities in a society. With respect to translation, the norm authorities *par excellence* are perhaps those members of society who are deemed to be competent professional translators, whom society trusts as having this status, and who may further be recognized as competent professionals by other societies also. "Competence" and "professionalism" are thus understood here to be intersubjectively defined: you are competent if you are recognized to be so by people who in turn are recognized by others to be competent to make this judgement; and so on. Henceforth I shall disregard the existence of non-competent professionals: for "professional" read "competent professional". And I shall assume that a "professional" is simply a full-time translator whose sole or at least main livelihood is indeed translation. (I know this assumption simplifies the situation!)

Professionals are the people who are largely responsible for the original establishment of the expectancy norms, in fact, for the products of their work naturally become the yardsticks by which subsequent translations are assessed by the receiving society. Their translation behaviour, in other words, is accepted to be norm-setting. Conversely, if a translation is accepted as conforming to the relevant expectancy norms, the translator of that text is *(qua* translator of that text, at least) accepted as being a competent professional. That is what final diploma exams and the like are about, after all.

Just as it is possible to distinguish a fuzzy subset of translations which are recognized as conforming especially closely to the expectancy norms (as argued above), so it is equally possible to distinguish (among the total set of people who translate literary or non-literary texts in a given culture) an equally fuzzy subset of translators who are recognized to be competent professionals. It is, then, the translational behaviour of this professional subset from which we derive the process norms of translation. For this reason, I shall call these translation process norms *professional norms*.

All professional translation norms can, I think, be subsumed under three general higher-order norms. They can be stated in an absolute form, but in real life they naturally tend to be followed only "as far as possible"; moreover, different translation tasks may require balancing acts between different priorities, a point that I overlook here. Note that the following formulations are not prescriptive in the sense that I would be laying down laws for translators to follow. They are descriptive: I hypothesize simply that these are kinds of norms that exist in the culture to which any translator belongs, and that insofar as the translator has internalized them, they help to account for translatorial behaviour. The norms themselves exert a prescriptive pressure – as any norms do. In other words, translators tend to behave as they think they ought to behave, and these norms represent an attempt to capture the nature of this "ought". True, a translator may also have reasons to disregard these norms or to set up particular priorities between them; such translators will feel they "ought" to translate in some different way, they interpret the norms in a way that is different from the majority view. Different interpretations may remain a minority opinion, or they may eventually become the majority view. – I formulate the basic process norms as follows (following Chesterman 1993).

(1) The *accountability norm:* a translator should act in such a way that the demands of loyalty are appropriately met with regard to the original writer, the commissioner of the translation, the translator himself or herself, the prospective readership and any other relevant parties.

This is thus an ethical norm, concerning professional standards of integrity and thoroughness. Compare the general language norm of sincerity, mentioned above (3.3). Translators behave in such a way as to be able to accept responsibility for their translations. A similar point has been made by Nord (e.g. 1991): she speaks of the translator being "committed" and "responsible", and of loyalty as a moral principle which is indispensable in human communication. (Compare also the ethical norm of the "true interpreter" in Harris 1990.) Formulated in this way, the norm nevertheless allows for various interpretations concerning which party should be given the primary loyalty in cases of conflict.

(2) The *communication norm*: a translator should act in such a way as to optimize communication, as required by the situation, between all the parties involved.

This is a social norm, which specifies the translator's role as a communication expert, both as a mediator of the intentions of others and as a communicator in his/her own right. Compare the general communication norm of language, mentioned above (3.3). Note that the norm does not necessarily presuppose a belief in an objectively fixed message, a signified, that must be communicated; the situation may be such that the intended communication is more like a shared sense of linguistic play, or an aesthetic experience. Communication is, after all, a sharing.

Neither the accountability norm nor the communication norm are specific to the translation process: translation theory merely applies them. But the third higher-order process norm is specific to translation and other rewriting processes: it in fact highlights the difference between these kinds of processes and other communication processes. It can be stated as follows:

(3) The *relation norm:* a translator should act in such a way that an appropriate relation of relevant similarity is established and maintained between the source text and the target text.

Defined in this way, in terms of a relation between texts, this is therefore a linguistic norm. It accounts for the assumption (argued for above) that equivalence as sameness is too narrow a concept, because of the wide variety of relations that actually exist between source and target texts. It is up to the translator to decide what kind of relation is appropriate in any given case, according to the text-type, the wishes of the commissioner, the intentions of the original writer, and the assumed needs of the prospective readers. One kind of relation might of course be "equivalence" or "optimal similarity" of some sort. One translation task might require a translation which gave priority to a close formal similarity to the original: legal contracts, for instance, which must correspond sentence to sentence. Another might prioritize stylistic similarity: a short story, perhaps a poem. Yet another might highlight the importance of semantic closeness: a scientific or technical article. And another might value similarity of effect above all these: a tourist brochure, an advertisement. Every translation task sets its own profile of "equivalence priorities", and it is part of the translator's job to assess the overall profile that would be appropriate. Simplified binary distinctions (form vs. meaning etc.) are only of limited use in this respect.

But, fundamentally, the question at issue here is broader and more complex. "Equivalence" (albeit inevitably partial) is only one kind of possible relation: recall the Wittgensteinian idea of family resemblance, with its infinite variation. In translation, such variation would also cover such parameters as degree of target-culture adaptation considered appropriate, addition or omission of information, relation to accompanying channels (lip movements etc. in film dubbing, melody and pitch in song translations), and so on. The above formulation of the relation norm seeks to capture precisely this potential range of valid resemblances between source and target text.

These three professional norms are partly validated by norm authorities: other professionals, teachers, critics etc., who are accepted as having norm-giving competence. But, like the expectancy norms, they are also validated by their very existence: that is, to the extent that they are accepted as governing the practice actually followed by such professionals. Furthermore, behaviour which breaks these norms is usually deemed deserving of criticism. This criticism might then be firmly rejected by the translator in question, and thus mark the beginning of an argument about how the appropriate norm should be interpreteted. Norms can always be argued about. The point of this chapter is to suggest what the main translation norms are, not to define how they should be universally interpreted.

A final comment: professional norms of course also govern the way a competent translator reads the source text, before actually translating anything, and the translator's own expectancy norms regarding the source language will affect the comprehension of the source text (cf. Dancette 1994). However, I shall not discuss this aspect of the overall translation process.

3.6 General translation laws and normative laws

3.6.1 Translation laws

We have seen that norms lie between judicial laws and conventions, in terms of their deontic force. At this point it will be helpful to clarify the distinction between norms and another type of law: empirical laws. In particular, what is the difference between professional norms (of translation behaviour) and behavioural laws (of the translation process)?

Let us call the latter type of behavioural laws "general translation laws". In keeping with the increasing current emphasis on translation as a process, Toury has argued in many contexts (e.g. 1991, 1995, 2012) that one ultimate aim of translation theory should in fact be to establish these laws of translation behaviour. We can gloss "law" in this sense as "observable behavioural regularity". Such translation laws are purely descriptive, and have the following general form:

Under conditions X, translators tend to do (or refrain from doing) Y.

Or as Toury puts it (1991: 186):

If X, then the greater/the smaller the likelihood that Y.

Provided that conditions X can be specified, such general descriptive laws of translation behaviour could in principle be set up at many different levels of generality: for all translators universally at all times, for translators in a given culture at a given time, for translators going from a given source to a given target language, for translators of certain text-types, for translators of a given degree of competence, etc. – In fact, at their most general, laws could be established to describe any behaviour (not necessarily "desirable" behaviour) which leads to something that is accepted as being a translation (but not necessarily a good translation). Translation laws as thus defined are, of course, probabilistic rather than absolute. But they are empirical, and falsifiable in the standard sense: they can be used as the basis for predictions, they can be tested, confirmed or disconfirmed. (See the comment on translation universals, in 2.10 above.)

Let us take some general examples. Perhaps the most pervasive of all translation laws is the law of interference (cf. Toury 1995: 274f.). This states that translators universally tend to be influenced by the language of the source text, in a wide variety of ways. Evidence for this law is particularly found in translated texts which purport to be covert translations but which are immediately recognized to be translations, for one reason or another. Such reasons include not only the occurrence of "grammatical errors" or "clumsy language", but also more subtly distinguishing marks such as the statistical distribution of grammatical or stylistic features. An early example of such work is Vehmas-Lehto (1989) on the quality of Finnish translations from Russian. The fact that this law is also applicable (to some extent) to the behaviour of competent professional translators merely underlines its pervasiveness.

Another tendency that has long been recognized is explicitation: translators tend to produce texts that are more explicit than the originals (see e.g. Toury 1980: 60; Blum-Kulka 1986: 19; Séguinot 1988; Toury 1991; Klaudy 1996; and Becher 2010 for a more recent critical view).

Closely related is the law proposed by Toury to account for a certain stylistic flattening that is particularly typical of literary translation. He formulates the law as follows (1991: 187): "textemes tend to be converted into repertoremes". A "texteme" is any sign which carries a textual function, and a "repertoreme" is any sign that forms part of an institutionalized repertoire. In other words, translators tend to replace text-specific items with institutionalized items: translations tend to be less idiosyncratic, more conventionalized, than their originals. Lefevere (1992:107) refers to a similar phenomenon as "flattening": "the illocutionary power of the original is sacrificed in favor of mere locutionary communication". Toury's later formulation (1995:267) calls this the law of growing standardization.

Interestingly, this law seems to run counter to the law of interference: whereas interference points to the dominance of the source language, the law of growing standardization points to the dominance of the target-language system at the expense of specifically source-text features. The two laws exert opposite pulls, and the translator can be swayed either way. The standardization law suggests that translators (at a certain level of competence, perhaps) tend to overreact to the risk of interference.

Some manifestations of the standardization law are purely statistical, and readily suggest hypotheses that can be empirically tested. To take a simple example: the occurrence of many textual features approximately follows a statistically normal distribution, a bell curve. If we plot the variation of sentence length in a text, for instance, we typically end up with a distribution showing a higher frequency of average-length sentences and a lower frequency of very short or very long ones. Such curves will of course vary somewhat depending on text-type. If the normal target-language distribution of this feature is then compared with its distribution in translated texts of the same type, we might hypothesize that various differences would emerge. Instead of a symmetrical bell curve the translations might show a skewed curve, showing an over-use of short or long sentences. But a more likely hypothesis is that we would find instances of normalization, showing over-use of the central, average range, and under-use of the two extremes. The translator would thus be "playing safe", making more use of the prototypical part of the range of distribution. The result would be a kind of "rhetorical flattening" similar to that observed by Toury. (We shall return to related matters of translation assessment in Chapter 5.)

At a lower level of generality, any teacher of translation will be familiar with the typical tendencies of translator trainees at different levels, both regarding their translation products and their translation process. One aspect of the process that has received attention is trainees' use of dictionaries and reference works, as compared to the practice of experienced professionals (see e.g. Jääskeläinen 1989): professionals use a wider range of reference works, and rely less on bilingual dictionaries, for instance. All such observations and research pertain to descriptive translation laws.

3.6.2 Normative laws

Within these general translation laws I would like to posit the existence of a subset of laws I will call *normative* translation laws. They are also descriptive, in accordance with the sense in which I am using "normative" throughout this book; however, they are not descriptive of the behaviour of all translators but only of some. They are only descriptive of the behaviour of competent professionals, of the same subset of all translators that is the source of professional norms. Normative laws, as thus understood, describe the behaviour of translators who conform to translation norms, and who actually set the professional norms. (Strictly speaking, of course, we are dealing with a continuum here, not an absolute distinction between "conforming" and "not conforming".)

A simple hypothetical example will illustrate the difference between general translation laws and normative laws. Assume that, in a given culture at a given time, there exists a communicative norm to the effect that, in a given text-type, source-language culture-bound terms are expanded or explained in translation, rather than preserved to add local colour or the like. We might discover a general translation law which revealed that, say, 70% of *all* translators (in this culture etc.) do indeed tend to explain such terms, but 30% do not. The 70% that do are thus following the norm. It may well be that the remaining 30%, by not conforming to this norm, expose themselves to criticism, if the opinion of their readers is that they should be conforming to it. But as we have seen, general translation laws are not sensitive to evaluative judgements, for they merely describe what is done, by good and less good translators alike.

Alongside this general law, however, we might also discover that, of all the *competent professional* translators studied, as many as 99% followed the norm; indeed, this would be evidence for our taking it to be a norm in the first place. If supported by subsequent research, this would suggest the existence of a *normative* law: that is, a law describing the typical behaviour of competent professional, norm-abiding translators, as opposed to *all* translators in the culture.

Again, we are not really looking at a binary distinction here, between competent professionals and "other translators": I have set up such an opposition for expository reasons only. What we expect to find is a correlation between "acknowledged translational competence", measured perhaps partly in years of experience, and the use of certain translation strategies such as, in this example, "explain culture-bound terms". It is partly by extrapolation from such an observed trend that we postulate the existence of the norm in question: good translators behave in such and such a way, which implies that they seem to follow guidelines of such and such a kind, i.e. norms.

One definition of "good translators", then, would be those who tend to follow normative laws, i.e. those who translate "like competent professionals". If we then ask by what criteria these professionals are to be defined, the answer is: not on intrinsic grounds but on extrinsic ones. That is, translators belong to the subset of "competent professionals" if they are acknowledged to do so by other members of their culture (or perhaps, more specifically, by members who are themselves acknowledged by yet other members as having the ability to make this evaluation). In other words, translator competence (on this view) is defined socially, not linguistically, in the same way as we have earlier defined what counts as a translation in the first place. Power relationships in society are thus also involved, inevitably.

It may be argued at this point that I am committing the naturalistic fallacy of deriving "ought" from "is". I question this fallacy, however (see further Chesterman 1993). With respect to translation behaviour, I think the "ought" does already exist in a perfectly genuine sense, in the translational behaviour of people who are acknowledged to be competent professionals, and in the social consciousness of norms. "Phylogenetically", within the community of translators, norms and translation laws (including normative laws) may change over time, they may differ between cultures, and even conflict within a given culture; but they certainly exist. Trainees entering the community of translators (ontogenetically, as it were) will naturally experience normative translation laws as being prescriptive (as "ought") vis-a-vis their own translation behaviour (cf. the similar point made in 3.3 on norms of language in general); but we can describe and investigate them as descriptive, empirical laws just as we can study any other laws of human behaviour.

3.6.3 Explanations

One function of scientific laws is to explain. Accordingly, we can expect translation laws to offer explanations to product questions such as "why does this translation, manifest the feature X?" or "why do translations of this type into this language tend to have the feature X?" or "why did certain kinds of translations at that time in that culture look like that?"; and also to process questions such as "why did this translator write X?" or "why do translators tend to do X?" or even "why do professional translators, faced with this sort of problem, tend to make decisions of such-and-such a kind?". The answers which general translation and normative laws offer represent various types of explanation. Any act, including acts of translation, may well have several explanations.

We might start by distinguishing causal from teleological explanations. Causal explanations explain by reference to a previously occurring phenomenon, such as the existence of the source text, whereas teleological explanations refer to intended final goals subsequent to the phenomenon being explained, such as the aim of the translation. Causal explanations here would include reasons, although reasons are usually defined as being agent-internal: for example, a translator's knowledge of P (e.g. knowledge of the client's aim) might be a *reason* for a translation decision Q.

A different account of various possible kinds of explanation is offered by Pym (1997: 85f.), who links them to Aristotle's four causes, approximately as follows:

> *Material cause:* the target language itself, out of which the translation is constructed; plus the source text; plus a computer and other aids.
>
> *Formal cause:* the translation norms which determine the ultimate form of a given translation, the appropriate relation with the source text.
>
> *Efficient cause:* the mind and body of the translator, including personal experience, emotional state etc.; plus the person of the client who initiates the act of translation.
>
> *Final cause:* the goal of the translation, as determined by the client and accepted or refined by the translator; plus perhaps the general aim of the translator to earn a living.

Pym's point is that acts of translation do indeed have more than one cause, and that a theory of translation must incorporate at least these types. Functional theories such as skopos theory, for instance, tend to give high priority to final causes at the expense of others. Some other theories, such as early linguistic ones, tended to focus exclusively on material (source-text) causes. Material causes concern the intertextual aspect of translation; formal and final causes the socio-cultural aspect; efficient causes the cognitive aspect; and formal, efficient and final causes the ethical aspect.

Another way of analysing potential explanations is to do so according to the normative laws describing the kind of translation behaviour which tends to conform to the various translation norms discussed above. The general form of the explanations runs as follows:

> A translator performs act A
> > or: translators tend to perform act A
> > or: a translation contains feature X
> > or: translations of a certain type and time tend to contain feature X
> because of
> > a particular normative law (or laws) of translation
> > or: a particular general law (or laws) of translation.

Normative laws of translation can be conveniently grouped under the various translation norms which give rise to them: normative laws, after all, describe behaviour that conforms to translation norms. Explanations which refer to these norms are in principle only formal causes, but if the translator is indeed *aware* of the norms they also suggest efficient causes, in that this awareness is part of the translator's state of knowledge. The translator conforms to these norms (a) because he/she knows what they are, and because (b) he/she wishes and intends to conform to them. (Alternatively, of course, a translator may decide *not* to conform to them: we are talking about tendencies, not universal truths or prescriptive commands. If enough translators decide not to conform, a new, competing norm may arise.) From the definitions of the general norms we can thus derive normative laws which offer explanations for translational acts, as follows.

1. *Professional translators tend to conform to expectancy norms.*
   A translator performs act A (or: a translation contains feature X, etc.) because of the target language expectancy norms regarding grammaticality, acceptability, appropriateness etc. for certain sorts of texts.
   Example: when translating journalistic texts from English to Finnish, translators currently tend to add titles and Christian names of international politicians.
2. *Professional translators tend to conform to the accountability norm.*
   A translator performs act A (etc.) because this act conforms to ethical principles which the translator accepts.
   Example: translators tend to check names or dates which appear suspect, double-check final drafts, ask other professionals for their opinion on a tricky point, stick to deadlines, etc. An appeal to ethical principles may also be offered for translations which go against prevailing expectancy norms (cf. e.g. Venuti 1995a).
3. *Professional translators tend to conform to the communication norm.*
   A translator performs act A (etc.) because this act conforms to overall communicative maxims, principles that are accepted as valid for any type of communication, not just translation. These would include readability, clarity and the like: the familiar Gricean maxims of quantity, quality, relevance and manner, in fact. In the case of literary texts, of course, the aim of the communication might be the creation of a particular aesthetic effect rather than (or in addition to) a given "message"; this might then justify apparent violations of communicative maxims. Nevertheless, the overall goal of the translation act is still to share an experience with the reader. (We shall return to the notion of clarity in Chapter 7.)

Example: for many kinds of texts, translators tend to clarify and improve awkwardly written originals.
4. *Professional translators tend to conform to the relation norm.*
A translator performs act A (etc.) because of the desired relation between the resulting target-text item or feature X and the source-text item or feature Y. In other words, a translator performs act A because the source text contained Y. Example: translating from German to English I write *seven per cent* – not "eight" or "seventeen per cent" – because the source text has *sieben Prozent*.

In accordance with our definition of normative laws, the above four are defined in terms of professional translation behaviour. This is not to say that they do not apply to non-professionals, but that they are truer of professionals as a subset than of all translators as a whole. Other sources of explanation, in turn, may be truer of translators as a whole than of the subset of professionals, and truer of trainees and non-professionals than of professionals.

One example would be the general translation law of interference: a translator performs act A (or: a translation contains feature X, etc.) because of interference from the source text or the source language. The result of such an act is sometimes a feature in the target text that can fairly be criticized, if it breaks some norm. Yet another source of explanation would be Toury's standardization law discussed above, describing how translators tend to be unduly influenced by conventionalized forms in the target language. And another would be the general tendency to explicitate, also mentioned earlier.

All the types of explanation outlined in this section are of course extremely general. In order to make them more concrete, and more applicable, we shall need the concept of the translation strategy: this will be the subject of Chapter 4. (For a more detailed discussion of the notion of explanation in translation research, see Chesterman 2008.)

3.7 Norms as constraints

As was mentioned above, norms serve to delimit the scope of acceptable deviance (of a process or product). In other words, they act not only as guidelines but also as constraints: constraints on freedom of action. In Popper's terms (recall Section 1.3), these constraints exist in World 3, and exert a "plastic control" on World 2 (subjective thinking and feeling) and consequently on the physical products existing in World 1.

In polysystem theory these constraints are seen as operating together as part of a system. Research here has tended to focus on literary translation, and consequently on the literary system of a culture, but the insights this research offers can also be applied to translation more generally.

I would now like to look at the work of André Lefevere (1992) in this respect, and relate the constraints he analyses to the kinds of norms we have been discussing above. Lefevere distinguishes five constraints which determine the way translators (specifically, literary translators) manipulate texts. These are:

1. *Patronage*: "the powers (persons, institutions) that can further or hinder the reading, writing, and rewriting of literature" (15).
2. *Poetics*: "an inventory of literary devices, genres, motifs, prototypical characters and situations, and symbols" plus "a concept of what the role of literature is, or should be, in the social system as a whole" (26).
3. The *universe of discourse*: this refers to the subject matter of the source text, the objects, customs and beliefs it describes (87). The point is that translators may feel some of these are unacceptable to the target readership, and hence adapt or bowdlerize passages thought to be "offensive" or the like.
4. The *source and target languages* themselves, and the differences between these (99).
5. The translator's *ideology*: this refers to the translator's personal set of values and attitudes, including his/her attitudes to the other constraints, e.g. whether he/she accepts them or not (41).

Let us consider first how these constraints relate to the translation norms. Patronage – which would include the influence of publishers and commissioners of translations – falls mainly outside the norms I have focused on, but would be covered by Toury's "preliminary norms" (see 3.5.1). To the extent that patrons are also readers of the target texts, however, their expectations will contribute to the expectancy norms.

The poetics constraint is also an obvious constituent of the expectancy norms, corresponding in literary translation to the expectancy norms for discourse patterns and text-types in non-literary translation.

The universe-of-discourse constraint has to do partly with the expectancy norms (what target readers will deem acceptable subject matter in a given situation), and partly with the accountability norm (the translator's own ethics: one might simply refuse to translate certain kinds of texts).

The language constraint affects the relation norm: the translator's choice of the appropriate relation between source and target is obviously restricted by the range of relations that are *possible* – and this range is defined partly by the intrinsic natures of the languages themselves.

The translator's own ideology is bound up with the accountability norm, and also with the communication norm, in that the ideology will affect what and how the translator chooses to communicate.

I suggested earlier that of these norms, the only one which is exclusive to translation is the relation norm: *mutatis mutandis*, the other norms apply to all modes of communication. That is, one normally purports to communicate effectively, relevantly, with integrity, in a manner broadly compatible with other people's expectations. (I say "normally", because one may of course wish to surprise or disrupt expectations…) The same point holds for Lefevere's constraints. Almost all writing, whether translation or not, is constrained by patrons (publishers, editors…), poetics (discourse conventions…), universe of discourse (what can be acceptably written about, to given addressees), and the writer's personal ideology (what do I want to say, what should I say, what do I believe I have the right to say…). The only constraint that seems exclusive to translation is the language constraint, the differences between the source and target languages.

However, even this constraint is less translation-specific than it might seem, and so is my relation norm, for both these actually apply more generally to any form of rewriting, whether across languages or within the same language, such as editing or paraphrasing, even summarizing. It is no coincidence that Lefevere's book on this subject is entitled *Translation, rewriting, and the manipulation of literary fame*. As this suggests, he looks at translation in the wider context of rewriting as a whole.

This observation raises two points that are worth stressing, both of which run counter to some current thinking on translation. The first concerns the relevance of contrastive analysis to translation theory. Supporters of the communicative approach to translation (cf. 2.6, above) tend to be highly critical of contrastive analysis (cf. 2.5): it is argued that contrastive analysis sees language as *langue*, whereas translation theory ought to look at language as *parole*. Yet it is obvious that a translator, when making *parole* decisions, can only choose from what is available, i.e. from *langue*. And the more the translator knows about what is available, the better the decisions are likely to be. Further, this knowledge of what is available must include a knowledge of how the possible choices relate not only to each other but also to the point of departure in the source text. In other words, the translator needs to know the relevance of each possible choice to his/her intentions, in order to be able to decide on an optimal version. This weighing up of the relative relevances of different options relies heavily on contrastive analysis, on the translator's knowledge of the differences and similarities between the two languages. Through the translator's mind there runs something like the following: given that (a) a source-text item means / carries the message / is interpreted as X; and that (b) I am aiming at a relation R between source and target; then:

(c) what options does the target language offer as possible translation solutions?; and (d) what would be the best / an optimal solution in this particular case, bearing in mind the prospective readership etc.? A knowledge of the similarities and contrasts between the two languages is an essential part of a translator's competence (see also Chesterman 1998).

The second point is often overlooked by scholars who focus on literary translation. Literary translators normally translate into the mother tongue; so do many non-literary translators, of course, but many non-literary translators actually translate out of their native language into one that they typically command somewhat less proficiently. (The fact that such non-native translations may subsequently be revised by target-language native speakers is beside the point here.) It would therefore be of interest to translation theory to study, rather more than has been the case to date, the relations between texts translated by non-natives and texts (in the same target language) not translated but written by similar non-native speakers. For English, for instance, we could be looking at "near-native" written English (see e.g. Ringbom 1993), and comparing it to English translations produced by non-native speakers of English (at equivalent levels of proficiency in English, of course). Do Finns writing English produce the same kind of English as Finns translating into English? After all, both groups are working under the same non-native-proficiency constraint; the distinguishing variable would be that the translators are additionally bound by the language-difference constraint (or the relation norm). It would be interesting to see what effect this had. Would there be interference differences, for instance, which could be explained by the fact that translators had an original Finnish source text in front of them whereas the other group (the free writers) had no such text, although they might also be expected to think in Finnish to some extent or be otherwise influenced by their native tongue? Free writers in a foreign language can exploit the "avoidance strategy" – avoid items they feel unsure about – and one might hypothesize that translators are allowed less leeway in this respect, being required to use a wider range of target items.

Moreover, although the much-maligned non-native translator presumably has, by definition, less proficiency in the target language itself, and thus tends to be less successful in conforming to the expectancy norms, there is no reason why non-natives should be any less proficient than natives with respect to other aspects of the translation process, in particular with respect to the communication and accountability norms. And if they are translating out of their native language they may be assumed to have a higher comprehension proficiency, which would be important for meeting the relation norm. This view is of relevance to the formulation of realistic standards in translator training and the granting of professional status. It may also go some way towards counterbalancing the pessimistic view that translators, and *especially* non-native translators, inevitably "make mistakes". (See e.g. Rydning 1991 and Pokorn 2005 for discussions of the special status of translation into a non-native language.)

3.8 On expectancy norms for English

This section will do no more than illustrate the kind of research that is relevant to the analysis of expectancy norms. The strictest English expectancy norms are "rules of English grammar" which are not normally expected to be broken: this is an obvious point.

Beyond these, and probably of more interest to the translator, are norms that are determined not by grammaticality but by acceptability and appropriateness: norms of usage, in other words. Some of these are qualitative, others quantitative. Both types are increasingly studied with the help of computerized parallel corpora.

Qualitative expectancy norms
Qualitative norms of usage, over and above grammaticality, incorporate what we might call "good style" (within a given text-type, as always). We could usefully distinguish here between "general" expectancy norms and "higher" expectancy norms: the latter would be embodied by texts that were acknowledged to be not only "native" but also "well written". Acknowledged by whom? For instance by a subset of readers who see themselves, or are seen by others, as norm authorities in this respect. Writers of style guides on good writing, or compilers of dictionaries for language learners, for example. Some readers, in other words, have higher expectations than others. Clear evidence of this is the very existence of books and courses (for native speakers) on how to write better, etc. These higher expectancy norms could be called "recommendable norms" (Vehmas-Lehto 1989: 22): recommended, because they make processing easier for the receiver.

These recommendable norms manifest at the textual level, in a variety of ways, the general pragmatic principles of co-operation. Examples of such norms for English are the following:

> *End weight*: heavier items tend to occur after lighter items (see e.g. Quirk et al. 1985).
>
> *End focus:* more informative or newsworthy items tend to occur towards the end of a structure (ibid.)
>
> *Iconicity*: structures where the form somehow reflects the content tend to be thought easier to process (see e.g. Haiman 1985; Enkvist 1991).

Cohesion: there is an expectation that (in written English) sentences should be linked cohesively to those around them, often explicitly (see e.g. Beaugrande and Dressler 1981). In this connection, Hinds (1987) has argued that written English manifests "writer responsibility" rather than "reader responsibility": the onus is on the writer to ensure clarity and fluent readability (as compared with e.g. Japanese).

More specifically, English expectancy norms (in certain text-types) might include the avoidance of stigmatized usage, i.e. such prescriptive-grammar chestnuts as the split infinitive (*to carefully observe that…*), dangling participles (*Using a telescope the stars seem pinker*), *due to* instead of *owing to*, and the like. Some dictionaries draw overt attention to such usage. Under *due to*, for instance, the Collins Cobuild Dictionary notes (among other points) the following:

> You can say **due to** to introduce the reason for something happening. Some speakers of English believe that it is not correct to use **due to** in this way. EG *Due to repairs, the garage will be closed next Saturday.*

In other words, this dictionary entry mentions the existence of a usage that (for some speakers at least) breaks a norm.

Quantitative expectancy norms
Quantitative expectancy norms fall into two large classes. First, there are expectancy norms for the distribution of features in a given type of text. Such features can be lexical, syntactic, or textlinguistic/discoursal. Computer corpora have made the study of these features fairly straighforward (see e.g. Kučera and Francis 1967; Ellegård 1978; Johansson 1978a; Francis and Kučera 1982).

Lexical features whose distributional norms have been studied include lexical density (ratio of lexical words to function words) and lexical variety (ratio of types to tokens), and word length (see e.g. Linnarud 1988 and the studies mentioned above).

Syntactic features include things like average sentence length, typical distribution of clause types, clause structures, structural complexity, noun phrase structures, word-classes, stative vs. dynamic verbs. The whole area of readability research is obviously relevant here, too.

From the computer-corpus studies mentioned above, for instance, we can derive information such as the following:

- the average length of an English sentence ranges from about 25 words for government documents to about 13 words for detective fiction, with an overall mean of about 19 words;

- the overall proportion of common nouns in informative prose is around 25% of all word-tokens;
- in scientific texts, relative clauses account for about 20% of all clauses; in more popular text-types, this proportion drops to about 9%;
- the overall frequency of the definite article *the* is about 6.9% of all word-tokens; slightly higher in scientific English and slightly lower in adventure stories.

Textlinguistic and discourse features include degree and kind of cohesion, use of metatext (Mauranen 1993), markers of involvement (Chafe 1982), distribution of thematization structures, scheme and trope density – in fact, macrostructural features in general (e.g. van Dijk 1988). Additionally, there will be norms for such things as illocutionary structure (e.g. Riley 1979), formality markers, closeness to the spoken language, etc. Such norms have mainly been studied for particular genres, such as the genre of academic or scientific English (e.g. Swales 1991). And much of the research interest here has been contrastive, coming from contrastive rhetoric (see e.g. Connor and Kaplan 1987; Purves 1988; Mauranen 1993; Connor 1996). For instance, these studies suggest that academic English tends to conform to norms such as the following:

- linear presentation;
- in contrast to some other languages, the main point is mentioned early in an article, rather than being kept to the end as a climax;
- in contrast to some other languages, academic English makes great use of metatext (markers of transitions, cohesion, textual signposts etc.); recall the point about "writer responsibility", above;
- wide and varied use is made of explicit markers of modality (hedges, signs of academic modesty);
- at least in some fields, as compared to certain other languages such as German, the general level of formality is lower in English academic writing (there is a growing acceptance of the first person singular, for example).

A brief caveat is in order here. Norms such as those mentioned above may appear at first sight to be loose tendencies rather than norms proper. However, recall that the crucial feature of a norm, as opposed to a convention or indeed a mere tendency, is that instances of non-conformation can be fairly criticized. A text (translated or otherwise) which had noticeably more relative clauses than the expected norm for that text-type, for instance, might raise irritated eyebrows among some readers – unless this deviation was somehow motivated. English scientific articles submitted to a journal for publication will indeed be criticized by the editor if they manifestly fail to conform to the appropriate discourse norms; they may even be returned for further rewriting.

The second class of quantitative expectancy norms has to do not with the absolute frequency of given items but their relative frequency, their distribution relative to that of other items. In other words, collocation. Here again, studies of computer corpora can provide a great detail of information about co-occurrence probabilities, about the adjectives that tend to occur before a given noun, etc. Such research can often be of relevance to a translator wondering which to choose from a set of near-synonyms: the preferred co-occurrence patterns may be different from those which might be expected on the basis of the apparent translation equivalents of individual items. For instance, in English "coffee" can collocate with "weak", but not in Finnish, where it is "thin" (*laihaa kahvia*).

Unlikely collocations are, of course, a well-known cause of irritation to readers of a translated text – unless they are persuaded that such deviation is motivated, e.g. in a literary text.

3.9 Update

This chapter originally ended with a brief look at some of the implications of a norm-based approach to translation. One was the relevance of contrastive studies, particularly in different genres, as a way of finding out more about the possibilities from which translators can choose. Such work has indeed continued, for instance in the series of conferences on contrastive research at the University of Ghent (e.g. Willems and Defrancq 2004), and the UCCTS series (Using Corpora in Contrastive and Translation Studies) based at the University of Lancaster (see e.g. Xiao 2010).

A second implication concerns the way norms are actually attained in practice, a topic to be taken up in the next chapter on strategies. But a third issue was also raised, concerning translators' attitudes to norms. A translator may choose not to follow a norm, and accept the risk of not doing so, perhaps with the intention of changing the norm. There may also be a gap between what a translator says about his/her attitude to a norm and what he/she actually does. This has been interestingly demonstrated for instance by Brownlie (2003), who also drew attention to the effects of translators' personal preferences on the way they translate. Norms are only one of the potential causal factors, after all.

Toury's revised version of his classic *Descriptive Translation Studies and Beyond* appeared in 2012. With respect to his proposals for what he calls translation "laws" (interference, and increasing standardization), some scholars have been reluctant to follow Toury's terminology and have preferred to speak of universals, or general tendencies (see the Update of Chapter 2). In retrospect, I think my own use of "law" in 3.6 above was not optimal. It would probably have been better to refer to these generalizations simply as tendencies or behaviour patterns.

Like Toury, I see norms as explanatory hypotheses. But finding evidence for the existence of norms is not a simple matter. We can start with an observed textual regularity, but this in itself does not prove the existence of an underlying norm, as it may have other causes, such as cognitive constraints over which the translator has no influence, such as lack of knowledge or particular task conditions. We also need text-external indicators of normative force, such as belief statements by the translator ("I think I should do this"), criticism of breaches of the assumed norm, perhaps even norm statements by relevant authorities ("Translators of such texts must do this"). Further, hypotheses about norms need to be tested, like any hypothesis. We can deliberately break a norm and see how people react. We can look for counter-evidence. We can elicit belief statements ("What do you think you should do in such cases?") or ask norm authorities or clients for an explicit norm statement. Appeals to such external evidence and test results will then be more or less convincing. Alternative explanations also need to be weighed up, such as personal preferences, cognitive constraints, and of course chance.

This chapter has highlighted the special status of competent professional translators. However, it is worth recalling that most translators throughout history have been non-professionals, in the sense that translation has not been their main source of income and they have not been professionally trained. One major development in translation practice over the past two decades has been the increasing appearance of new kinds of non-professional work, sometimes of high quality. Practices such as fansubbing and crowdsourced translation have spread, and so has the use of volunteer activist translators (who may of course also be professionally trained). Translation scholars are now paying more attention to this phenomenon, which also raises interesting questions about the role of translator training. (See e.g. the special issue of *The Translator*, vol. 18 no. 2, 2012, on non-professional translation and interpreting.) Perhaps professionally trained translators of the future will need to specialize in more demanding work such as literary, legal or medical translation – and also in postediting, in the light of the improving quality of machine translation for common text-types and language pairs.

The point that translation itself is a fuzzy notion has come in for further attention since 1997. There have been important contributions by Halverson (1999 and several subsequent publications), arguing that translation is a prototype concept, and Tymoczko (2006), who argues that it is a cluster concept, like Wittgenstein's family resemblances between different kinds of games. However one conceptualizes it, it is evident that the notion of translation has fuzzy borders; that these borders vary to some extent according to time and place; and that we have sometimes found it hard to separate the idea of a translation *per se* from the narrower, evaluative idea of a *good* translation.

Claims about general features of translations may turn out to hold only for certain types of translations, and thus be less general than first assumed. Furthermore, in 3.7 above I raised the issue of whether some of the claims made about translation tendencies might be not specific to translation but also shared by other forms of discourse such as rewriting, and thus be more general than first assumed. This line of inquiry has been continuing. Ulrych (2009), for instance, found many common features (e.g. explicitation) between translation and other kinds of mediated discourse, such as transcriptions from oral to written. And Lanstyák and Heltai (2012) have argued that so-called translation and language contact universals are only a subset of a more general class of features of "constrained communication", similar to those found in the speech of bilinguals and in language contact situations. It has thus become important to be clear about the level of generality that is claimed for the tendencies we investigate, so that these claims can be tested appropriately.

CHAPTER 4

Translation strategies

4.1 General characteristics of strategies

I have suggested that some memes of translation become norms. But there are other kinds of translation memes, too: translation strategies are also memes. They are memes, that is, insofar as they are widely used by translators and recognized to be standard conceptual tools of the trade. Trainee translators learn them, and they are thus passed on from generation to generation as a meme pool: not fixed for all time, however, but open-ended and amenable to adaptation, variation and mutation. This chapter looks at some of the main strategies in the current pool.

The term "strategy" has many different senses in psychology, sociology, linguistics and applied linguistics, and translation theory. Different kinds of distinctions have been made between strategies, tactics, plans, methods, rules, processes, procedures and principles etc. (see e.g. Lörscher 1991): the result has been considerable terminological confusion. (And see Update below…)

Within applied linguistics, there have been studies on language learning strategies and on communication strategies. Language learning strategies are understood as being typical of good language learners: they include metacognitive, cognitive and social strategies such as self-monitoring, self-talk, inference-testing, co-operation etc. (see O'Malley and Chamot 1990). Communication strategies are ways of solving communication problems: the two main classes are reduction strategies (changing or reducing the message in some way, such as topic avoidance) and achievement strategies (attempts to preserve the messsage but change the means, such the use of paraphrase, approximation, restructuring, mime etc.). (See e.g. Faerch and Kasper 1983.) Both these areas of research are relevant to translation theory. Translators are, after all, people who specialize in solving particular kinds of communication problems; and translator trainees are interested in learning how to become good translators. In both cases, there are kinds of problems to be solved.

This chapter is less concerned with strategies as theoretical concepts than with their practical application; I shall not, therefore, give much space here to an exploration of the debate on their theoretical status and definition (for a review of this, see Jääskeläinen 1993, and the Update below). Instead, I shall first outline the points that seem most relevant to the way I shall use the term in this book, before shifting the discussion to a more practical level.

A process

Let us start with the idea that strategies are ways in which translators seek to react to norms: primarily, but not necessarily always, to try to conform to them. Note: not necessarily to achieve maximum equivalence, but simply to arrive at the best version they can think of, what they regard as the optimal translation. A strategy is understood here first of all as a planned way of doing something. To speak of translation strategies is to look at translation as an action, to place it in the wider context of action theory. This is precisely what a number of scholars have been doing over the past decade or so, particularly those associated with what I called the Communication stage of translation theory (see 2.6, above).

One such analysis is that of E. Steiner (1988). Steiner is concerned not just with translation but with language use more widely. He sets out to place language activity as a whole in the context of a general description of any human activity. In his model, any human activity has a hierarchical structure. General activities (such as translating) are composed of smaller actions, and these in turn are made up of smaller operations still. Some of the things we would like to say about translating apply to translation practice at a general level, but other things – such as, precisely, strategies – concern lower levels.

Textual manipulation

It should be stressed that the overall framework here is behavioural rather than neural. I make no claims about psychological reality, beyond the observation that strategies (in the sense used here) do appear to have the *prima facie* validity of being useful conceptual tools.

Furthermore, strategies (in the present sense) describe types of *linguistic* behaviour: specifically, text-linguistic behaviour. That is, they refer to operations which a translator may carry out during the formulation of the target text (the "texting" process), operations that may have to do with the desired relation between this text and the source text, or with the desired relation between this text and other target texts of the same type. These relations in turn are of course determined by other factors, such as the intended relation with the prospective readers, social and ideological factors etc.

Strategies, in the sense I shall use the term, are thus forms of explicitly *textual* manipulation. They are directly observable from the translation product itself, in comparison with the source text. I am therefore excluding here such translatorial actions as looking something up, accessing a database, checking a reference, reaching for the phone, going for a walk... (For a discussion of strategies from the more general point of view of creativity and problem-solving in translation, such as the use of divergent and convergent thinking, see Kußmaul 1995; also Lörscher 1991.)

Goal-oriented
Steiner stresses the teleological nature of human activity: actions of different kinds have objectives, goals. In this chapter, the kinds of goals we are interested in have to do with translation norms, of all kinds. So one criterion of a strategy is that it is goal-oriented.

Problem-centred
If a goal is the end-point of a strategy, what is the starting point? The simple answer is: a problem. A strategy offers a solution to a problem, and is thus problem-centred.

One of the results of think-aloud protocol research on translation has been that translators of all kinds tend to proceed in jerks: there are smooth, "automatic" patches of activity, interrupted by pauses, problem points where the translator appears to have to think in a non-routine manner: this is Lörscher's (1991) distinction between "non-strategic" and "strategic" behaviour. Further, these jerks do not proceed linearly, from beginning to end of a text; the process is more of a spiral one, with constant switching back and forth in the text, going back to an earlier problem again, and so on. It seems reasonable to assume that it is mainly at the problem points that translators have recourse to strategies, as ways of overcoming temporary hitches in the translation process. Kiraly (1995) draws on experimental evidence to arrive at a similar conclusion. He distinguishes between more controlled (more aware, "strategic") and less controlled (less conscious, more intuitive) processing. In Kiraly's model, tentative translation solutions emerge from the "intuitive workspace" (104f.) and are then monitored by the "Relatively Controlled Processing Center" for target-language acceptability and source-text relation; any problems arising are also processed by the same centre.

Jääskeläinen (1993) makes a similar distinction between "unmarked processing" and instances of "marked processing" indicated by "attention units", where the translator's conscious focus of attention shifts to a particular task. Apart from verbal protocols, eye-movement studies can also show the existence and location of such problem-points (see e.g. Tommola 1986, and more recently Jakobsen 2011).

However, Jääskeläinen prefers to extend the concept "strategy" to cover very general principles (such as "texts need not be translated word-for-word") which also govern unmarked processing, or which pertain to the translation task as a whole (such as the requirements set by the translation skopos). A similar approach is taken by Hönig and Kußmaul (1982), who use the term "strategic" to describe a translator's higher-level decisions concerning general reader-orientation and the like: these decisions determine both how and what the translator translates, in the attempt to convey as much of the original information as is relevant to the function of the text and to the needs of the reader. Jääskeläinen's definition of translation strategies reflects this broader conception: "they are a set of (loosely formulated) rules or principles which a translator uses to reach the goals determined by the translating situation in the most effective way" (1993:116).

It therefore seems helpful to distinguish between two levels of strategy, as Jääskeläinen does (116), following Séguinot (1989). At the more general level, where the problem to be solved is something like "how to translate this text or this kind of text", we have "global strategies". An obvious example of a global strategy is the translator's initial decision about the general nature of the appropriate relation between target and source texts, about how freely to translate, about what kinds of intertextual resemblance should be given priority. Another example might be the general issue of dialect choice: whether (and how) to represent source-text dialects. And another might concern decisions about whether an older source text should be modernized or historicized in translation (see e.g. Hochel 1991).

At the more specific level, on the other hand, the problem to be solved is something like "how to translate this structure / this idea / this item"; here we have "local strategies". Henceforth, my concern in this chapter will be with local strategies, and thus with local problems.

Potentially conscious
A further characteristic of strategies that is relevant to the distinction between global and local ones is that they are conscious, or at least potentially conscious; although deciding what is or is not conscious, and explicating possible degrees of consciousness, is a tricky business. One might suppose that global strategies are normally less conscious, to an individual translator at a given moment in translating, than local ones. On the other hand, many things can be *made* conscious, for instance in response to a question.

Lörscher's definition of a translation strategy takes explicit account of this: "a translation strategy is a potentially conscious procedure for the solution of a problem which an individual is faced with when translating a text segment from one language into another" (1991:76). This requirement – that a strategy should be potentially conscious – will be of particular relevance to Chapter 6, below.

In Steiner's analysis mentioned above, higher-level actions are defined as being conscious, in the sense that "the actor can report on [them]" (1988:148). For example, I can report to a friend that I am currently writing a book. But lower-level operations (fast typing, say) are mostly non-conscious; however, they may be consciously planned, for instance in less routine situations requiring explicit conscious attention (when I need to type in German I go more slowly and make more mistakes, which then need to be corrected). Conversely, conscious actions can become automatized and thus unconscious "as a consequence of 'facilitation' or practice" (148). Accordingly, we can think of strategies as problem-solving processes which are potentially conscious. Whether a given strategy is in fact conscious or unconscious, to an individual translator at a given moment, might have quite a bit to do with that translator's degree of professionalism: an argument we shall come back to later (6.1).

Intersubjective
As Jääskeläinen also argues, strategies tend to be "loosely formulated" rather than given explicit formal definitions. This is largely because of their intersubjective character: like other memes, strategies (as shared concepts) exist in Popper's World 3. As they spread through the community of translators – which they indeed tend to do, partly as a result of formal translator training – and thus continue their existence, strategies are typically formulated in non-formal, rule-of-thumb mode. This makes them learnable, and hence "portable" and readily accessible. They are, in effect, intersubjectively known to be "tried and tested procedures" (Lörscher 1991: 68) for achieving particular goals: proven conceptual tools.

In other words, strategies constitute easily accessible descriptive knowledge concerning a certain kind of procedural knowledge.

4.2 A classification

In the first place we need to distinguish between comprehension strategies and production strategies (cf. Gile 1992, 1995). Comprehension strategies have to do with the analysis of the source text and the whole nature of the translation commission; they are inferencing strategies, and they are temporally primary in the translation process. Production strategies are the results of various comprehension strategies: they have to do with how the translator manipulates the linguistic material in order to produce an appropriate target text. I shall be concerned here with production strategies only.

Given the nature of strategies as operationally defined above, it will be apparent that the kind of classification we can set up for production strategies must be a linguistic or text-linguistic one (rather than, say, a cognitive one, which would be more appropriate for comprehension strategies). At its simplest, such a taxonomy might consist of a single strategy only:

  Change something.

This would well illustrate the domain in which strategies operate: the space between source and target texts. "Change something" could be informally glossed as follows: if you are not satisfied with the target version that comes immediately to mind – because it seems ungrammatical, or semantically odd, or pragmatically weak, or whatever – then change something in it. The "being not satisfied" is thus evidence of the existence of a translation problem. (I shall not take up here the point that different translators may thus experience different problems; but see Chapter 6.)

This grand overall strategy also suggests that one way to look at strategies in more detail is in fact to see them as kinds of changes. Of course, the source text is "changed" anyway in an obvious sense when it is translated into another language; but change as a strategy begins to apply beyond the scope of this obvious change from one language to another. The changes in focus here are those that involve a choice between possibilities. This means we are not concerned with changes that are obligatory for obvious grammatical reasons, like adding a definite article in English when translating from a language which does not use one.

Such a view has led to a number of classifications of changes which have traditionally been thought of as various kinds of transfer operations or formal shifts from source to target text. Among many sources, probably the most influential has been that proposed by Vinay and Darbelnet (1958), despite much criticism. Their "procedures" were: borrowing, calque, literal (but grammatical) translation, transposition (change of word-class), modulation (change of point of view), "équivalence" (total structural change), and adaptation. Other sources from which I have drawn are Catford (1965), Nida (1964), Malone (1988) and Leuven-Zwart (1989/1990). (See also Update.)

Some of the classifications proposed have been extremely simple, such as Nida's with four classes only: change of order, omission, change of structure, addition. Nida then refines these by assigning different weightings, but his scales seem very ad hoc. Others are more complex, even dauntingly so, and hence less "portable": Malone's approach in particular, which uses a highly idiosyncratic terminology, would seem difficult to use in practice without a long apprenticeship.

The classification I shall propose is a heuristic one. It seems to work in practice; it uses accessible terminology; it seems to differentiate enough, but does not get bogged down in "unportable" detail; and it is flexible and open-ended. It comprises three primary groups of strategy: mainly syntactic/grammatical (coded as G), mainly semantic (S) and mainly pragmatic (Pr). (The point of the codes will become evident in Chapter 6.) It acknowledges that these groups overlap to some extent; that pragmatic ones usually involve semantic and syntactic ones as well, etc.; and that strategies of different types often co-occur. It also acknowledges that the strategies listed can themselves be broken down into sub-groups in a variety of ways. But no claims are being made here about the formal or theoretical status of these strategies or their grouping. In this context, if the strategies provide useful conceptual tools for talking about translation, for focusing on particular things that translators seem to do, and for improving translation skills, then that is justification enough.

The classification does, however, also represent an attempt to structure various proposals made by other scholars into an overall framework. Many of the strategies listed have obvious subtypes, but I shall not develop these in any detail here. I would also like to stress that the point of this chapter is not to explore particular translations in any detail, but simply to present a set of strategies that professionals tend to use. The level of analysis is thus fairly superficial: we are displaying a set of linguistic tools, not pondering here on exactly why they are used, nor on their various possible effects. Yet an analysis of this kind represents a necessary first stage towards further research that would dig deeper into the reasons why particular translators choose particular strategies under particular circumstances.

In principle, these strategies are not language-pair-specific, although many of them can be readily adapted to yield prototypical rules-of-thumb along the lines of "if the German source text has feature X, try Y in the English translation". I will use German-to-English translations to illustrate the strategies, mostly from an Austrian Airlines flight magazine. (The full texts used from this magazine are given in the Appendix.) The examples are therefore limited, and often rather simple.

4.2.1 Syntactic strategies

These may be thought of as involving purely syntactic changes of one kind or another. Larger changes obviously tend to involve smaller ones too. Syntactic strategies primarily manipulate form. The main ones are these:

G1: Literal translation
G2: Loan, calque
G3: Transposition
G4: Unit shift
G5: Phrase structure change
G6: Clause structure change
G7: Sentence structure change
G8: Cohesion change
G9: Level shift
G10: Scheme change

G1: Literal translation
I define this rather loosely, as meaning "maximally close to the SL form, but nevertheless grammatical". For some theorists (such as Newmark, and also Vinay and

Darbelnet), this strategy has the status of a default value. On this view, one only needs to deviate from literal translation if for some reason or other it does not work (recall the previous section). Example:

> ST: Wir wünschen Ihnen einen guten Flug mit Austrian Airlines.
> TT: We wish you a pleasant flight with Austrian Airlines.
> [I disregard here the slight semantic difference between *guten* and *pleasant*.]

G2: Loan, calque
This strategy covers both the borrowing of individual items and the borrowing of syntagma. Like the other strategies, it refers to a deliberate choice, not the unconscious influence of undesired interference.

In the above example, the English term *Austrian Airlines* has actually been adopted as the official name of this Austrian company. It therefore already represents a loan in the German.

Standard examples of calques are German *Übermensch* → English *Superman*; and English *the man in the street* → French *l'homme dans la rue*. Newmark (1988: 84) points out that calques are frequently used in the translation of the names of international organizations: *Communauté Économique Européenne* became *European Economic Community*.

The German term *Check-in-Bereich* for English *check-in area* combines both forms of loan.

One variant of this strategy is what Pym (1992a: 76) calls "double presentation". This means including both SL and TL versions in the target text, so that one acts as a gloss of the other. This strategy has interesting ideological implications, as Pym discusses: the SL form tends to be attributed a higher value, inherent in the SL words themselves. A classic example, also involving transcription, is to be found in sentences like: *This is the true sense of logos, the Word*. An example analysed in detail by Pym is ... *the phenomenon known as 'La Movida'* ('*The Happening*') from a Newsweek article. The late 1980s saw similar examples in texts dealing with *perestroika* (or *restructuring*) and *glasnost* (literally 'openness') and the like: the form of the double presentation varies.

Another variant is the introduction of a loan-based neologism as a translation solution. The first time a loan-word appears in a target language, it is in fact a neologism in that language. Others are created afresh from the target language itself, perhaps even by the democratic vote of language users. In Finland in the 1990s a weekly magazine held a competition to find a good Finnish term for the CD-ROM, so that people would no longer have to refer to a *CD-rom*, a loan translation. The most popular suggestion for a Finnish term turned out to be *romppu*, obviously based on the translation loan but given a natural Finnish form (neatly related to the earlier word denoting a floppy disk, *lerppu*). This neologism was adopted in informal use, but it did not displace *CD-rom* in formal contexts.

G3: Transposition
I use this term (from Vinay and Darbelnet) to mean any change of word-class, e.g. from noun to verb, adjective to adverb. Normally, this strategy obviously involves structural changes as well, but it is often useful to isolate the word-class change as being of interest in itself. Examples:

> ST: Es sind dies *informativ* gestaltete Hinweise auf ... [adverb]
> TT: Both deal in a highly *informative* way with ... [adjective]

> ST: Durch *Einbeziehung* von Mietwagenfirmen ... [noun]
> TT: Car rental companies have been *incorporated* ... [verb]

G4: Unit shift
This is a term from Catford (1965). The units are: morpheme, word, phrase, clause, sentence, paragraph. A unit shift occurs when a ST unit is translated as a different unit in the TT: this happens very frequently, of course, and subclassifications can be set up for unit shifts of different types. Examples:

> ST: Wir akzeptieren folgende Kreditkarten und ersuchen Sie, jene, mit der Sie Ihre Rechnung begleichen wollen, anzukreuzen.
> TT: We accept the following credit cards. Please mark the one which you would like to have charged.
> [One sentence to two; German clause becomes English sentence.]

> ST: ... eine Dienstleistung, die wir *gemeinsam* mit Swissair anbieten
> TT: ... a service which we are offering *in conjunction* with Swissair
> [German word to English phrase; this also incorporates a transposition, from adverb to noun.]

> ST: ... eine Dienstleistung, die wir gemeisam mit Swissair anbieten. *Es handelt sich um das Vielflieger-Programm "Qualiflyer".*
> TT: ... a service which we are offering in conjunction with Swissair: *the frequent-flyer program "Qualiflyer"*
> [German sentence to English phrase.]

G5: Phrase structure change
This strategy, or rather group of strategies, comprises a number of changes at the level of the phrase, including number, definiteness and modification in the noun phrase, and person, tense and mood in the verb phrase. The unit itself may remain unchanged, i.e. an ST phrase may still correspond to a TT phrase, but its internal structure changes. Examples:

ST: Die *Produkte* auf den JET SHOP Seiten sind ...
TT: The *merchandise* depicted on the JET SHOP pages is ...
[Plural to singular, count to non-count.]

ST: Dies Ausgabe von SKY LINES *enthalt*...
TT: In the present issue of SKY LINES *you will find* ...
[German third-person verb phrase to English second-person, involving a change of subject. Also, English adds the premodifier *present* whereas German has a demonstrative.]

ST: Details über "Qualiflyer" *finden Sie* auf Seite 97...
TT: For details of the "Qualiflyer" program, *turn* to page 97...
[German indicative to English imperative mood.]

G6: Clause structure change
Under this heading I group changes that have to do with the structure of the clause in terms of its constituent phrases. Various subclasses include constituent order (analysed simply as Subject, Verb, Object, Complement, Adverbial), active vs. passive voice, finite vs. non-finite structure, transitive vs. intransitive. Examples:

ST: Zu den Neuheiten im Produkt *kommen* weitere Verbesserungen unserer Dienstleistungen.
TT: The enlargement of our destinations list *is supplemented by* further improvements in our range of passenger services.
[German active intransitive to English passive voice.]

ST: *Diese Ausgabe* ... enthalt...
TT: *In the present issue* ... you will find...
[The semantically locative item (i.e. what a Case Grammar would mark as Locative) appears as subject in German and as an adverbial in English; this entails a change of clause structure from S+V... to A+S+V...]

ST: "Qualiflyer" ist auf den kombinierten Streckennetzen von Austrian Airlines and Swissair gültig.
TT: "Qualiflyer" is valid on the route networks of both Austrian Airlines and Swissair.
[The German clause structure S+V+A+C goes to English S+V+C+A.]

ST: ... und die Versandspesen dadurch relativ hoch *sein können*.
TT: ... which *makes* overall dispatching costs relatively high.
[The italicized change is from intransitive to transitive.]

ST: Artikel- und Preisänderungen *vorbehalten*.
TT: We *reserve the right to make* alterations to articles and prices.
[German non-finite (finite verb ellipted) to English finite.]

G7: Sentence structure change
This group of strategies affects the structure of the sentence unit, insofar as it is made up of clause units. Included are changes between main-clause and sub-clause status, changes of sub-clause types etc. Examples:

> ST: Schon der Name signalisiert ein sorgfältig durchdachtes Qualitätsprogramm...
> TT: As its name suggests, this is a painstakingly devised quality program...
> [German main clause to English sub-clause plus main clause.]

> ST: Durch Einbeziehung von Mietwagenfirmen und First-class-Hotels können Qualiflyer-Mitglieder auch am Boden Dienstleistungen zu besonderen Konditionen in Anspruch nehmen und zugleich Meilen-Guthaben buchen.
> TT: Car rental companies and first-class hotels have been incorporated into the "Qualiflyer" program, so that members can take advantage of its money-saving services on the ground too – and at the same time add more miles to their total.
> [The German is a single main clause, with one finite auxiliary verb and two co-ordinated infinitives; this is changed to English main verb + two co-ordinated sub-clauses.]

> ST: Wir möchten Sie weiters darauf aufmerksam machen, daß in einigen Ländern zusätzlich Zölle eingehoben werden und die Versandspesen dadurch relativ hoch sein können.
> TT: We should also like to remind you that some countries levy import tariffs, which makes overall dispatching costs relatively high.
> [The German has main clause + nominal sub-clause + co-ordinated nominal sub-clause; this changes to English main clause + nominal sub-clause + relative sub-clause.]

> ST: Denn wir sagen unseren Fluggästen gerne "Dankeschön".
> TT: Because we are happy for any opportunity to say "Thank you".
> [The German is a main clause; this is changed to a "free-standing" sub-clause in English.]

G8: Cohesion change
A cohesion change is something that affects intra-textual reference, ellipsis, substitution, pronominalization and repetition, or the use of connectors of various kinds. Examples:

> ST: *Diese* Ausgabe...
> TT: In *the present* issue...
> [The German reference to "proximity" is made through a demonstrative; this changes to definite article + adjective.]

ST: Hamburg wird im Linienverkehr angeflogen. *Ebenso* mit Beginn des Winterflugplanes werden die Kurse nach Amman ... und Minsk ... aufgenommen.
TT: The Vienna-Hamburg route will be one of our *new* scheduled services. *Other innovations* in the winter timetable will be ...
[German inter-sentence cohesion is via an adverb; this changes to English cohesion via the ordinal *other* plus the semantic repetition of *new* and *innovation*.]

ST: Zu den Neuheiten im Produkt kommen weitere Verbesserungen unserer Dienstleistungen. Besonders erwähnenswert ist der neue Terminal 1...
TT: The enlargement of our destinations list is supplemented by further improvements in our range of passenger services. The most notable *of these* is the new Terminal 1...
[The German uses no explicit connector between the two sentences; English adds a demonstrative.]

ST: Es sind dies informativ gestaltete Hinweise auf neue Ziele von Austrian Airlines im Winterflugplan 1992/93.
TT: Both deal in a highly informative way with Austrian Airlines destinations which will be making their debut in *the airline's* 1992/93 winter timetable.
[The German does not repeat *Austrian Airlines* in the premodification of *Winterflugplan*, presumably because the previous mention of the Airlines is so close and the definite article in *im* is considered sufficient to clarify the reference. In the English version, there is more of a gap between the mention of the Austrian Airlines and that of the winter timetable, and the translator perhaps thought that merely writing *the winter timetable* would be insufficiently clear, and chose to repeat *airline*.]

G9: Level shift

By levels I mean phonology, morphology, syntax and lexis. In a level shift, the mode of expression of a particular item is shifted from one level to another. An obviously influential factor here is the types of languages concerned, whether they are more analytic or more agglutinative, for instance. Another factor is the role of intonation: in some languages (e.g. English) this can express meaning (such as "interrogativeness") which other languages express through morphology (e.g. Finnish), or wholly or partly through word order (e.g. German). Examples:

ST: Wir ... *ersuchen Sie,* ... anzukreuzen.
TT: *Please* mark ...
[German expresses the sense of "polite request" here via lexis (a particular verb) plus syntax (main verb plus infinitive); English uses only the lexical item *please*.]

ST: ... nur eine kleine Auswahl unserer JET SHOP *Produktpalette*
TT: ... only a small selection of the JET SHOP *articles available*
[Compound nouns are one kind of lexical item; the English here chooses an ellipted relative clause instead.]

G10: Scheme change
This refers to the kinds of changes that translators incorporate in the translation of rhetorical schemes such as parallelism, repetition, alliteration, metrical rhythm etc. Initially, the translator can choose between three basic alternatives here (a–c).

(a) *ST scheme X → TT scheme X*. That is, if the ST scheme is judged to be relevant to the translation task, it can be (to some extent) preserved (e.g. ST alliteration → TT alliteration): in fact, no change.

In the airline texts referred to above, one rhetorical scheme that seems to be used deliberately is the repetition of key words such as Austrian Airlines, JET SHOP, Qualiflyer. For obvious reasons, the translator has chosen to preserve these unchanged.

For a literary example of alternative (a), consider these lines from Goethe's *Römische Elegien* 1.5):

> Oftmals hab' ich auch schon in ihren Armen gedichtet,
> Und des Hexameters Mass leise mit fingernder Hand
> Ihr auf dem Rücken gezählt.

The hexameter metre here is obviously intended iconically, since it manifests the very rhythm that is being described. A translation might thus seek to preserve this if possible, as being an intrinsic feature of the text. A suggestion (from Chesterman, ed. 1989: 178):

> Often have I composed poems even in her arms,
> Counting the hexameter's beat softly with fingering hand
> There on the back of the beloved.

(b) *ST scheme X → TT scheme Y*. That is, the ST scheme can be changed to another scheme that is deemed to serve an appropriate or similar function in the TL (e.g. ST parallelism → TT chiasmus). The following example comes from a Vienna City Guide.

ST: Es gibt ein Wien fur jedermann. Ein Wien für Kulturfans, die die weltberühmten Philharmoniker hören wollen; für Architekturliebhaber, die Wiens Jugendstilbauten oder das Hollein-Haus bestaunen können. Ein Wien für Gourmets, die sich an Wiener Schnitzel und Sachertorte gütlich tun, und eines für Souvenir-jäger, die Trachtenmode und Augarten-Porzellan mitnehmen wollen.

> TT: There's a Vienna for every taste. Culture vultures will long rave about hearing the famous Philharmonic, and architecture buffs will stand enthralled before the Jugendstil buildings or Hollein's house on Stephansplatz. Gourmets will relish the legendary "Schnitzels" and "Sachertorte", while souvenir hunters will snap up costume fashions and Augarten porcelain.
> [The basic rhetorical device used in the ST is that of a single main verb followed by a list, a series of postmodified noun phrases some of which function as independent clauses; the items of the list are arranged in pairs. The translator has foregrounded the notion of rhetorical pairs and opted for a parallelistic pattern. The second and third sentences have a parallel structure, and the two finite clauses in each sentence are also parallelled.]

(c) *ST scheme X → TT scheme Ø*. That is, the scheme is dropped altogether. For instance, in the previously quoted example the German ST makes some use also of asyndeton: note the lack of any connector between the sentences, and between the two parts of the second sentence. The translator has dropped this rhetorical feature.

To these three basic alternatives, we can also add a fourth possibility:

(d) *ST scheme Ø → TT scheme X*. Here, the translator opts to use a rhetorical scheme of some kind, although not prompted directly to do so by the ST. E.g.:

> ST: Kulturfans
> TT: Culture vultures
> [The TT could have selected e.g. "culture lovers", but has preferred to add the rhetorical element of phonological similarity in this established collocation; from the Vienna City Guide, see above.]

4.2.2 Semantic strategies

Under semantic strategies I group kinds of changes which mainly have to do with lexical semantics, but also include aspects of clause meaning such as emphasis. Semantic strategies manipulate nuances of meaning. Several of these strategies derive from Vinay and Darbelnet's concept of modulation. We will look at:

S1: Synonymy
S2: Antonymy
S3: Hyponymy
S4: Converses
S5: Abstraction change
S6: Distribution change
S7: Emphasis change

S8:   Paraphrase
S9:   Trope change
S10: Other semantic changes

S1: Synonymy
This strategy selects not the "obvious" equivalent but a synonym or near-synonym for it, e.g. to avoid repetition. Example:

> ST: Diese *Ausgabe* von SKY LINES...
> TT: ... the present *issue* of SKY LINES
> ST: ... auf Seite 97 dieser SKY LINES *Ausgabe*.
> TT: ... page 97 of this *magazine*.
> [The English uses two near-synonyms for the single German term, within the same text.]

S2: Antonymy
The translator selects an antonym and combines this with a negation element. Example:

> ST: Alle Preise inklusive MWSt., jedoch *exklusive* Nachnahmegebühr und Porto.
> TT: All prices include V.A.T. (value added tax) but *do not include* the C.O.D. (cash on delivery) fee and mail charges.

S3: Hyponymy
Shifts within the hyponymy relation are common. In principle, this strategy comes in three subclasses:

(a) *ST superordinate → TT hyponym*, i.e. specification. Example:

> ST: zahlreicher anderer *Gesellschaften*
> TT: numerous other *airlines*
> [The translator chooses a hyponym of the superordinate *companies*.]

(b) *ST hyponym → TT superordinate*, i.e. generalization. Example:

> ST: das mitteleuropäische *Luftdrehkreuz* Wien
> TT: Vienna ... a Central European *interchange*
> [A *Luftdrehkreuz* is a kind, a hyponym, of *Drehkreuz*: the translator has moved up to the corresponding superordinate.]

(c) *ST hyponym X → TT hyponym Y (of the same superordinate)*. To see how this subclass (c) strategy works, consider what Austrian Airlines actually sells. We might roughly divide its products (the superordinate) into two (hyponyms): actual flights, and the various subsidiary services attached to these. In the ST we are using, the term *Verkehr* is used to describe the flight routes, as in the compound *Nachbarschaftsverkehr*, which is translated *routes linking...* Some near-synonymous expressions are also used, such as *Streckennetzen* and *Angebot* translated as *route network(s)*, and *Kurse* translated as *scheduled flights*. For the services concept, the German uses *Dienstleistung(en)*, or simply *Leistung*, which are translated as *services, passenger services*. So far, the hyponym relation is clear, in both languages: two classes of product, consistently distinguished by different lexical hyponyms, *route* and *service* in the TT. But at one point the hyponyms are switched:

> ST: Linienverkehr
> TT: scheduled services
> [Here, the translator has selected to shift from the "route" hyponym to the "service" hyponym.]

S4: Converses

Converses are pairs of (usually) verbal structures which express the same state of affairs from opposing viewpoints, such as *buy* and *sell*. An example from the Airlines text:

> ST: Bitte beachten Sie, daß zu den angegebenen Preisen noch Porto und Nachnahmegebühren *verrechnet* werden.
> TT: Kindly note that the prices quoted are *exclusive of* postal charges and collection fee.
> [The German states that B is added to A, the translation that A is exclusive of B.]

S5: Abstraction change

A different selection of abstraction level may either move from abstract to more concrete or from concrete to more abstract.

> ST: aus aller Welt
> TT: from all corners of the globe
> [The TT is more concrete, both in the addition of *corners* and the choice of *globe* rather than *world*.]

> ST: Charter-*Tochter*
> TT: charter subsidiary
> [Here the TT selects a more abstract term.]

S6: Distribution change

This is a change in the distribution of the "same" semantic components over more items (expansion) or fewer items (compression). Expansion "dilutes" the text somewhat. Example:

> ST: Selbstverständlich können wir Ihnen die Unterlagen auch *zusenden.*
> TT: We can, of course, also *forward* the documentation to you *by mail.*

Compression has the opposite effect, with a denser distribution:

> ST: ... jene, mit der Sie *Ihre Rechnung begleichen* wollen
> TT: ... the one which you would like to have *charged*

S7: Emphasis change
This strategy adds to, reduces or alters the emphasis or thematic focus, for one reason or another. Examples:

> ST: informativ
> TT: in a *highly* informative way [Emphasis added.]

> ST: ... daß damit das mitteleuropäische Luftdrehkreuz Wien fur Gäste aus aller Welt noch interessanter und bequemer geworden ist.
> TT: ... that this added degree of convenience will make Vienna even more attractive as a Central European interchange to visitors from all corners of the globe.
> [The ST emphasizes the quality of the new interchange, syntactically the subject complement; the translator has chosen to emphasize the range of visitors. Other strategies too are in evidence here.]

S8: Paraphrase
The paraphrase strategy results in a TT version that can be described as loose, free, in some contexts even undertranslated. Semantic components at the lexeme level tend to be disregarded, in favour of the pragmatic sense of some higher unit such as a whole clause. An example from the airline text:

> ST: Wenn Sie sich entschließen, die Vorteile zu nutzen...
> TT: If you decide to become a member of the scheme...

This is a typical strategy for the translation of idioms, for instance, for which no corresponding idiomatic expression can be found in the TL.

S9: Trope change
This strategy, or rather set of strategies, applies to the translation of rhetorical tropes (i.e. figurative expressions) in the same way as strategy G10 above applied to the translation of schemes. Correspondingly, we can first distinguish three main subclasses of strategy here (a–c):

(a) *ST trope X → TT trope X.* For instance, a ST metaphor is retained as a metaphor in the TT. Further subclasses can obviously be set up at this point (i)–(iii):

(i) The TT trope is the same trope in terms of its lexical semantics. In the case of a metaphor, for instance, both tenor and vehicle (in the sense of Richards 1936) would be preserved, as in:

TT: MD-81 / MD-82: Das Rückgrat der Austrian Airlines-*Flotte*
ST: MD-81 / MD-82: The mainstay of the Austrian Airlines *fleet*
[The naval metaphor of "fleet" is preserved, and is in fact strengthened by the choice of *mainstay* rather than *backbone*.] Other examples:

ST: Qualiflyer
TT: Qualiflyer
[This semi-pun, which is itself a loan into German, has been retained unchanged in the TT.]

ST: *Das Museum ... dokumentiert* die Stadtentwicklung
TT: *The ... Museum documents* the city's growth...
[The TT retains the personification trope of the ST, in the same lexical form; example from a feature article on Hamburg.]

(ii) The TT trope is of the same type as the one in the ST, but is not semantically identical, only related. We might say that the image comes from the same source, the same general area of experience (cf. Rissanen 1971). E.g.:

ST: ... dessen einfacher Abwicklung wir uns von Mitbewerbern *abheben* wollen.
TT: ... whose distinguishing features ... should *give it a clear edge over* rival programs.
[The translator has retained a metaphorical expression but changed it slightly: both texts have the image of something being higher than something else, but the viewpoint of each is different; the TT is also somewhat more concrete (cf. strategy S5).]

(iii) The TT trope is of the same type, but not related lexically to the ST one: the source of the image is different.

ST: Als Kaiserin Elisabeth ... Kaiser Franz Josephs *ein und alles* (war)...
TT: In the days [when] ... the Empress Elizabeth ... was still *the apple of Emperor Franz Joseph's eye*...
[Both versions (from a guide to Vienna) use metaphorical expressions, but these are lexically unrelated.]

(b) *ST trope X → ST trope Y.* Here, the general feature of figurativeness has been retained, but the realization of this feature is different, so that for instance an ST metaphor might be translated as one based on a different tenor, or as some other trope altogether. E.g.:

> ST: Ein komfortabler *Europäer*, der Kontinente verbindet.
> TT: European *comfort* which spans continents.
> [This is a headline describing a class of airbus. The image underlying the ST is an equative metaphor: the airbus *is* a comfortable European which… The TT image is constructed differently: the underlying idea is that the airbus *has* a European comfort which…, and it is this comfort that is then personified. The strategy also affects the emphasis here.]

(c) *ST trope X → TT trope Ø*. Here the figurative element is dropped altogether. E.g.:

> ST: Herrliche Leihgaben aus öffentlichen und privaten Sammlungen machen das New Yorker Museum of Modern Art zu einem *Mekka* für alle Fans des Moderne-Klassikers Henri Matisse.
> TT: Devotees of Henri Matisse won't want to miss the current show at New York's Museum of Modern Art, which is made up of magnificent items on loan from public and private collections.
> [The translator drops the metaphorical use of *Mekka*.]

To these, as in G10, we can also add:

(d) *ST trope Ø → TT trope X*. That is, a trope is used in the TT but not in the ST, as in:

> ST: Damit können weltweit Meilen-Guthaben *gesammelt*… werden.
> TT: This means that passengers can *clock up* "Qualiflyer" mileage worldwide…
> [The ST expression is not figurative; the TT uses a metaphor.]

The following example, from elsewhere in the same magazine, also adds a trope:

> ST: Paris im Picasso-Fieber.
> TT: Picasso fever has seized Paris.
> [The German personifies *Paris*; the English translation does so too, but also personifies the fever.]

(For detailed discussion of these and other options, see e.g. Newmark 1981; van den Broeck 1981; Königs 1990; Toury 1995: 81f.)

S10: Other semantic changes
These would include other modulations of various kinds, such as change of (physical) sense or of deictic direction, as in:

ST: besonders *erwähnenswert*
TT: the most *notable*
[Change from oral to visual sense.]

ST: Ihr besonderes Augenmerk dürfen wir auf eine Dienstleitung *lenken*
TT: We should also like to *draw* your attention to a service
[The German steers attention from "here" to "there", the English beckons it from "there" to "here".]

4.2.3   Pragmatic strategies

By pragmatic strategies I mean those which primarily have to do with the selection of information in the TT, a selection that is governed by the translator's knowledge of the prospective readership of the translation. I do not enter here into any wider discussion of the place of pragmatics in translation more generally, but propose a set of strategies comparable to the syntactic and semantic ones mentioned above. Pragmatic strategies tend to involve bigger changes from the ST, and typically incorporate syntactic and/or semantic changes as well. If syntactic strategies manipulate form, and semantic strategies manipulate meaning, pragmatic strategies can be said to manipulate the message itself. These strategies are often the result of a translator's global decisions concerning the appropriate way to translate the text as a whole. My set is:

Pr1:   Cultural filtering
Pr2:   Explicitness change
Pr3:   Information change
Pr4:   Interpersonal change
Pr5:   Illocutionary change
Pr6:   Coherence change
Pr7:   Partial translation
Pr8:   Visibility change
Pr9:   Transediting
Pr10: Other pragmatic changes

Pr1: Cultural filtering
This strategy is also referred to as naturalization, domestication or adaptation; it describes the way in which SL items, particularly culture-specific items, are translated as TL cultural or functional equivalents, so that they conform to TL norms. The opposite procedure, whereby such items are not adapted in this way but e.g. borrowed or transferred directly, is thus exoticization, foreignization or estrangement (see Jones 1989). House (1981) speaks of a "cultural filter" in this context.

(See also Florin 1993, on ways of translating realia. The larger ideological issues involved in the selection of this strategy are discussed e.g. by Venuti 1995a; see also Chapter 7, below.) Examples:

> ST: Familienname
> TT: Surname
> [On an order form; compare the exoticized "Family name".]

> ST: Flughafen Wien
> TT: Vienna *International* Airport
> [By adding *International* the translator has adapted to the name by which this airport is indeed officially known in English.]

> ST: Vorstandsdirektor / Vorstandsdirektor-Stv.
> TT: President / Chief Executive Marketing & Sales
> [These titles, of the executives who have signed the airline magazine editorial, have been adapted to American-English norms.]

Pr2: Explicitness change
This change is either towards more explicitness (explicitation) or more implicitness (implicitation). Explicitation is well known to be one of the most common translatorial strategies (cf. 3.6.1). It refers to the way in which translators add inferrable information explicitly in the TT, information which is only implicit in the ST. Examples:

> ST: Bei *Versand* in das Ausland ...
> TT: ... when *merchandise is dispatched* abroad
> [The translator makes explicit *what* is sent.]

> ST: ... die bestellten Artikel werden *Ihnen* mit der Post per Nachnahme zugesandt.
> TT: The articles which you order will be sent cash-on-delivery (COD) by post *to your address.*
> [Explicitation of *Ihnen.*]

> ST: Artikel- und Preisänderungen vorbehalten.
> TT: *We* reserve *the right to make* alterations to articles and prices.
> [The italicized items are all explicitated.]

> ST: ... *dort* in einem eigenem Check-in-Bereich
> TT: ... its own check-in area *in the new terminal*
> [Explicitation has the effect here of increasing the level of specificity; the TT version is also more concrete (cf. S5).]

Implicitation is the opposite change: bearing in mind what the readers can be reasonably expected to infer, the translator leaves some elements of the message implicit. Examples:

> ST: ... so wenden Sie sich, bitte, ... an unsere Mitarbeiter beim Check-in oder an unsere *Flugbegleiter an Bord*.
> TT: ... our check-in staff or the *flight attendants* will be glad to be of assistance.
> [The translator opts to leave "on board" implicit.]
>
> ST: bei Redaktionsschluß *dieses Bordmagazins*
> TT: At the time of going to press
> [The italicized element is left implicit.]

Pr3: Information change
By this I mean either the addition of new (non-inferrable) information which is deemed to be relevant to the TT readership but which is not present in the ST, or the omission of ST information deemed to be irrelevant (this latter might involve summarizing, for instance). An example of addition:

> ST: Hamburg wird im Linienverkehr angeflogen.
> TT: The *Vienna*-Hamburg route will be one of our new scheduled services.
> [We are flying Austrian Airlines, but at this point in the text we have not yet had any mention of the fact that the company is based in Vienna. For some readers, this might be relevant information, and the translator adds it here.]

Omission is the opposite process. Strictly speaking, omitted information in this sense cannot be subsequently inferred: it is this that distinguishes this strategy from that of implicitation. Elsewhere in the same magazine, for instance, we find a list of the mail-order merchandise, which includes the following item:

> ST: Spielesammlung (Dame, Mühle etc.)
> TT: Games compendium (checkers etc.)
> [The translator has omitted the second game, presumably because it is not commonly played in the English-speaking world.]

Pr4: Interpersonal change
This strategy operates at the level of the overall style: it alters the formality level, the degree of emotiveness and involvement, the level of technical lexis and the like: anything that involves a change in the relationship between text/author and reader. In our main source text here, the second person plural is used, and this in itself is a syntactic indicator of formality that English lacks: in this respect, the translator had no choice. But in other respects interpersonal changes seem to be chosen deliberately. An example:

ST: Damit können ... Meilen-Guthaben *gesammelt* ... werden.
TT: This means that passengers can *clock up* "Qualiflyer" mileage...
[The choice of a phrasal verb, rather than "collected" or "registered", makes the TT slightly less formal.]

Or compare the two forms of address:

ST: Sehr geehrte Fluggäste!
TT: Dear passengers,
[The German norm here stresses the high status of the addressee, while the English one rather expresses solidarity.]

Pr5: Illocutionary change
Illocutionary changes (changes of speech act) are usually linked with other strategies too. For instance, changing the mood of the verb from indicative to imperative (cf. G5 above) also involves an illocutionary change from statement to request.

Other such changes might involve, for instance, the use of rhetorical questions and exclamations in texts, such as the following example from a magazine text on why Dr Zamenhof invented Esperanto:

ST: Beweggrund war seine Sorge über den Unfrieden zwischen Polen, Russen, Deutschen und Juden in seinem Geburtsort Byalistok.
TT: *His motive?* The unrest between Poles, Russians, Germans and Jews in his native town of Bialystok.
[The translation introduces a rhetorical question, to produce a more dialogic text.]

There can also be changes within particular classes of speech acts. For example, within the class of acts known as representatives (such as stating, telling, reporting), a translator may choose to shift from direct to indirect speech.

Pr6: Coherence change
Whereas the cohesion change strategy listed under G8 has to do with formal markers of textual cohesion, coherence changes have to do with the logical arrangement of information in the text, at the ideational level. (See e.g. Blum-Kulka 1986.)

An example: the original German of the airline text starts with an introductory paragraph of a couple of sentences, and the second paragraph then focuses on the route innovations (see the Appendix). But the translation has no paragraph break here, after the introductory sentences. In other respects the translation follows the overall information structure of the original. The effect of this strategic change is to link the introductory sentences with the route innovations into one whole information unit, separate from the services innovations that follow in the next paragraph. The change also affects the status of *Hamburg*, which is given subject-position at the beginning of the second paragraph in the ST but receives less emphasis (as a mid-paragraph modifier) in the TT.

Pr7: Partial translation
This covers any kind of partial translation, such as summary translation, transcription, translation of the sounds only, and the like. Classical examples are, for instance, the "symbolist" translations of literary texts, such as:

> ST: My heart leaps up when I behold
> A rainbow in the sky.   (Wordsworth)
> TT: Mai hart lieb zapfen eibe hold
> er renn bohr in sees kai.   (Jandl)

Pr8: Visibility change
This refers to a change in the status of the authorial presence, or to the overt intrusion or foregrounding of the translatorial presence. For instance, translator's footnotes, bracketed comments (such as explanations of puns) or added glosses explicitly draw the reader's attention to the presence of the translator, who is no longer "transparent" (see Venuti 1995a). The translator is thus visibly interposed between original author and reader, and the author is accordingly backgrounded (temporarily). (See Schiavi 1996; Hermans 1996.)

A curious and extreme example of this change in translator's transparency is furnished by a postmodern Russian novel by Jevgeni Popov, translated into Finnish as *Aaton aattona* (literally, 'On the eve of the eve') by Jukka Mallinen, himself a well-known literary figure in St. Petersburg circles. At one point in the novel, the hero travels from Russia to Helsinki, which is portrayed as a haven of peace and opportunity and personified in the figure of one "Uncle Jukka". The point is that this Uncle Jukka is without a doubt Jukka Mallinen, the translator, whom Popov has thus incorporated as a character in the very novel which Mallinen will translate. To many of the original Russian readers, this postmodern role-play is presumably absent; but to many Finnish readers the translator is most obviously "present", "visible", not transparent. (The novel is reviewed by Pesonen, 1993.)

Pr9: Transediting
This is a term suggested by Stetting (1989) to designate the sometimes radical re-editing that translators have to do on badly written original texts: it includes drastic re-ordering, rewriting, at a more general level than the kinds of changes covered by the strategies so far mentioned.

Pr10: Other pragmatic changes
One example would be layout: in the original of the first airline text (text A, see Appendix), the layout was in two parallel columns on a single page, with the German on the left. The German signature was right-justified and the English one left-justified, so that the page ended with both signatures aligned in the centre.

Another example here is the choice of dialect, in particular British vs. American English: the translator of the airline texts opts for American, perhaps because of official company policy. This counts as a pragmatic change in that the source text is not readership-specified in this way.

4.3 Motivation

The motivation underlying a translator's choice of strategy derives ultimately from the norms of translation discussed earlier. Consider how a translator might answer the question: why did you use that strategy here, why did you write X? Following Section 3.6.3, the possible answers can be initially outlined thus:

1. Desire to conform to the expectancy norms of the target-language community.
2. Desire to conform to the accountability norm.
3. Desire to conform to the communication norm.
4. Desire to conform to the relation norm.

Underlying these first-level explanations we can of course suggest others: a translator wishes to conform to a given norm because of various political or cultural or social pressures, because of personal ideological reasons, instinct, and so on. For instance, Lefevere (1992: 59f.) discusses examples where translators of Anne Frank's diary tended to omit or change information which was considered to breach certain target-culture norms of propriety, certain political or sexual taboos. This use of what I would call information-change or implicitation strategies is presumably motivated by the translators' understanding of the expectations of the readers and of the client; by the cultural and political climate of the time of translation; by the influence exerted over their choices by the client; and perhaps by the translators' own ideology insofar as this is in agreement with the expectancy norms: if they are members of the target culture, they themselves may not have wished to go against these norms.

Another example: when Faulkner's novels were first translated into Finnish it was at a time when modernist techniques in Finnish literature were still in their infancy. The early translations tended to conform to the prevailing stylistic norms of Finnish, which meant that they split up Faulkner's long sentences (strategy G7), made much use of paraphrases (S8), little use of literal translation (G1), and very little use of stream-of-consciousness and free indirect speech, which were not yet current in Finnish prose (illocutionary changes, Pr5), etc. (Randell 1986). The reasons for these choices are to be found in the prevailing interpretation of translation norms (priority given to expectations of fluent target style, the duty of the translator to make necessary changes in order to achieve this, etc.), and also in the state of poetics and literary development in Finland at the time. Later, Saarikoski's norm-breaking translation of Salinger's *Catcher in the Rye* helped to loosen the dominant poetic constraints and open up other choices for subsequent translators, who were thus able to select a different range of strategies (e.g. Robinson 1987).

As already noted, therefore, the overriding motivation is not inevitably "in order to achieve equivalence", or at least "maximum equivalence". The overriding motivation is the intention to arrive at the best possible translation in the given circumstances. This general motivation obviously covers a multitude of more specific reasons, most of which have been mentioned or implied in the preceding chapter; but some additional comments can be made here.

4.3.1   The significance threshold

To a large extent, expectancy norms are straightforward matters concerning the grammaticality and acceptability of the target text, at all levels from morphology and syntax to text and discourse. As argued above (3.8), some of these expectancy norms are qualitative and others quantitative. One additional aspect that has not so far been mentioned is what I call the *significance threshold*: this varies from culture to culture, and can have quite an effect on the choice of pragmatic strategy. (I do not refer here to the strict statistical sense of this term.)

The concept of the significance threshold arises by analogy from that of the silence threshold, which is a well-known phenomenon in contrastive research: some cultures have a higher tolerance of silence, a higher silence threshold, than others (see e.g. Tannen and Saville-Troike 1985). We can define the silence threshold as follows: the silence threshold marks the point above which speakers feel it necessary to say something. The *significance threshold* is defined thus:

> The significance threshold marks the point above which something is felt to be worth saying.

Whereas the silence threshold marks the lower edge of the felt need to say *anything at all*, the significance threshold marks the point at which *a given message or meaning* is felt to be worth uttering. The higher the significance threshold, the more meaningful something must be in order to get uttered. Things below the significance threshold are deemed "insignificant", not worth saying.

If this significance threshold is at a different level between source and target culture, translators need to exploit strategies to take account of this difference. Going from Finnish to English, for example, translators occasionally seem to feel a need to "strengthen" the English text in some way, to add emphasis, emotiveness, concreteness, even colloquialness, in order for the target text to meet the expectancies of the readership. In Finnish, a little seems to go a long way, as it were; in English, you need more to achieve the "same" effect, the "same" distance above the significance threshold. (Compare the notions of "global preference" and "global recrescence" in Malone 1988: 50.)

There is an example which seems to illustrate a similar difference between German and English in the airline text we have been looking at:

> ST: Es sind dies informativ gestaltete Hinweise auf neue Ziele von Austrian Airlines im Winterflugplan 1992/1993.
> TT: Both deal in a *highly* informative way with Austrian Airlines destinations which will be making their debut in the airline's 1992/93 winter timetable.

The translator has used the pragmatic strategy of addition (Pr3), adding an element which increases the emphasis (strategy S8), and I suggest that the motive has been precisely this felt difference in the significance threshold: the translator evidently thought that without the addition, the English would appear to have been "written too quietly", as it were.

In a study of the way translators edit journalistic texts from French to English, Séguinot (1982) found that the overwhelmingly most frequent motivation mentioned (accounting for 50% of all editorial changes) was the desire to increase readability. This would fall under our communication norm, together with values such as clarity and explicitness. Séguinot's results are also interesting in the light of the significance threshold. The second most frequent motivations (21% each) were the desire to adapt the text to the target audience (cf. my pragmatic strategy Pr1), and the felt need to reduce emotive and figurative language. This suggests that, on the basis of her data at least, the significance threshold of English is perhaps lower than it is for French: the texts needed to be "toned down" somewhat to meet the target culture's different tolerance of rhetorical display. Interestingly, a similar conclusion is reached by Vehmas-Lehto (1989) with respect to journalistic translations from Russian to Finnish: the Finnish also needed to be toned down, in order to meet the appropriate conditions of its higher significance threshold, otherwise the translations were felt to be "over-written".

4.3.2 Compensation

A final additional point concerns the notion of compensation. This is a well-known motive underlying many strategies. Its validity rests on the understanding that what is translated is a whole text, not any smaller unit of language. If, therefore, the translator chooses to do something (add, omit, change etc.) at one point in the text, this action in itself may be sufficient justification for a compensatory strategy at some other point in the text. Further, such compensation may even work retrospectively: a choice made at a later point in a text may then prompt the translator to back-track to an earlier point and make a compensatory change there.

The idea has long been a commonplace meme among translators. Dryden ([1680] 1975) thus justified his own translation method, claiming that he had dared to add new touches of stylistic elegance at some places in the text, in order to make up for those he had lost elsewhere.

Of the examples we have looked at so far, the strategies concerning scheme and trope changes (G10 and S9) can also illustrate compensation. The loss of a scheme or trope, or the impossibility of an identical one, can often be compensated for by adding another type, perhaps even elsewhere in the text. (For an extended discussion of compensation as a strategy rather than as motivation, see Harvey 1995.)

4.4 Update

Arguments about how best to conceptualize translation strategies seem never-ending. Gambier (2008) gives a critical analysis of several proposals, including my own in this chapter and a later article (2005b), others mentioned in this chapter, and also those by Newmark (1988) and by Molina and Hurtado Albir (2002). He reminds us of the military origin of the term "strategy", meaning a general plan to reach a defined objective, comparing it with "tactic", meaning a specific action carried out in accordance with a given strategy. He shows the terminological confusion around this topic, with some terms having several senses (such as adaptation) and other senses having several near-synonymous terms (such as paraphrase, descriptive equivalence, explicitation). He points out that the criteria for many of the categories proposed are unclear. Gambier's own proposal is that we keep "strategy" for general, global decisions about how to translate a whole text, i.e. a synonym of, or replacement for, "method". "Tactics" are then the ways of local problem-solving that this chapter has discussed, either conscious or automatized. He suggests using "solutions" (replacing Catford's "shifts") for the classification of the resulting differences and similarities between source and target texts. In my own later paper (2005b) I proposed using "techniques" for the local textual changes I have in this chapter called "strategies", so that "strategy" could be kept for the global sense of a problem-solving plan. Apologies for contributing to the confusion!

One later contribution not mentioned by Gambier is the work of Schreiber (e.g. 1998); it is, however, discussed in Pym (2016). Schreiber relates his proposed procedures (*Verfahren*) to what he sees as the main translation methods: text-restricted (a method that preserves relevant features of form and content), context-sensitive (preserving intended meaning and function), and adaptation (translating more freely, with bigger changes of form and content). His listed procedures are partly versions of those by Vinay and Darbelnet (1958), but also include change of word order, explicitation, addition and omission, and helping procedures (*Hilfsverfahren*) such as translator's notes, forewords, glossaries. As Pym notes, Scheiber's list includes obligatory and routine changes (like adding a necessary definite article) as well as problem-solving options.

The latest proposal I am aware of is Pym's new monograph entitled *Translation Solutions for Many Languages – Histories of a Flawed Dream* (2016). This is an impressively broad historical and critical survey of many proposals, showing how concepts and terms have spread and become adapted under different conditions (like memes, in fact!). There are telling criticisms of typical and specific weaknesses in the various taxonomies discussed (including mine), concerning the ways categories are often set up and illustrated, and about the lack of adequate organizing principles. It concludes with Pym's own proposal, for what he calls "solution types" (following Zabalbeascoa 2000). These concern problem-solving, not routine or obligatory changes. They fall into three groups: Copying, Expression Change, and Content Change. The number of actual "solution types" is only seven, which Pym argues is a teachable and memorizable set. But each solution type can be realized in many ways. Pym's list is as follows:

Copying:
    Copying words (or sounds, morphology…)
    Copying structure (fixed phrases, text structure…)
Expression Change:
    Perspective change (focus, voice, word-class…)
    Density change (generalization/specification, explicitation/implicitation, multiple translation, resegmentation…)
    Compensation (new place in text, e.g. note, shift of level between lexis and syntax…)
    Cultural correspondence (corresponding culture-specific terms…)
Content change:
    Text tailoring (correction, omission, addition…)

Pym comments that all these solution types are potentially possible for all problem types. I'm not sure about this: as he points out himself, Text Tailoring (cf. transediting, Pr9 above) is not likely to solve translation problems in legal texts, for instance. He also notes that the top-down order of his solutions represents increasing effort by the translator (as did the classic list by Vinay and Darbelnet, who also had seven categories). But he adds that this effort must be related to risk: in cases of high risk, which threaten loss of trust or breakdown of communication, more effort is obviously justified. On compensation, his view differs from mine: as illustrated above in 4.3.2, I see the wish to compensate as a motivation for making a change, whereas Pym takes compensation as a kind of change in itself. Pym has tested the applicability of his categories in translation classes and seminars in different countries and between different language pairs, and refined his taxonomy accordingly, which is greatly to his credit. Although he states that the aim of his classification is pedagogical, not as an aid to descriptive research, it will no doubt also be used and tested by researchers in descriptive analysis.

CHAPTER 5

Translation as theory

5.1 Tentative Theory, Error Elimination and translational competence

Recall the Popperian schema introduced in Chapter 1:

P1 → TT → EE → P2

We have so far (in Chapter 2) used this schema as a way of structuring the history of translation theory, but we can now use it to illustrate the nature of the translation process itself. For the translator, the initial problem (P1) is "how to translate this text / this sentence / this stylistic feature / this item?" The Tentative Theory then corresponds to the first draft of the translation. It is convenient that TT stands not only for Tentative Theory but also Target Text: the two coincide here. Translation strategies (both comprehension and production) are used in the process which derives TT from P1. They thus contribute to hypothesis-creation.

A translation is therefore a theory: the translator's theory, posed as a tentative solution to the initial question of how to translate the source text (cf. Toury 1995: 77). In accordance with the etymology of the word, too, the translator's theory thus represents a *view* of the source text, the translator's view. The translation is a representation of how the translator *sees* the source text: "sees" also in the sense of "understands, interprets". Discussing the different translations of Proust into English, Craig (1993: 24) remarks revealingly:

> The translator's choices, despairing or triumphant, may shock us, but not only because they are crass or leaden. In the best, they are nothing of the kind, but they still shock because they are other ways of seeing, of hearing the original: new beams of light into a partly dark ground.

Popper's schema was originally proposed to represent the growth of scientific knowledge. After a Tentative Theory has been proposed, there then occurs the phase that is crucial to science, that of Error Elimination. The theory is subject to critical examination, tested in various ways, checked out by peers, refined etc. As pointed out above (1.4), a theory does not become "true" by virtue of having its possible errors eliminated: it may become more "truthlike", it may approximate closer to "the truth", but at bottom it remains a hypothesis, however well supported or corroborated it may be. The evolution of scientific knowledge leads not to ultimate truth, but to new problems, and these in turn to new theories. Knowledge is never final, on this view.

There is a sense in which a translation is never final, either. Like any other theory, a translation of a given source text has the status of a hypothesis, to be tested and refined as long as anyone is interested in doing so. It is thus quite natural that certain texts (usually canonized ones) should be translated over and over again, as new generations have different views and different expectations of what a translation should be. Recall Goethe's notion of the various stages a translation goes through (see 2.4).

This is a view that coincides exactly with Popper's idea of scientific progress. Other theorists, too, evidently have this kind of conception of the translation process: to take just one example, compare Delisle (1988), who distinguishes the processes of comprehension, reformulation, and verification of tentative translation solutions. A classic example of this approach is to be found in Bly (1984), who demonstrates "from the inside", as it were, as many as eight stages in the translation of a single Rilke poem: seven drafts and seven revision processes before a final version is arrived at.

This chapter focuses on how translations are assessed as tentative theories. To assess something is to examine its quality, and "quality" is a usefully ambiguous term. In one sense it can mean 'nature, characteristics', and in this sense assessment is purely *descriptive*: a statement is made to the effect that a given translation is of such-and-such a type, that it has such-and-such features, that it has such-and-such an effect on the target culture or on intercultural relations more generally, etc. In Toury's view, for instance, the aim of a descriptive translation analysis is to infer the translator's concept of equivalence by looking at the kinds of decisions made during the translation process (1995: 36f.); alternatively, one can start with a concept of equivalence that is assumed or known to have been prevailing at the time of the translation, for this kind of text etc., and then use this to justify a translator's decisions. The focus of interest is on describing what the translator has decided to do and why. Segments of the target text (solutions) are paired with segments of the source text (problems) – i.e. various textual correspondences are defined – and then the relationships between the pairs of corresponding segments are examined.

In terms of Popper's schema, this kind of descriptive analysis looks at the relation between P1 and TT, at the way the Tentative Theory (Target Text) comes to be justified and proposed as a solution for the initial problem. This aspect of the translation process has become a major focus of attention for scholars working in the tradition of culture studies. It leads to an examination of the social and cultural conditions under which translations are produced, of the ideological and other values which motivate a translator's decisions, and of the effects which these decisions then have on texts, readers and cultures. A further step taken by some scholars is then to compare the values apparently held by a given translator or group of translators with those held by the scholar himself or herself. A discussion then ensues about whose values are better, such as the argument about the merits and demerits of the value of target-language fluency (see e.g. Venuti 1995a; Pym 1996). Purely descriptive analysis merges here into social or cultural criticism, or even into prescriptive pronouncements about what translators should do. There is a shift to the second sense of "quality" as an *evaluative* term, not just a descriptive one.

In this evaluative sense of "quality", assessment is made in terms of how good or bad the translation is, whether it conforms to required standards, particular values etc. This is of course the way the term is used in quality assurance systems in a translation agency, and in the translation industry as a whole. Such evaluative assessment can obviously be either negative or positive. In terms of the Popperian schema, we are now looking at the Tentative Theory from the Error Elimination perspective. Both descriptive and evaluative assessment will be relevant to the discussion in this chapter. In critical practice, both types of assessment tend to co-occur.

Before examining various ways of actually carrying out translation assessment, let us first consider how the whole process of theory production and error elimination is part of a translator's competence.

Pym (1992a: 175ff.) comes very close to Popper in this respect. Pym argues strongly that translators inevitably theorize, and that this theorization is an intrinsic part of translational competence. His definition of this competence can be summarized as follows. Translational competence consists of two skills:

a. The ability to generate a series of possible translations for a given source text or item.
b. The ability to select from this series, "quickly and with justified (ethical) confidence" (175), one version considered to be optimally appropriate.

The first ability (a) is a generative one: the more possible translations you can come up with, the more competence you have (divergent creativity). Popper's initial schema can thus be expanded as follows:

$$P1 \rightarrow TT1 \rightarrow EE \rightarrow P2$$
$$TT2...$$
$$TTn$$

Pym points out that this definition explicitly incorporates a recognition "that there is more than one way to translate" and a refusal of "any notion of exclusive correctness" (175).

The second ability (b) is a critical, selective one. It pertains exactly to the Error Elimination process: it is the ability to assess each of the proposed possibilities and select the one which appears (at that moment) to be the best, given the overall nature of the translation commission, prospective readership etc. (convergent creativity).

The definition thus also incorporates the ability to improve a translation: in the first place, to improve one's own proposals, the tentative theories that come to mind. The picture it gives is of a series of possible versions, each of which is submitted to examination and rejected or refined until an appropriate one is arrived at. (As mentioned above, the process is not a simple linear one: previous decisions can be altered later, etc.) This overall ability to generate, manipulate and assess tentative hypotheses is, as Pym says, something fundamentally theoretical.

The critical ability to assess alternatives is not only a requirement for individual translators, of course. It is – or should be – also the basis of translation criticism. On this view, one which Pym endorses too, if a proposed translation is rejected, the critic should suggest something better in turn, a better Tentative Theory. It is thus not only translators who inevitably theorize; translation critics do so too.

Pym's model of translational competence (and my Popperian adaptation of it) is primarily a model of a translator's linguistic competence. However, during the production of a tentative target text and also during the Error Elimination process a translator will naturally resort to other activities as well, such as documentation research, consultation with the client or other experts, and so on. A similar overall model is proposed by Gile (e.g. 1992, 1995). Gile starts with the comprehension phase: the translator generates hypotheses about the meaning of the source text, and then tests these for plausibility. A TL draft version is then proposed, and this in turn is tested, both against the source text for fidelity and against target norms for acceptability. The process is repeated for each item translated, each translation unit, and then for the text as a whole. Gile stresses that the testing process involves not only instinct, language proficiency etc., but also documentary research and knowledge of the world. Sager's (1994: 237f.) model of translation also highlights the revision process. Gile's "testing" corresponds to Popper's Error Elimination, as do several of Sager's algorithmic questions (Sager 1994: 219). The picture that emerges is of a repeated, cyclical process, switching back and forth constantly from hypothesis-generation to hypothesis-testing. Gile argues that a model of this kind can be usefully applied in translator training – cf. Chapter 6, below.

The Error Elimination process typically starts with a recognition of "errors" that thus need to be eliminated. During the translation process itself, this elimination takes place within the translator's head as part of normal text-processing and revision. The moment at which a translation is submitted or published represents a cut-off point that is imposed by external circumstances, deadlines etc. In the best case, it may coincide with the point at which the translator can find no more errors to eliminate, no more refinements to make. The Tentative Theory is then submitted to public scrutiny. But there is nothing theoretically final about this stage: it may well be that other people can still find errors or suggest improvements, or even that the translator can too, some weeks later. From this point of view, evaluative translation assessment is no more than a continuation of the overall translation process but involving more people.

Problem: what is a translation error? Nord (1991: 169f.) argues for a functional view according to which errors are not defined on intrinsic criteria such as correctness. Instead, a recipient classifies as errors those features of the translation that do not meet a given norm or standard, which frustrate the recipient's expectations for instance because the translator has failed to follow the task instructions in some way. (However, features that *exceed* expectations are naturally not regarded as erroneous.)

Nord's definition is broad enough to be applied in different methodological approaches. We can add that the translator him/herself is the first "process-internal" recipient, and thus the first to react to prospective target versions. Generalizing slightly, let us say that an error is anything in the form of the translated text that triggers a critical reaction in a reader. This definition can cover anything from grammatical mistakes or the mistranslation of technical terms, to a translator's choice of overall approach (e.g. target-language fluency rather than non-fluency, or vice versa). The definition is also a relative one: errors are relative to readers and readers' expectations. But readers are different: some have access to the source text, others do not; some may be familiar with the source culture, others not; readers may read with different purposes; and so on. Readers in one culture may respond differently from readers in another culture to one and the same translation. The definition is also relative in the sense that recognition of errors, as thus defined, may well vary over time, so that features considered as erroneous or non-erroneous at one point in time may be differently received at some other point. Indeed, even at the same point in time, one reader's criticism may be another reader's praise: this raises the important question of which readers count more in the overall assessment. And this in turn leads to questions of authority, status and power, and to questions about competing values within and between cultures. All this goes to show that, like translations themselves, evaluative assessments too are ultimately not final or absolute but relative to particular people and places and times.

A functional definition such as the one suggested above also has some pedagogical use, as I will try to show.

Reactions that are intended to be negative or critical, i.e. going against and/or falling below the expectations of the translator or the critic, take many forms. Here are some examples:

- X doesn't mean the same as the corresponding source text item.
- X is the wrong term for this concept.
- The style seems quite different from the original.
- Compared with the original, it's too emotive / too marked / too flat...
- X doesn't sound right.
- There is something strange about the style which I don't like, but I can't quite put my finger on it.
- It sounds old-fashioned.
- X is ungrammatical; it could never have been written by a native speaker.
- I think the client would reject this.
- I am the client, and I do reject this.
- This text could never be published in this form: there are far too many signs of carelessness, misprints etc.
- This reads like a translation, it's full of interference from the original.
- This reads very naturally, but it thereby hides the otherness of the original, which I would like to have seen.
- The language is unnatural, clumsy, irritating, difficult to read.
- I wouldn't say it like that.
- I wonder what this bit means? It doesn't make sense.
- This sounds amusing, but I guess it isn't supposed to be.
- You mean this is supposed to be funny?
- You mean this is meant for children??
- Well, I followed these translated instructions, but the machine still didn't work.
- I wonder what on earth the translator was thinking of when he/she wrote that.
- The translator has acted unethically in translating in this way : he/she is simply serving the ideological needs of the target/source culture, with no respect for the autonomy of the source/target culture.

Such are the symptoms that may betray the presence of an error, a weakness (they may not do so, of course, if the expectations are different – e.g. that a translation of this kind of text *should* indeed read like a translation). These reactions also reveal different kinds of assessment, different kinds of expectation about how translations can or should be assessed. The rest of this chapter will examine five such assessment models. These rarely occur in isolation, but they do provide a conceptual framework in which different emphases in assessment can be specified and compared.

5.2 Retrospective assessment

I call the first approach retrospective because it focuses on the relation between the target text and its source text: on the relation norm, in fact. This relation has been given various technical terms in the literature, some of which are unfortunately used in quite other senses by other scholars (a good example is the polysemy of the term "adequacy"). Perhaps the most common one is simply "equivalence", insofar as practitioners of this mode of assessment typically praise the TT for being "equivalent" or criticize it for not being "equivalent" enough (but recall the critical discussion of equivalence in 1.2.2). Such practitioners, by definition, form a subset of those readers who also have access to the source text. Most readers of the target text, of course, do not have this access.

A descriptive assessment of the source-target relation will simply state what this relation is, typically in terms of such parameters as free-vs-literal, degree of preservation of various aspects of the original text (meaning, form, style…), whether the relation meets the expectations of the readership or not. An evaluative assessment will pronounce judgement on the relation. If this assessment is negative, the translation is declared to be e.g. too free, or not free enough, or the features of the original that have been preserved are argued not to be the features that *should* have been preserved. See for instance Kundera's critical response to various French translations of a sentence from Kafka, which he compares negatively to his own proposal (in Kundera 1993: Part Four). Kundera's initial expectation is that a literary translation should be as close as possible to the form and style of the original, preserving every element possible. Strategies other than literal translation are therefore criticized.

In other words, we can start by distinguishing between a relationship that appears to be as expected – it is as it should be, i.e. conforms to the norm – and one that is not as expected. Thus far, such assessment is descriptive. If the relation is not as expected, we can then evaluate it as being better or worse than our expectations. These expectations, for instance, may incorporate certain requirements, which may or may not be met. In keeping with the relativistic definition of "error" introduced above, this kind of assessment is thus relative to the expectations of a given reader or group of readers, or to the requirements of a given client or communication situation. The assessment of the relation between TT and ST is thus subjective insofar as it is based on the opinions and expectations of the readers; but it is intersubjective insofar as such expectations and requirements exist as observable norms in a given society, and are recognized to exist as such. However, the assessment is not objective in the sense that there is assumed to be some kind of objective, absolute standard to which all translations must conform, such as "equivalence", for instance.

Perhaps the most influential exposition of this kind of assessment has been House (1981), although she is not concerned only with this viewpoint. Starting with the assumption that the goal of a translation is functional and interpersonal equivalence, she sets up a series of functional-stylistic categories based on Crystal and Davy (1969): geographical origin, social class, time, medium, participation, social role relationship, social attitude, province. ST textual correlates are established for these, and the resulting ST text profile is then compared with that of the TT. House explicitly states that this ST profile is the "yardstick" against which the translation is measured. Mismatches between the two profiles are designated as "covertly erroneous"; breaches of the target-language system – ungrammaticality etc. – are "overtly erroneous", as are mismatches of denotative meanings (i.e. obvious semantic mistranslations). After applying this model to a number of test cases (German-English), House concludes that functional equivalence only makes sense as a desirable criterion when the text to be translated is not "linked" to the source culture and can thus be translated "covertly". "Overt translation", where the translation is indeed transparently a translation and quite validly so, cannot be assigned functional equivalence as a goal.

Against this latter argument we might claim, however, that literary texts are normally translated "overtly", and yet stylistic and functional equivalence is often expected of literary translations. In fairness to House, though, it must be added that she is not primarily concerned with literary translation. In fact, her approach to style is made rather narrower than a study of literary translations would warrant, by her exclusion of Crystal and Davy's dimensions of "singularity" and "individuality", i.e. features which represent an author's personal style, whether deliberately or unconsciously used.

Furthermore, one typical arena where this retrospective model of assessment is practised is precisely the translation criticism of works of literature. Where the translation exhibits a TT-ST relationship which is as the critic expects, comments are not usually made. But if the relationship is felt to be either "better" than expected, "not" as expected or even "worse" than expected, comments are felt to be in order.

Here is a typical example: in a Times Literary Supplement review, Roger Huss (1993) is comparing two English translations (by Francis Steegmuller and Geoffrey Wall) of Flaubert's *Madame Bovary*:

> Steegmuller sometimes has the edge on Wall in his understanding of the original ("jeunes gens" are "young men" not "young people, the "lampion" Emma wears at the carnival is not a paper lantern but a cocked hat). [...] Yet Steegmuller's impressive ability to communicate a sense of naturalness in English pulls him towards lexical and syntactic normalization even where the original is deviant. [...] Steegmuller often supplies links absent in Flaubert and collapses isolated clauses

into the flow of a longer sentence. [...] Although always intelligent, Steegmuller's drawing out of implicit meaning also makes for a more digestible and subtly affable text than Flaubert's original. [...] By contrast, Wall's greater literalness makes him rather more successful in rendering Flaubert's meticulous verbal patterning.

Huss draws attention here to several aspects of the TT-ST relationship: the semantics of ST and TT items (i.e. House's overt mismatches), the degree of markedness of the syntax, and the overall style (cf. singularity). The assessment is made more complex, of course, by the fact that Huss also wishes to gauge the quality of the two translations vis-a-vis each other, not only vis-a-vis his own expectations of what an optimal translation of the novel ought to look like. Rather than making overall value judgements, Huss rather seeks to characterize the different strategies that each translator seems to prefer, and shows what the results of these strategies are: i.e. the assessment is primarily descriptive. Judging by this review, one translator has evidently placed more priority on literal translation and the preservation of rhetorical schemes etc.; the other has given more weight to the pragmatic strategies of explicitation and perhaps even adaptation. The two translations will thus relate differently to the current English literary polysystem and its subsystem of translated works. Huss does not prefer one above the other in general, but recommends the Steegmuller version for first-time readers and the Wall version for a second reading. Huss's assumption thus seems to be that initial readers will expect a more fluent rendering, one that makes the original more accessible. (Compare Goethe's first two stages as opposed to his final one, mentioned above in 2.4.)

Translation strategies can thus be useful and relevant to translation assessment. Another example is an analysis by Nylander-Tuominen (1992) of French and English translations of some traditional Finnish folk lyrical poems (from the Kanteletar). Her analysis is a semiotic one, but her argument returns again and again to the fact that the French version uses more hyperonyms than the English, and both use more than the original. In effect, she is criticizing the French translator for giving too much weight to one kind of semantic hyponymy strategy (my strategy S3b).

Similarly, a review of a translated biography of Václav Havel (Rosenberg 1993) comments that:

> The book is often hard to follow – it has been well-translated from the Czech language but not from the Czech milieu. Kriseova [the author] throws in names, places and events without explaining them and focuses on issues perhaps more interesting to Czechs and Slovaks than to foreigners.

In other words, the translator is criticized for not making more use of cultural filtering (Pr1), explicitation (Pr2) and information change (Pr3). The reviewer has expected a more domesticating rendering, one that would make the reading easier for a less knowledgeable target audience. This expectation may of course clash with the conscious aims of the translator, who may have deliberately chosen a different overall method.

I will now illustrate this assessment model in more detail, with a comparative (descriptive) analysis of three English translations of a Latvian poem. The original poem is a *daina*, a traditional folksong in regular trochaic metre, and runs as follows:

> *Dziedot dzimu, dziedot augu,*
> [sing+PRES.P. born+PAST+1SG sing+PRES.P. grow-up+PAST+1SG]
> *Dziedot mūžu nodzīvoju;*
> [sing+PRES.P. life+ACC live+PAST+1SG]
> *Dziedot gāja dvēselīte*
> [sing+PRES.P. go+PAST+3SG soul+DIMINUTIVE+NOM]
> *Dieva dēla dārziņā.*
> [God+GEN son+GEN garden+DIMINUTIVE+LOCATIVE]

The translations are:

(a) Singing, I was born; singing, I grew up;
Singing, I passed through life;
Singing, my soul entered
The garden of the Son of God.
(Trans. Ruth Spears, in J. Andrups and V. Kalve (1954) *Latvian Literature*. Stockholm: Goppers, p. 17.)

(b) I was born singing, I grew up singing,
I passed through life singing;
And, singing, my soul ascended
Into the garden of the Son of God.
(Trans. Aleksis Rubelis, in A. Rubelis (1970) *Baltic Literature*. Notre Dame, Indiana: University of Notre Dame Press, p. 107.)

(c) I was born singing, I grew up singing,
I lived my life singing.
My soul will go singing
Into the garden of God's sons.
(Trans. Pauls Raudseps, in A. Lieven (1993) *The Baltic Revolution*. New Haven and London: Yale University Press, p. 109.)

The retrospective kind of assessment prompts a number of comments on what has been preserved and what has been changed. The ones I will mention relate to points where the translator had a genuine choice, not those where the grammatical norms of English force a change.

With respect to the form of the poem, none of the translations preserve a regular trochaic metre, although the first half of (a) comes closest (cf. the scheme change strategy, G10). Version (b) is the only one that preserves the punctuation and hence the relative strength of the break between the two couplets: (a) downgrades this break by introducing two semi-colons and three extra commas earlier; and (c) upgrades the same break into a full stop, thus separating the two halves of the poem more clearly (cf. the sentence structure change, strategy G7). On the other hand, all three versions preserve the line divisions, the repetition of *singing (dziedot)*, and the enjambement at the end of the third line. Translation (c) has changed the tense of the verb in line 3 (strategy G5), and the number of sons in line 4. The tense change also affects the speech act (strategy Pr5), since the future tense suggests more a prophesy than a report.

On the semantic and pragmatic levels, versions (b) and (c) choose an unmarked word order in the first two lines and thus change the emphasis somewhat (S7). Version (b) chooses the rather formal *ascended* (line 3) in contrast to the plainer verbs in the original and the other two translations (cf. strategy Pr4); this could also be seen as a hyponym of the more general concept *go* (cf. strategy S3). None of the versions preserves the diminutive aspects of *soul* and *garden*.

Perhaps the most striking choice is the one that affects the capitalizing of *Son* in translations (a) and (b). The original poem has a pagan background, not a Christian one. The decision to capitalize the son thus serves to adapt the poem to a Christian culture (naturalization: cf. strategy Pr1). It is perhaps the desire to preserve a pagan reading and obviate a Christian one that has motivated the third translator to use the plural *sons*, with no capital.

To look forward to another assessment model we shall examine below, the overall *effects* of these three translations are thus somewhat different, as a result of the different strategies chosen. Translation (a) seems to me to celebrate the actual act of singing most strongly, and is in fact the closest to the original in this respect; (b) comes across as a statement of joyous belief in a Christian heaven to which souls biblically ascend; and (c) seems an expression of jubilant pagan confidence in life.

5.3 Prospective assessment

The retrospective approach was heavily criticized by Nida (1964) and Nida and Taber (1969), who argued that it laid too much emphasis on the assumption of formal equivalence. They (and others) also pointed out that in real life, few readers of translations actually have access to the original text.

In place of the retrospective mode, Nida proposed a model of assessment based on "dynamic equivalence", i.e. not sameness of form but sameness of effect. I call this "prospective" assessment, because it looks forward from the target text to the effect this has, or is designed to have, on its readers, rather than back to the source text. The centre of attention becomes the communication norm rather than the relation norm.

The origins of this model of assessment lie largely in one tradition of biblical translation. Here, after all, the effect that the translation is supposed to have (i.e. its skopos: see 2.6) is relatively easy to define: to convert the readers to Christianity, or to confirm them in their faith, or the like. Further, in this kind of translation it is relatively easy to see that the intended effect of the translation is indeed "the same" as the effect of the original. The effects of the text are thus fairly well circumscribed, in principle at least (but see further, below).

In the review of the two translations of Flaubert I referred to above, there are several points which illustrate this kind of assessment, which thus occurs here in conjunction with the retrospective model. Huss writes (1993):

> Searching for an equivalence of effect, Wall also makes one glaringly unhappy choice: when Homais quotes English ("That is the question" and, more bathetically, "Yes"), most existing translations make the fact explicit. Wall, however, supplies an arbitrary sense of foreignness by putting "Yes" into German ("Jawohl").

Desired effects, then, do not always turn out to be actual effects. Again:

> [When Steegmuller adds cohesive links] [t]he effect is more often than not fluently elegant, but it attenuates the various moods suggested by Flaubert's laconic manner and respected by Wall: melancholy, perplexity, dismissiveness, or the bruised inability to articulate pain.

Huss's comments on the effects of a translation are, of course, primarily the effects the translation had on *him*. Let me take another personal example. On the bathroom door of a hotel room in Vienna I find the following bilingual text:

> Liebe Gäste!
> Täglich werden in Hotels zahllose Handtücher unnötigerweise gewaschen.
>   Wenn Sie neue Handtücher benötigen, werfen Sie bitte die Gebrauchten in die Badwanne. Wenn nicht, dann lassen Sie sie bitte auf dem Handtuchhalter hängen.
>   Mit dieser einfachen Massnahme helfen Sie dabei, Wasser und Waschmittel zu sparen und dadurch unsere Umwelt wesentlich zu entlasten.
>   Vielen Dank fur ihre Mithilfe!

Dear guests!
Every day, numerous towels are being washed in hotels without the real need.
    If you need a fresh towel, please throw the used one into the bathtub; if you don't, please leave it hanging on the hook, or on the towel-rack.
    With those simple measures, you contribute greatly to the rational use of water and washing powder, and actively help preserving the nature.
    We thank you for your co-operation!

It is often difficult to define a translation's intended effect or skopos adequately. But here the skopos of the source (German) text is clear: the immediate intended effect is stated explicitly within the text itself, readers are asked to behave in a specific way, to perform certain actions. (A longer-term effect is also suggested: that the text should influence readers' attitudes in a particular way.) And it is reasonable to assume that the skopos of the translation is the same here.

What *actual* effect is this translation likely to have on its readers? My own first subjective reaction was to respond in the manner desired, and not throw the towels out unnecessarily. The intended effect was achieved perfectly satisfactorily. From the point of view of a prospective assessment, then, I can say that this translation worked fine, for this one reader at least.

But of course my overall reaction is more complex. As a native speaker of English, I note almost unawares that the English is a bit odd in places, clearly not written by a native (*without the real need, those simple measures, actively help preserving the nature, we thank you a lot for your co-operation*). I admit, further, to being even slightly amused by the somewhat naive touch in the English style, and by the syntactic oddities. Why didn't they get a native speaker to edit it? This reaction is then followed by one of linguistic curiosity: this would be a good illustrative text for my chapter on translation assessment, I'll copy it down. Such mixed reactions are no doubt common among native readers of non-native texts around the world; I would guess, too, that some of them at least would be shared by other native readers of this particular translation.

In other words, *part* of my reaction is indeed the desired one: my reaction to the message content. But part of my reaction is to the form of the message, and these secondary reactions were scarcely part of the skopos of the translation. What we seem to have is an intended effect (achieved, in this case), plus a number of unintended side-effects. A descriptive assessment would state what these side-effects are. An evaluative one would have to say that, because they are unintended, they point to weaknesses in the translation: as a piece of English, the translation obviously falls short of native norms in several places.

Notice that even this kind of simple analysis nevertheless implies high demands on the standard of a translation: not only must the effect be the intended one, but also there must be no unintended side-effects. In particular, we might claim that if a translation is not intended to draw the attention of its readers to the form of the target text, and if it in fact *does* do so, then the translation is less than optimal. ("Readers", here, must of course be construed as excluding translation scholars, who tend to subject *any* translation they come across to a formal examination.)

My examples of prospective assessment have so far been subjective ones. For a more objective view we must turn to different methodologies within this approach. Several methods of assessing effect have been suggested e.g. by Nida and Taber (1969) and used by them and other scholars. Vehmas-Lehto (1989: 42–44) calls them "response-based" methods. They include the following:

(a) The use of Cloze tests on source and target readers, as a test of comprehensibility.
(b) Explicit elicitation of target-reader reactions to various alternatives: subjective assessment. (The examples above have illustrated this method for one alternative and one reader.)
(c) Reporting tests: the translation is read aloud to TL speakers, who are required to relate what they heard to a third person (the idea being to see what speakers tended to change in the retelling).
(d) Speakability tests: having TL speakers read the translation aloud and observing where they tend to stumble or hesitate.
(e) Comprehension tests: matched bilingual subjects answer questions either on the source text or on the target text, and the answers are compared.
(f) Performance tests (such as following instructions in the source and target languages) to see whether the performance varies with the language).
(g) Comprehensibility experiments based on reading time, comparing results for source and target texts.
(h) Identifying texts as either original or translated.
(i) Readability tests (other than Cloze tests).

Many of these methods have also been criticized. They only measure part of the overall effect of a text, and not always very validly at that. It is often exceedingly difficult to specify precisely what is meant by the "effect" of a text. Another problematic issue is whether we mean the author's intended effect or the actual effect. If we mean the intended effect, can this always be determined? If we mean the actual effect, actual effect on whom? All readers? Impossible. Typical readers? Who are the typical readers? Native speakers of the target language, or not? And besides, the same text may affect people in very different ways.

Yet such observations also point to one strength of this mode of assessment: its sensitivity to the reader, to who the reader is. After all, native speakers of the target language will react differently from non-native speakers, they will notice different things about the translation. Both native and non-native readers will no doubt react to a text's function, but non-native readers (naive, non-professionals, that is) are obviously less likely than natives to react to its form. Some readers will be speakers of both the languages concerned and others not, and this too may affect reactions. Some may even have access to the source text and make their own evaluations accordingly. And readers even react differently according to whether they know if the translation was by a TL native speaker or not: judgements may be made differently according to the kind of translator, in other words.

Criticism has also focused on weaknesses in the experimental design of these methods: too few subjects are often used, non-relevant variables are not excluded, reliability is poor, key concepts such as comprehensibility are too loosely defined.

Interestingly, these methods of assessment have also been criticized for lacking all reference to the source text (e.g. by House 1977) – a criticism that rather misses the point of this whole assessment model. (It has not, I think, been suggested that this model – or any other, for that matter – can suffice *alone* for an adequate overall assessment.)

Insofar as the prospective approach rests upon the assumption that the effect of the translation is expected to be *the same* as that of the original (as evidently in Nida's work), the approach is also open to the counter-argument presented most cogently by Gutt (1991): if the receivers of a message vary, the effect *cannot* be *exactly* the same on all of them. This is basically because receivers interpret any utterance in terms of their own knowledge of the world, their own current cognitive state; and since no two people, even within the same language community, have exactly the same knowledge of the world, no two interpretations can ever be absolutely identical.

A better foundation for this assessment type might therefore be the looser notion of the skopos of the translation. Although effects cannot be identical, skopoi of course may be; on the other hand, the skopos of a translation may well be different from that of the source text. Whatever the skopos, it can be compared to the actual reactions of a number of readers – to the extent that both skopos and reactions can be defined and described.

Perhaps the most effective use of the prospective model is therefore to combine several of the methods proposed above in a carefully designed empirical analysis, one that is aware of its own limitations but nevertheless able to provide interesting information about the kinds of effects translations have on their readers.

Puurtinen (1995), for instance, used a variety of methods in her assessment of two Finnish translations (both published in 1977) of Frank Baum's *The Wizard of Oz*. She used a Cloze test of readability, a speakability test and a subjective assessment of style, all designed to capture various differences between the two translations. It turned out that one is more formal than the other, with more complex, non-finite and left-branching constructions and a style characterized as static. The other translation prefers a simpler, more dynamic style, which seems easier to process and sounds more like contemporary spoken language; this translation scored higher on the Cloze test.

However, the speakability tests showed no significant difference between the two translations, and the subjective assessments indicated a great deal of individual variation. This last is an interesting result: it actually furnishes further evidence against the idea of a homogeneous readership in terms of which some ideal "effect" can be defined. People react to texts in very different ways, even when they are sociologically matched to some extent (Puurtinen's 28 subjects were all trainee translators). In Puurtinen's experiment some subjects reacted positively to colloquial, everyday style, others preferred a more literary style and even relished the occasional archaism. Some gave readability a high priority, others placed it below aesthetic values. There was no significant difference in the overall evaluative assessment of the two translations, but Puurtinen concluded that the whole concept of acceptability is a slippery one. Individual judgements of acceptability are of course influenced by each person's personal experience of the text-type in question, personal life history, family values, and so on ad infinitum: cf. Gutt's argument, above.

5.4 Lateral assessment

In view of the criticisms directed against the concept of dynamic equivalence, and the difficulty of defining and measuring effects, some scholars have advocated a different model of assessment which we can call lateral. The label denotes that the point of view here is sideways, towards other texts already existing in the target culture; the emphasis is on the extent to which the translation fits into the appropriate set of texts in the receiving language, whether it bears an adequate family resemblance to them. Where the retrospective model focuses on the relation norm, and the prospective model primarily on the communication norm, the lateral model thus focuses mainly on the expectancy norms. In lateral assessment, the translation is lined up not alongside the source text, nor alongside aims, effects or reactions, but alongside authentic (untranslated) texts in the target language that are of a similar type: texts that have come to be called "parallel texts" (see e.g. Neubert 1981), or comparable texts. Lateral assessment avoids some of the limitations of the previous two models and is more objective than either, being strictly text-based.

A major influence on this mode of assessment has been Toury's work (cf. above, 2.7 and 3.5), particularly his distinction between source-oriented and target-oriented translation. Lateral assessment is obviously target-oriented.

As discussed earlier (3.8), expectancy norms are both qualitative and quantitative. When qualitative norms are broken, the result is typically an ungrammatical form, a non-native expression, or other such "overt error". If quantitative norms are broken, this is manifested in "covert errors" such as non-typical distribution or frequencies of items, differences which may only become evident after statistical analysis. (Recall the normalization hypothesis mentioned in 3.6.1.) This statistical approach is not a new one: it was advocated long ago by Grimes (1963), for instance, as a method for measuring the naturalness of Bible translations.

Here is an example of a statement implicitly based on a lateral type of assessment, from a review of a translation of *Fima* by Amos Oz (Rawson 1993: 28):

> The translation of *Fima* is by Nicholas de Lange. I know no Hebrew, but the best compliment I can pay to his many translations of Oz is that they don't read like translations. When one reads one of his other translators, decent though they are, one knows it.

The example illustrates the close relation between this model and the prospective one: a breaking of expectancy norms leads (or may lead) to unwanted side-effects. The reviewer makes his own assumptions about the expected translation quality quite clear here.

As we have pointed out before, norms (both qualitative and quantitative) are relative concepts. They represent a range of acceptability, from "preferred usage" through "unusual but acceptable" to "disturbingly deviant" and "definitely unacceptable". In empirical research, expectancy norms must therefore be defined operationally, as covering a specified range of variation. Quantitative differences (between a translation and an expectancy norm) can then be stated in terms of their statistical significance.

Let us take a simple example (based on Chesterman 1994b): a study of the relative distribution of the English article *the* and the use of "no article" with common nouns, in translations from Finnish and in parallel texts. (By "no article" is meant the use of zero before indefinite plural and mass nouns like *papers, ink*, plus the lack of an article before singular count nouns in expressions such as *hand in hand*.)

Before looking at translations we first need to establish what the expectancy norm is. In the Brown corpus (Francis and Kučera 1982; Ellegård 1978) the overall percentage (i.e. of all word-tokens) of *the* is 6.9%; the equivalent figure for the LOB corpus (Johansson and Hofland 1989) is 6.7%. Corresponding figures for "no article" are not directly accessible from these corpora.

But expectancy norms are of course largely genre-specific. And the relative occurrence of *the* does indeed vary to some extent according to genre, because of the variation in noun and pronoun distribution overall and the syntax of the noun phrase in particular (Brainerd 1972; Johansson 1978a). Ellegård (1978) reports that the average frequency of *the* in learned and scientific writing is 8.4%, compared with 7.6% for belles lettres, 7.5% for press reporting and 6.4% for adventure stories.

The data for this particular mini-study came from a quarterly English-language magazine issued by the University of Helsinki entitled Universitatis Helsingiensis (hereafter HEL), and the equivalent Cambridge University magazine CAM. Both are very similar in layout, content and readership, except that HEL is of course for the minority of non-Finnish-speaking members of Helsinki University whereas CAM has a larger readership. The articles in HEL are translated by professional Finnish translators and then checked and edited by native English speakers before publication. One would expect, then, that the relative distributions of *the* and "no article" would be very close in the two magazines.

However, it turned out that there was a surprising (and, at the .005 level, statistically significant) difference between the two. On the basis of admittedly limited data (2500 words from each magazine, spread across five extracts with matched subject matter), the overall frequency of *the* in HEL (9.8%) was noticeably higher than it was in CAM (7.5%). The CAM figure is close to the expected norm (cf. above), but the HEL figure is higher even than that for rather more formal, academic texts. The figures for "no article" were the reverse: CAM 8.3%, HEL 7.3%.

Both sets of data had approximately the same overall percentage of nouns (CAM 21.4%, HEL 22.5%), and when the occurrence of *the* and "no article" is calculated as a percentage of the total number of nouns the difference becomes very clear:

CAM: *the* 35%, "no article" 39%
HEL: *the* 44%, "no article" 33%

These Finnish translators thus appear to overuse the definite article and underuse "no article". They tend to "overspecify", whereas native writers are content to leave more of the specification to the reader to infer. Perhaps this is an instance of the general translation law of explicitation (cf. 3.6.1). There may also be other reasons for this difference, of course, but further discussion will not be relevant in this context.

A much more comprehensive application of the lateral type of assessment is illustrated by Vehmas-Lehto (1989), who combined it with methods in the prospective mode as well. Her material was journalistic texts translated from Russian to Finnish. Finnish readers usually recognized the translated texts to be translations (they were grammatically correct but felt to be clumsy or obscure etc.), and Vehmas-Lehto explored the reasons for this. Using a combination of reaction tests and lateral comparisons with parallel texts, she pinpointed a variety of quantitative features in the translations which break expectancy norms; these include the relative frequency of co-ordinated constructions, emotive words and clichés, sentence length, clause length, noun phrase length, noun and adjective frequency, and connective frequency. The study shows clearly that Finnish journalism had different discourse norms from those of Russian journalism (at the end of the Soviet period), and that translators did not take adequate account of these norm differences.

There are of course problems with this method of assessment. One is the difficulty of holding all other variables constant apart from translated vs. non-translated text. Texts that are *exactly* parallel are hard – sometimes even impossible – to find. And even if one finds some, it is not always easy to show that they are themselves "typical" and therefore can reasonably be taken to represent a norm. Computer corpora can provide data on the quantitative distribution of morphological, lexical and syntactic features, but tagging is often less sensitive to textual or discourse features, which makes it more difficult to establish norms in these areas. (See also above Update, 2.10.)

On the other hand, norms are not laws, they are not absolute. We are concerned with relative differences only. In most cases, a translator's aim should presumably be to produce a text that is perceived to bear at least a Wittgensteinian family resemblance to the set of target-language texts into which it is designed to fit.

5.5 Introspective assessment

All the methods of assessment mentioned so far share one characteristic: the criteria upon which they are based lie outside the translator's own mind. We have assessed by looking at the source text, at target-reader reactions, at parallel texts, but we have not yet delved into the translator's own decision-making processes. In keeping with some recent developments in translation theory more generally (see 2.8), translation assessment too has turned its attention to introspective data.

It has even been suggested (e.g. by Wilss 1977) that the only way to assess a translation fairly is to take account of the translator's own internal decision-making process – not in isolation, admittedly, but in combination with other models of assessment. In other words, we need to know why a translator has made certain decisions before we can reasonably assess the results of these decisions. Ideally, in fact, we need to reconstruct the whole translation process.

Although we cannot actually enter the translator's head directly, there are various situations that can be set up from which at least some inferences can be made. One is the think-aloud protocol method, where translators are asked to give a verbal commentary on what is in their minds as they translate. One refinement of this approach (suggested e.g. by House 1988) is to have subjects in pairs, giving running commentaries to each other: this has the advantage of being a more natural situation. Yet another is to interview translators immediately after the translation task, asking them why they wrote this, why they rejected that, what options occurred to them at this point, and so on. A further variant is to ask translators to write notes on their own translation process, as they translate. And there are also a number of computer applications that have been experimented with (e.g. Tommola 1986, and above, Update 2.10).

Such methods allow only indirect access to mental processes, and oral protocols in particular have come in for some sharp criticism (discussed e.g. in Lörscher 1991). But in what way can the results of such research be relevant to translation assessment?

I think we need to return here to the distinction made above between descriptive and evaluative assessment. Insofar as protocol studies of various kinds do provide information about mental processes, they may well be relevant to a purely descriptive assessment. This, then, would not only state what a translator does textually, but also what he or she does mentally. Such an assessment would seek to trace the mental decisions which precede and accompany "texting". In this sense, all protocol research into translation is relevant to descriptive translation assessment in the introspective mode. We can thus describe, for instance, the way in which professionals think about and use reference material, in comparison to the attitudes and practices of trainee translators (Jääskeläinen 1989); or look at the different decision criteria used by professionals and non-professionals (Tirkkonen-Condit 1990); or analyse what is felt by different translators to be a translation problem (e.g. Krings 1986).

However, this research does not directly constitute evaluative assessment. Regardless of *how* a translator arrives at a final product, regardless of the decisions made or the attitudes held, the final product will be judged evaluatively on its own merits. Good translations may (in theory, at least) come from quite misguided decisions, by chance, as it were. What matters in the long run – evaluatively speaking – is whether the translation works for the readers it was intended for. By their fruits you shall know them, surely.

This said, it must be added that protocol research nevertheless does have obvious evaluative applications: if non-professionals know what professionals do, they can learn to imitate them and perhaps improve the quality of their own work – see the section below on pedagogical assessment.

In terms of translation norms, the introspective mode of assessment is most closely associated with the accountability norm. In looking at the ways translators make decisions, in getting them to describe, explain or justify their choices, we are implicitly focusing also on ethical aspects of translatorial behaviour. We are stressing that translators are responsible for what they do. From this point of view alone, the introspective assessment model has a significant role to play in translation research.

5.6 Pedagogical assessment

In real life, much translation assessment is pedagogical. It is carried out by teachers or professionals, and is applied to translations produced by translation trainees or language students (or perhaps other professionals). It typically takes place as part of translator training, and differs from the previous approaches (although it may incorporate and apply any of them) in that its main purpose is not descriptive but evaluative. Its aim is to provide feedback that will enable the translator to improve the quality of future translations. A related aim is accreditation, to certify whether the translator in question has reached a predetermined standard.

Both these kinds of evaluation start with a diagnosis, either implicitly or explicitly. This typically focuses on an analysis of what are felt to be errors in the translation. As argued above, errors are deviations from norms: strictly speaking, they are unwanted deviations – we can exclude for the moment instances of norm-breaking that exceed expectations. In pedagogical assessment, what constitutes a deviation that is "unwanted" will depend partly on the level of competence of the translator: assessors may well "accept" deviations in the work of beginners that they would not accept from more advanced trainees, for instance. "Unwantedness" also partly depends on who is doing the wanting: in my experience of professional pedagogical assessment, target-language native assessors often tend to be more tolerant of deviance than non-native assessors, because they naturally have a wider range of language competence in terms of which translations can be evaluated. Here too, we see that errors are relative, not absolute. The relevant norms are also relative: elastic, as it were.

All the translation norms are relevant here. Perhaps the ones most frequently appealed to in this respect are the expectancy norms: when these are broken, or deviated from, the result is what Wilss (1977) calls errors of expression. When the relation norm is broken the result is either an error of comprehension manifested as "wrong meaning" in some sense, or a translation that is felt to be "too free" or "too literal", etc. When the communication norm is broken we get poor readability, inappropriate effects, puzzled reader-responses and the like. And when the accountability norm is broken we have a translation that is manifestly careless, inaccurate or deceptive.

In all pedagogical translation assessment, furthermore, one problem that cannot be avoided is that of *error gravity*. There has to be some reason for saying that this error is worse than that one, that the general level of error in this translation places it above or below a given standard, and so on. Let us look at briefly some of the approaches here.

Wilss (1977) focuses on the concept of the norm itself, drawing attention to its relative nature. He distinguishes between various levels of norms: (a) norms of the language system *(langue)*, (b) usage norms in a given speech community, (c) usage norms with respect to appropriateness and social roles, and (d) usage with respect to individual *parole*. A similar view, with some variation of emphasis and terminology, is offered by Vehmas-Lehto (1989: 17f.): at the most basic level she places (a) conformity with the target-language system – i.e. grammaticality; this is followed by (b) conformity with the norms of acceptability, (c) with the functional style of the target language (appropriateness), and finally (d) with "the recommendable norms", having to do with official sanction and readability, with "well-written texts" rather than just any native target-language texts.

Both these views presuppose a notion of "norms" that could be pictured as a series of concentric circles of target-language usage. Deviations occurring towards the centre are implied to be "more serious" than those occurring more towards the outer perimeter, although the actual definition of this perimeter varies. Both these views place the highest value on grammaticality as such; alternative priorities, however, might also be suggested, perhaps with acceptability or appropriateness at the centre.

With respect to expectancy norms, several criteria of error gravity can be proposed; but the trouble with these is that they often conflict with each other. One is: errors affecting a higher unit are worse than those affecting a lower unit. (Units are here understood as paragraph, sentence, clause, phrase, word, morpheme.) For instance, an incorrect clause structure is more serious than an incorrect phrase structure. An alternative formulation of this point is that global errors are worse than local ones. Another possible criterion is generality: if a grammatical rule is broken, is this rule one that applies very generally (such as verb concord in English), or does it apply only in a few or exceptional cases (such as the structures following particular verbs, e.g. the *ing*-form after *avoid*)? The breaking of more general rules is more serious. A third criterion might be frequency: breaking norms applying to frequent items (English articles, for instance) would be more serious than those applying to less-used items. A fourth could be the degree of systematicity: repeated occurrences of the same deviation would be more serious than isolated occurrences. Fifth, generative grammarians might argue that errors traceable to earlier derivational stages should be worse than those traceable to later stages (such as inflections). And a sixth might be rule-boundness: all errors of grammar would be worse than errors of lexis, on this count, since grammar is more amenable to description by systematic rules; but some areas of grammar (articles?) seem less explicitly rule-bound than others (e.g. concord). Similarly, all deviations of grammar might be felt to be worse than deviations of style, since stylistic features are presumably outside the central core of norms and allow for more variation.

With respect to the relation norm, we can usefully apply some of the proposals scholars have made concerning various types of equivalence (cf. 1.2.2). Our interest here is not in equivalence as such, but in aspects of the source-target relation. One approach is to evaluate various aspects of the source-target relation separately, and evaluate the extent to which each relational aspect is in accordance with the expectations or requirements for the text-type in question. Such aspects can be defined as (a) the formal relation, (b) the semantic/stylistic relation, and (c) the pragmatic relation. Error gravity also enters the picture when this assessment takes into account the expected relative priorities of these various relational aspects, for the translation in question. For many text-types, pragmatic and semantic considerations are paramount; in such texts, therefore, deviation from the expected pragmatic and/or semantic relation would be more serious than deviation from the expected formal relation. In other text-types, such as legal contracts for instance, the formal relation might have a higher priority.

With respect to the communication norm, we can make use of research into the effects of various types of errors. Johansson (1978b) reports a series of experiments testing the way in which different error-types affect the comprehensibility of the text and the degree of irritation of the reader. This research suggests, for instance, that (for English) errors in verb complementation are more disturbing than those of concord, but that concord errors are worse than some types of word-order errors. Lexical errors disturb communication more than syntactic ones, as one might expect. Kußmaul (1995: 128f.) agrees that error assessment in professional translator training should focus on the communicative function of the item in question, but he points out that this should be related to the translation specification and its overall purpose.

It might well be argued, however, that the most serious errors of all are those that break the accountability norm: cases where the translator has falsely represented the message, confused technical terms, miscopied figures or names, failed to check things that don't seem to make sense, etc.

What the assessor can do, then, is to indicate the points in the text where some norm seems to have been broken, and note further which norm this is. In a feedback situation, the translator can then either propose a revised version or defend the original proposal.

Whatever system of error gradation is used in pedagogical assessment, one further element still needs to be added: explanation. Ideally, when feedback is given to a translator, an attempt should be made to discover why the translator wrote the unwanted form in the first place. And it is at this point that the relevance of the introspective model of assessment becomes clear. Translators should be encouraged to introspect, to justify their choices, to state objectively what their motivation had been for the strategies selected, why other possible strategies or alternatives had been rejected, and so on.

What we end up with, then, is a picture of pedagogical assessment that involves all kinds of translation norms, and also all the other types of assessment. Furthermore, in addition to drawing attention to points where these norms have been broken, it is of course also encouraging to give feedback on places where reader expectations have been exceeded, where the translation is unexpectedly good.

In this way, the feedback process becomes a continuous loop: drafts are produced, tested, perhaps rejected or reconsidered, new proposals are made and refined in their turn, and so the process continues. If a translation product is a theory, literally a view, of the source text, the translating process does not end there: first views are followed by revisions, in a (theoretically) endless process inspired by the ideal of the "perfect translation" (i.e. optimal in a given situation). As we have seen, this conforms exactly to Popper's schema of the evolution of scientific knowledge, inspired by the ideal goal of "truth". The ultimate unattainability of both truth and perfection is irrelevant: both are what Popper (1972: 237; following Kant) calls "regulative ideas"; they serve as guiding lights in these forms of human endeavour, and without them we should be floundering around even more in the dark than we are.

5.7   Mind the gap!

Any mode of translation assessment, then, is normative, in that it examines the extent to which translations conform to norms and values. However, not all instances of norm-breaking are equally important, and some might even be desirable. We can set up three basic categories of norm-breaking, according to different relations between form and function.

(a) *Function-enhancing*. Some norm-breaking is done deliberately, to enhance the function (skopos) of the translation. Translations of advertisements or poetry, for instance, may deliberately exploit deviant spellings or structures or word orders (indeed, this happens so often that we might even see such deviations *as* the norm for such text-types, and so in this sense the norms would not in fact be broken; a translation might then become deviant by returning to the previous non-norm-breaking norm…). Recall the marked, phonetic translation of Humpty Dumpty into French (cited in 3.4), for instance.

Another way in which norm-breaking can enhance the function of a text is when the translator deliberately improves the text (e.g. via transediting) in order to make it better than the expected norm: one might cite certain types of bureaucratic or academic texts, for instance, which tend to come fairly low down on the reader-friendly scale in many languages. If translators then decide *not* to follow the perhaps clumsy style in which such texts are often written in the target language, this shows that they have given priority to other norms than expectancy ones: to the communication and accountability norms, in fact. In other words, there is a conflict of norms. We shall return to this point in the last chapter.

(b) *Function-preserving*. Translations which break norms but nevertheless preserve functions (i.e. preserve the skopos) are often the work of non-native speakers of the target language. Formal expectations are not always met, but the message is generally clear enough. A good example is the Vienna hotel text cited above, which communicates clearly and well despite the signs of non-nativeness.

(c) *Function-changing*. This refers to unintended changes of function, not to changes that form part of the translation commission. Instances of norm-breaking that fall into this category are of course more serious. They crop up in the work of both native and non-native translators, for different reasons.

Non-native translators may produce texts that are so far away from expectancy norms that they cause laughter or scorn, or some other totally inappropriate reaction. A badly translated advertisement or company brochure obviously gives the impression that the company itself is inefficient and its products below standard. Here are some extracts from an English advertisement by a Finnish publisher, whose face we will save by calling it X:

> X has its customers now in whole Scandinavia… Children are familiar with our teaching materials throughout their school years. We also publish illustrated guides and other books for hobby and leisure… X is a reputed publisher of business and management books which deal with actual topics… Now X has its audience in other Scandinavian countries too. In the summer of 1992 we acquired company Y, which enables X to deliver its books to an increasingly large marget [sic].

Such a text, with its non-native word orders, ungrammaticalities (*whole Scandinavia, books for hobby*), mistranslations (*actual* is intended to mean 'topical, current') and misprints, gives a sloppy image of a careless company: far from the intended function of the advertisement.

Native speakers of the target language also occasionally produce translations which change the intended function in quite unacceptable ways. The reason here is often a misunderstanding of the source text. A delightful example comes from the published translation of a Finnish short story ("Hilda Husso") by Maria Jotuni (let the translator remain anonymous). The text is a monologue, one side of a telephone conversation between Hilda Husso, a middle-aged cleaning lady, and her ex-lover, now a head waiter. She tells him that she is thinking of getting married to a Swede and moving to Sweden, and asks him to keep an eye on their son, who is being brought up by foster parents in the country. At one point in the conversation, the lady explains why she has apparently decided to take the Swede's offer of marriage, although it is clear that she still has a soft spot for her ex-lover. She says, in rather colloquial Finnish:

> ST: Arvelin ottaa miehen, kun on sopiva. On asioita, jotka puhuvat sen puolesta. Jalat ja vanhuus.
> Literal translation: I thought to take the man, since he is suitable. There are things which speak in favour of it. Legs and old age.

In other words, she feels that because she is getting on a bit and her legs are giving her problems, she might not get a better offer. An appropriately colloquial translation, with some explicitation, might therefore be: "I thought I'd take him, he'll do all right. There are other reasons, too – my legs are beginning to play me up, and I'm not as young as I was." Jotuni's underlying point is that people get married for many reasons, that there are many forms of love apart from the romantic one, that romantic love is not the only good relationship between people.

Unfortunately, the published translation misses this point entirely and substitutes another, totally inappropriate one. It reads:

> TT: I've been thinking of saying yes to him. He will do. There are a few things to be said for him. His legs and his oldness.

This raises roars of laughter in most readers: as if anyone – let alone the kind of person Hilda Husso is – would marry a man because of his legs! The error comes about because two syntactic features have been misread: in the second sentence, *sen* can mean either 'him' or 'it', but pragmatically it must mean 'it' here, i.e. the getting married; and (as is common in colloquial Finnish) the possessive suffix has been omitted from the two nouns in the last sentence because the possessor can be inferred to be the speaker, an inference that the translator has missed.

The published translation has thus broken the relation norm at these points; it has also broken the communication norm, in that the message and effect are not what was intended; and it has broken the accountability norm, in that one wonders why the translator did not get his text checked by anyone before going into print, to guard against possible misreadings of the original: where was the Error Elimination stage? Furthermore, although the translator is a native speaker of English, even the expectancy norm seems to have been disturbed a bit, in the choice of the lexical item *oldness*. All in all, it is undesirable and in fact irresponsible to break norms in such a way that functions are also unacceptably altered.

Some stations on the London Underground are built on a curve, so that the platforms do not line up precisely parallel with the trains. When a train arrives at one of these stations, a voice over the loudspeakers intones: Mind the gap! This is a good image for translators who are subjecting their Tentative Theories to Error Elimination. Compare Hervey and Higgins (1992:24): translators seek to "minimize dissimilarities".

There are several gaps to mind. One is that between source and target text. There must be, and remain, something of a gap: no train can actually touch the platform, but the usefulness of platforms is that they make it easier for people to get on and off trains. The nature of the inevitable gap must therefore be such as to optimize the flow. In information-theory terms, minding the gap thus corresponds to reducing "noise". There will also be an inevitable gap between the translation and its readers, just as there is one between any text and its readers. Here again, the point is obviously to minimize it, so that people do not fall through. And there are gaps too between translated texts and authentic non-translated TL texts, again to be minimized in many kinds of translation. There are even gaps between translators' own aims and their achievements, between the ideal and the real, between what I know I ought to do and what I actually do. Finally, there may be ideological gaps between the values that have governed the translator's work and those that govern the assessor's; no translation criticism is, after all, value-free. Interestingly enough, there are also serious ethical and philosophical reasons for focusing on gaps; we shall return to these in Chapter 7.

We assess texts; implicitly, we also thereby assess those responsible for the texts, we asses the translator's expertise. The following chapter discusses how this expertise develops, and how it can be developed.

5.8 Update

One clear gap in this chapter has been the lack of any discussion of revision procedures, which by definition are concerned with Error Eradication, although mention was made of Bly (1984). One reason might be that a wider interest in this topic is a relatively recent phenomenon. During the past two decades many important empirical studies have been published. Some of these focus on textual studies of what Toury calls "interim solutions" (e.g. Toury 1995: 181f.), i.e. the series of drafts which translators make, and the various changes made at each stage. Others take a more sociological view of the revision process as part of the workplace procedures of a team. The growing interest in revision was further encouraged by the publication in 2006 of the first official EU standard on translation services, CEN 15038. This has since been superseded (in 2015) by the international standard ISO 17100. One of the most influential scholars on this topic has been Brian Mossop, whose handbook on revision and editing gained a wide readership (Mossop 2007a). Mossop also published a useful summary of the main empirical research on revision up to that date (2007b).

Some of the research has been purely descriptive. For instance, Englund Dimitrova (2005) is interested in testing the literal translation hypothesis, according to which translators tend to come up first with a more literal version, and then move to less literal versions as they correct their drafts. The hypothesis was largely supported in her study. But many of the studies have taken an applied view, looking for the optimum revision system. (See e.g. Horguelin and Brunette 1998; Breedveld 2002; Brunette 2000; Brunette et al. 2005; Robert and Van Waes 2014.) There has also been recent work on applying usability heuristics to translation, as a way of improving quality (e.g. Suojanen et al. 2015).

Among the questions that have been investigated are the following. Is other-revision (i.e. revision by others) better than self-revision? Is revision on paper more reliable than revision on screen? Is it financially worth investing in two stages of revision: first with relation to the source text, and then with relation to target function? On this point, the CEN and ISO standards mentioned above seem to assume that a double revision is sometimes better. They make a terminological distinction between the *reviser*, who checks the translation against the source, and the *reviewer*, who does a monolingual check on the translation, looking e.g. at terminology and adherence to the conventions of the relevant domain. Translation scholars have noted that the CEN standard (on which the ISO standard is based) has evidently been influenced by the work of Christiane Nord (especially Nord 1991): a good example of the way academic work can have useful practical effects!

Attention has also been paid to the problems that can arise in revision. Over-keen revisers may provide instances of hyper-revision (unnecessary changes), under-revision (where errors are not corrected) or even over-revision (the revision itself can introduce a new error). These terms are from the work of Künzli (e.g. 2007).

The question of how descriptive scholars should deal with what look like errors has also received attention. If a descriptive scholar says of an item in a translation "X is an error, it should be Y", it sounds as if they have changed hats and are now acting in the role of a translation critic, prescriptively. So they might just be content to say "this is indeed a puzzling solution…" A descriptive scholar might of course contact the translator (if this is possible), and draw his attention to the item in question. The translator might then say "oops, that's a slip, it should of course be Y", and this is then good descriptive evidence of a mistake. But if the translator sticks by the original translation, are we left only with a difference of opinion between the translator and the critic? And what if the translator cannot be contacted? This issue is discussed, with some interesting evidence, by Malmkjær (2004), who proposes a way of distinguishing between deliberate choices and errors by investigating the systemacity of the assumed error in question. A systematic use of a given word, for instance, looks more like a deliberate choice than if it is used only once. But, one wants to add, couldn't the systematic use of the word perhaps also indicate a systematic gap in the translator's knowledge, rather than a deliberate choice?

A very different line of research has been the revision, by human translators, of texts translated by machine: what is known as post-editing. The first major monograph on this topic was Krings (2001), and the Internet now shows ever more seminars and guidelines on the topic, particularly with respect to localization. The website of the Association for Machine Translation in the Americas (http://www.amtaweb.org/mt-for-translators/) says post-editing is now "one of the hottest most discussed topics in the translation industry". (I feel I want to revise that quote and insert a comma after "hottest"…) See also O'Brien and Simard (2014).

The concept of translation quality has also been expanded to include the ethical quality of the working conditions of the translators themselves (see especially Abdallah 2012). This will be discussed in the Update to Chapter 7.

CHAPTER 6

The development of translational competence

6.1 Stages of expertise

The contemporary conception of the professional translator's role is that of an expert, someone with expertise, i.e. with translational competence. The focus of this chapter is on how this expertise is acquired. We shall first look at a theory of how human expertise develops, and then apply this to how people grow as translators, both by being taught and by learning on their own. A parallel will also be suggested with the growth of translation theory itself.

In their critique of artificial intelligence, Dreyfus and Dreyfus (1986) set out five steps defining the process from "novice" to "expert" in the acquisition of any skill. (Their fundamental purpose is to argue that human expertise has features that can never be imitated by computers, but this particular argument is not relevant to our present concern.) The steps are the following.

Stage one: novice. The trainee learns "to recognize various objective facts and features relevant to the skill [in our case, the skill of translation] and acquires rules for determining actions based upon those facts and features" (1986: 21). The key points here are "recognition" and "rules". Features which are to be recognized are defined so explicitly that they appear to the trainee to be "context-free", and the rules to be applied to these features are therefore context-free rules. The authors call the manipulation of such rules "information processing". An example is the way a novice driver learns to change gear at given speeds: the relevant speeds are defined free of context, and the appropriate gear-changing rule is applied accordingly. At this level, say the authors, the trainee lacks a overall sense of the task at hand, and judges performance mainly by reference to these explicit rules. Behaviour is thus fully conscious, easily verbalized, and atomistic.

Stage two: advanced beginner. After more experience of real situations, trainees begin to recognize not only relevant situational features that have been previously defined but also ones that have not been so defined; these may even be such that neither instructor nor learner can in fact define them explicitly, although they are mainfestly relevant to the task at hand. This more advanced kind of recognition is based on the trainee's ability to perceive similarity with prior examples. Features thus recognized are "situational" as opposed to context-free (22–23). Drivers at this level, for instance, learn how to change gear in accordance with the way they hear the engine noise, albeit not in any way that they could define explicitly, acoustically as it were. Behaviour is conscious, but less easily verbalized and less atomistic.

Stage three: competence. As experience grows, and as the number of recognized relevant features of the situation therefore also grows, it becomes increasingly difficult to retain all the features in consciousness. It thus becomes necessary to develop a sense of priorities, and this is the crucial aspect of this phase. People learn "a hierarchical procedure of decision-making" (24). This entails the ability to see the situation more as a whole, to formulate a plan, and select the set of factors which are most important for the realization of the plan. A competent trainee has a conscious sense of the goal of the task, and it is this goal-awareness that determines the selection and prioritizing of the situational features deemed to be relevant. At this level, the learner is more of a "subject" than earlier, actively reviewing an array of situational facts and selecting from them in accordance with a conscious goal. The picture, therefore, is not one of information processing alone; it also involves problem-solving. One of their examples is of someone driving fast in an emergency, choosing the shortest possible routes, deliberately breaking norms or traffic rules wherever possible, driving with a very specific goal in mind.

The authors stress that this stage involves the conscious choosing of an appropriate plan of action, and this necessity to choose affects the learner's behaviour in that it introduces an element of personal responsibility. The learner is no longer simply reacting to a defined or undefined set of situational features, but overtly ranking these features and drawing conclusions about requisite action: in a word, solving a problem. Moreover, although the mental attitude during the process of recognition and selection is still what the Dreyfuses call "detached", analytical, learners do feel responsible for the outcome of their actions, and emotional involvement thus enters the picture at this stage.

Rational problem-solving is one recognized form of intelligence; but much of our behaviour manifests still higher levels of expertise.

Stage four: proficiency. Up to this point, argue the Drefuses, learners have been consciously following rules, processing information and making choices. At the level of proficiency, however, decisions are made less because of objective rules etc. and more because of personal experience. The recognition of certain situational features as being more salient than others is based on experience, on perceived similarities between the current situation and previous ones. The authors call this "know-how" or "intuition", not in any irrational or mystical sense but to describe "the sort of ability we all use all the time as we go about our everyday tasks" (29). They speak of "the intuitive ability to use patterns without decomposing them into component features" (28). In other words, this kind of understanding is not atomistic but holistic.

But analytical thinking is still involved. "The proficient performer, while intuitively organizing and understanding his task, will still find himself thinking analytically about what to do" (29). It is as if the proficient performer wavers between intuitive understanding and rational, deliberative action, alternately involved in "the world of the skill" (29) and detached from it. Their example is of an experienced driver approaching a curve on a rainy day, intuitively realizing he is going too fast, and then rationally deciding whether and when to remove his foot from the accelerator or apply the brakes.

Stage five: expertise. At this final level, intuition takes over. Conscious deliberation is superseded, and nonreflective involvement is dominant. "An expert's skill has become so much a part of him that he need be no more aware of it than he is of his own body" (30). "The expert driver becomes one with his car" (30). If any deliberation does occur, the authors say, it is not a matter of problem-solving but rather "critically reflecting on one's intuitions" (32). Expert performance is beyond analytical, "calculative" rationality. It is "arational" (36) in that it gives priority to intuition, but it is also said to be characterized by "deliberative rationality", which involves the testing and improving of intuitions.

As described by the authors, this kind of rationality seems close to our Popperian paradigm: examination of the salient features of a situation, and observation of differences and similarities with past experience, lead intuitively to tentative solutions, and these are then submitted where necessary to scrutiny by deliberative rationality. This is not a simple question of following rules or algorithms, but a process of self-reflection, a kind of monitoring which can be switched on at will, the aim being the overall improvement of the performance of the task.

To sum up: "[i]nvolvement is essential for the holistic similarity recognition of proficient and expert performers. But if learning is to occur, some part of the mind must remain aloof and detached" (40). What the Dreyfuses call a "monitoring mind" is responsible for "fine tuning" in order to ensure "more effective guidance of future behavior" (40). Yet in between such moments of deliberative monitoring, expert performance proceeds as a "flow", accompanied by a feeling of "euphoria".

This "flow" describes what happens "when things are proceeding normally" (30). Yet the range of what is normal is experienced differently by different people. We are all experts at breathing, and do it perfectly fluently most of the time, without thinking about it and without euphoria; but in less usual situations we may well become conscious of it, and deliberately seek to control it, for instance when swimming, or in a very hot sauna (when one may deliberately try to breathe slowly, through cupped hands, to avoid scorching one's throat). For experts in a particular field, of course, such situations are not unusual, not "problems", and unlike the rest of us they will react appropriately without thinking. As the Dreyfuses put it (156):

"skill in any domain is measured by the performer's ability to act appropriately in situations that might once have been problems but are no longer problems and so do not require analytic reflection." Within a given field, then, we might say that the wider the range that is felt to be normal and problem-free, the greater the expertise.

This view of the overall process of skill acquisition is thus one of gradual automatization: it goes from atomistic to holistic recognition, from conscious to unconscious responses, from analytical to intuitive decision-making, from calculative to deliberative rationality, from detached to involved commitment. Stage by stage, we have:

1. recognition of predefined features and rules
2. recognition of non-defined but relevant features
3. hierarchical and goal-oriented decision-making
4. intuitive understanding plus deliberative action
5. fluid performance plus deliberative rationality

Let us now see how this view of learning can be applied to the acquisition of translational competence.

6.2 The significance of memes

Many practising translators may feel that translation *theory* is a waste of time and only hinders fluent access to intuition. Theory, it is commonly thought, exists solely in order to help practice, and if it doesn't do this we are better off without it. (See e.g. the opening debate in Chesterman and Wagner 2002.) I think such a reaction reveals a rather narrow view of theory, and also a reluctance to introspect, a mistrust of deliberative rationality, and perhaps a suspicion about consciousness-raising as a pedagogical principle. Those who reject theory would claim that we learn best through developing procedural knowledge, not declarative knowledge.

But consider this claim in the light of the Dreyfuses' five stages in the growth of expertise. If the Dreyfuses' argument holds good, conscious awareness plays a crucial role at two points. First, in the early stages of novice, advanced beginner and competent performer, where task situations are analysed for specific features and explicit "rules of behaviour" are learned and applied. And second, in the higher stages of proficiency and expertise, when performance results or behaviour need to be monitored and fine-tuned. In the earlier stages, consciousness is "switched on" all the time, but in the later stages recourse is made to conscious deliberative reflection only intermittently.

Recall, too, Steiner's distinction (1988; see 4.1 above) between conscious actions, readily accessible to verbal report, and more automatic ones. In Dreyfusian terms, behavioural or cognitive procedures at the early stages of performance skill are conscious, but they typically become unconscious at higher levels of expertise, and normally unconscious procedures can be made conscious at these higher levels if the situation requires. An expert performer, by this definition, has the ability to manipulate the monitoring mind at will, to switch between automatic and deliberative actions as the occasion demands (cf. also Kiraly's model, 1995: 99f.).

Insofar as translating is seen as a skill, an expert translator is thus someone who works largely on intuition, who has automatized a set of basic routines, and who can draw on deliberative rationality when the need arises, in the solving of unusual problems or in the comparison and justification of possible solutions. Translation tasks will naturally vary in the degree to which they require deliberative rationality. Translating poetry, for instance, may involve the monitoring mind from start to finish, with no possibility to exploit ready routines. A translator who is deliberately setting out to break a prevailing norm, to surprise readers (for whatever reason), is in a similar situation: critical conscious engagement may be required throughout. At this end of the continuum, indeed, we can query whether translation can properly be called a "skill" at all. At the other extreme, a translator of routine documents or certificates may be able to operate automatically for most of the time. One mark of the expert professional is presumably the ability to judge precisely when deliberative rationality is needed and how it should be used.

What does this have to do with memes? Precisely this: memes are conceptual tools. Useful memes are aids to thought. And as such they are also aids to skilled performance. This book has discussed various kinds of memes. We first introduced some universal supermemes of translation theory, and then looked at certain historical memes illustrating how concepts of translation and of the translator's role have changed over the centuries. I pointed out that translation norms are also kinds of memes, insofar as they are indeed recognized to be norms. Translation laws are also memes of a kind, to the extent that they are known. And so are widely-used translation strategies. All such memes constitute a pool of concepts at the disposal of translators who wish to improve their expertise.

In the Dreyfus model, during the beginning stages, these memes will be perceived and used consciously; but when translators grow in expertise memes sink below the threshold of awareness, yet remain accessible to deliberative rationality when required. Their relevance is thus fourfold: to the novice and beginner becoming aware for the first time of the wide range of thinking about translation; to the competent or proficient practitioner needing to explain or justify choices and decisions made; to the expert wishing to fine-tune tentative intuitive solutions; and finally to the teacher, critic or assessor of translation skills.

An awareness of what I called supermemes stakes out the basic co-ordinates of the whole business of translation. Awareness of the historical memes enables translators to see their own social role in a historical context, and perhaps clarify their own attitudes towards this role. Awareness of those memes that have become translation norms establishes "regulative ideas" which then guide translational behaviour. Awareness of general translation laws can also regulate translational behaviour, in a different sense: if one is aware that translators tend to explicitate, or to succumb to interference or stylistic flattening or normalizing, one can guard against this. And awareness of common strategies can help to automatize frequently used translation routines, as the following section illustrates. Indeed, awareness of theory in general, of the explanatory power of theoretical concepts, is widely accepted as an important part of professional training in any field, and scarcely needs to be justified separately in translator training (but see Gile 1995: 13f., nevertheless).

It is not, then, that a declarative knowledge of memes is an obstacle to fluent procedural knowledge. On the contrary: such declarative knowledge is surely a necessary prerequisite to expertise. Once acquired, such knowledge does not need to be retained constantly in consciousness, as the Dreyfuses' stages of expertise illustrate; yet even experts can profit by having access to it when required. This is not a particularly original point, of course. Arguing along similar lines, Kußmaul (1995: passim) also gives great prominence to a translator's self-awareness and the need to cultivate this.

We can also note in passing that the importance of awareness, of reflectivity in learning, of learning to learn, is a crucial element in pedagogical approaches such as experiential learning (Kolb 1984) and applications of action research (e.g. Kemmis and McTaggart 1988).

6.3 Suggestions for teaching

This section is addresssed primarily to teachers and trainers of translation skills. If the Dreyfuses are right in their understanding of how expertise grows, the process is one that starts with an explicit focus on salient aspects of the translation situation, a focus on consciousness-raising, in fact (see Shlesinger 1992, for an interesting report on a consciousness-raising exercise that seemed to have a clear effect on the translation process). But it does not stop there: the ability to recognize relevant situational features and to choose appropriate response strategies becomes increasingly automated and intuitive as expertise grows, until conscious awareness itself becomes a tool which an expert can resort to at will, via deliberative rationality. Consider now how this approach can be applied in developing an awareness of translation strategies and norms.

Exercises with strategies
Exercises one can do with translation strategies can follow the Dreyfuses' stages of expertise quite closely. At the novice stage, typical strategies such as those discussed in Chapter 4 can be introduced and defined, and students can be taught to recognize certain predefined strategies when comparing source texts with their published translations. The strategies are thus learned as concepts, as rules of thumb. A typical instruction might be: find three examples of a transposition strategy in this paragraph.

At the advanced beginner stage, students can be asked to examine a translation alongside its original and list the strategies they observe. The assumption here is that the basic strategies will be familiar concepts by this time, and that students now have the ability to recognize them in context, situationally. Practice can also be given in the use of specific strategies: students can be asked to use a given strategy in translating certain marked passages of a text (or a number of separate sentences). The rubric could be: translate the following sections using the converses strategy. Or: translate the following sentences in such a way that the clause structure changes from passive to active. Or: translate the following, for such-and-such a readership, adding whatever information you think necessary. Another type of exercise is to mark a source text right through with code numbers indicating certain strategies, as guidelines for the students. A mark G8 in the text, for instance, would suggest: think about making a cohesion change here. One such practice text might focus exclusively on syntactic strategies, another on semantic ones and a third on pragmatic ones.

At the competence stage, with its focus on analytic decision-making, a primary focus is on the question "why?" Students can be asked to analyse published translations, and suggest reasons why the translator used certain strategies, what priorities or goals the translator has evidently had in mind at this point. Alternatively, as a pretranslation exercise, they might be asked to state what strategy they would use at a particular point, and why.

At the proficiency stage, the aim is to move away from analytical thought and towards intuition. Students can be asked to translate a text under some time pressure, following their intuition about the appropriate strategies and not stopping too much for detached thought. When the task is completed, time can then be given to a rational analysis, comparison and evaluation of the strategies selected. Group discussion might also be based on comments each member makes about the intuitive work of other members. Practice of this sort might also bring to light new strategies that the group had not yet considered, deriving from spontaneous translating activity. Alternatively, students could be explicitly encouraged to invent new strategies from their own experience. Another way to underline the intuitive element is to use texts the students have written themselves (see below).

It has also been pointed out (e.g. by Séguinot 1991) that translators who have got beyond the analytic decision-making stage tend more to be guided by higher-level factors such as the overall nature of the translation commission. Lower-level decisions are then made more automatically, unconsciously even, leaving the mental monitor free to focus on more global aspects of the task. This point might also be made use of in teaching at this stage: explicit attention can be drawn to the way in which higher-level goals affect lower-level choices. (See also below.)

At the stage of true expertise, teaching is scarcely necessary, by definition.

Exercises on accountability

The accountability norm is something that can be drawn attention to early in translation training: an awareness of the ethical responsibility of a translator is fundamental. A number of practical exercises seem useful in this respect.

One is "personal translation" into the non-native language. This is an exercise designed to trigger emotional, subjective feelings about one's own writing, to see how one is answerable for one's own text. Trainees write a short essay in their native language; this can be on any topic, but ones that involve some subjective, impressionistic element generally work best. They are not told at this stage how the exercise will proceed, so that they can write "naively", naturally. Pairs are then asked to translate each other's texts into the target language. These translations are then returned to their original writers, who are given the task of evaluating the translation of their own text, giving feedback direct to the translator. Seeing one's own text in another language arouses powerful subjective responses, and these in turn lead to fruitful discussions. The whole exercise thus stresses the importance of being personally involved in the translation process. Receiving immediate feedback from a real authority – the original writer, who is just as bilingual as the translator in this case – enhances this effect.

Another exercise focusing on accountability is summary translation. This stresses the translator's responsibility for selecting what needs to be translated and structuring it appropriately. A summary translation is naturally more like the translator's "own" text than an "ordinary" translation is, since in some sense the translator is also producing (mentally, or in the form of notes) the source. This exercise also overtly stresses the way in which translators do indeed "manipulate" texts.

Both these exercises are thus useful at the beginning stages of expertise, when the emphasis is on the raising-to-consciousness of crucial concepts and behaviour patterns.

An additional technique that underlines accountability for one's text is process writing. Because this underlines not the end-product but the process which leads to it, writers are forced to take the responsibility for constantly moulding and manipulating their texts; the texts remain "alive", responsive and dynamic, not static. Process-writing methods can obviously be used in translation teaching as well as composition teaching: time can be given for drafting and redrafting, responding to feedback, final revision etc., in a heuristic process that exactly matches our Popperian schema.

Gile (1994) makes a similar point, stressing the usefulness of focusing on the translation process rather than the product, both in training and in feedback or assessment, particularly during the early phases of training. Gile further notes that providing feedback in the form of questions rather than criticism can help to stimulate students to improve their own working methods. Questions provoke introspection, and hence relate to accountability too.

Exercises on the communication norm
Similarly, there are a number of ways of focusing on the communication norm. One is discussed by Jakobsen (1994b) under the rubric of "starting from the (other) end". The idea here is that students should be given more practice in *writing* texts in the target language before they get round to actual translating. They will then have a better view of what the desired end-product of a translation should look like, and avoid the pitfalls of interference or translationese. Practice in original text production, argues Jakobsen, also emphasizes that both writing and translating start with the *need* for a text, and thus underlines the importance of the extra-textual factors creating this need. Such work also stresses how the skopos of any text affects the way it is put together.

An obvious application of this idea is to exploit the use of target-language parallel texts as models when constructing a text of a given type: students are thus sensitized to the idea of matching texts against a text-type template.

Another application is to vary the way in which background information texts are introduced to support the writing of original texts. These background texts can be first in the target language, but then increasingly in the source language as well, so that students need to process more and more from one language to the other. Original target-language writing gradually merges into actual translation.

Furthermore, a text that is being written for a genuine communicative purpose is experienced as being "warm", in that the writer feels "involved" in its production. In this respect, "starting from the other end" also focuses on accountability.

The communication norm can also be the main focus in exercises that start from the source-text end. One form of practice here is source-text rewriting. This is a kind of pretranslation exercise that focuses on the importance of transediting when necessary. A badly-written source text is rewritten over and over again, for instance by successive members of a group, until the whole group is satisfied with it as a source text, satisfied that it meets agreed criteria of clarity, logic, readability etc. If the source text is in fact in the native language of the trainees, this sensitizing to style will perhaps develop more easily.

Source-text rewriting also prepares translators to cope with the frustrations of being faced with source texts in real life that are indeed clumsy or obscure. Such rewriting (mentally or physically) is all too often a normal part of the translator's work, and should not come as a surprise. After all, not everyone is a language expert.

Building on this, students can then be given target-language texts (not necessarily translations) which could also be "cleaned up" and edited in a similar way. This exercise has the further advantage of representing the kind of work that translation-trained language experts often have to do: polishing target-language texts written by someone else.

Such exercises thus emphasize that the translator should be an expert in communication, not in theory but in practice. A declarative knowledge of the kind of editorial changes one often needs to make should then transfer into procedural knowledge, along the lines outlined by the Dreyfuses.

Exercises on the relation norm
As regards the relation norm, the main problem seems to be a question of attitude. After secondary school, students and trainees typically have a very narrow view of what the relation between source and target should be. They perhaps have some idea of equivalence, based on the kind of translation work they did at school. This idea is often couched in terms of absolute "sameness" in some way or other: there is an assumption that the translation must have the "same meaning", "same content" or "same style" as the original, that it should convey the "same message" or have the "same form". It usually goes hand in hand with an undifferentiated tendency to translate rather literally. This assumption often continues to be held even in some professional circles: a good example of an unusually persistent meme! However, as I have argued earlier, I do not believe it is a useful notion, nor even a theoretically tenable one.

In my view, the aim of translation training in this respect should therefore be to broaden trainees' concepts of what a translation can be; in other words to increase trainees' awareness of the wide variety of relations that can legitimately hold between a source text and its legitimate translation. Such exposure should develop a flexibility of attitude and response, and this in turn should enhance the "fluid" performance that is characteristic of expertise.

Several general teaching procedures seem to be applicable here. One is to present trainees with a wide variety of texts that are fairly claimed to be translations and to study the kinds of source-target relations which they manifest, comparing originals with their translations. These text-pairs should be of all possible types. Attention could then be focused on possible correlations between relation-type and text-type, or between relation-type and translation-skopos. This is actually another kind of pretranslation exercise, in that the focus is entirely analytical, looking only at existing translations as products.

A second procedure is to focus more on translation as a process: to take a single source text and examine how it either has been, or would be, translated in different ways depending on the audience, skopos etc., in order to see in practice how the source-target relation does actually vary. This variation is different from the purely idiosyncratic differences between one translator and another translating the same text for the same readership. To take a very brief example: in my own translation of Karlsson's textbook on *Finnish Grammar* (1983), I gave very literal (but not morphemic) glosses of the various example sentences, following the basic constituent order as far as possible, sometimes even resorting to ungrammatical English, in order to illustrate the Finnish structure. So for instance

> ST: Mistään maasta ei tule enemmän edustajia kuin Suomesta.

was translated as

> TT: From no country are there coming more representatives than from Finland.

I claim that, for the skopos of this particular translation commission, this is a legitimate translation (not the only one, granted: some readers might prefer a morpheme-by-morpheme version). But I would of course translate the same sentence rather differently in a different target context.

A third approach is to examine stated assumptions about the desired source-target relation that are clearly inappropriate in certain cases. One such is provocatively discussed by Vuorinen (1994), who criticizes the blanket statement in the guidelines laid down by the Finnish Association of Translators and Interpreters, to the effect that translators should seek to preserve the content and style of the original. Vuorinen sets this injunction against a text containing a number of stylistic obscurities, and where the author made a claim – that patents are not subject to strict discourse norms – which any translator would presumably reject. Most professional translators commissioned to translate such a text, argues Vuorinen, would feel free to tidy up the argument; furthermore, they would perhaps either check with the original writer whether the claim about patents was really what was intended, or even omit this item from the text's list of "freer" kinds of texts, and thereby save the original writer from an embarrassing slip. To make such changes, and hence to manipulate and alter the relation between source and target, is to take true responsibility for the translation. Translatorial accountability thus means balancing the interests of all the various parties involved, not simply giving priority to source-text content without question.

Exercises on expectancy norms
Expectancy norms are of course taught anyway, via attention to grammaticality, acceptability and appropriateness. In addition, students can be made aware of many of the basic text and discourse norms of the target language by comparing distributions of features in their own translations with distributions in parallel texts. Parallel texts are obviously worth studying in detail as pretranslation exercises, too.

There is a further pedagogical point to be made here, which derives from our earlier discussion of norm validation (cf. 3.5.2 and 3.8). It was pointed out there that some texts conform to general expectancy norms in the sense that they do indeed meet the expectations of most of their readers, but that a subgroup of these readers (norm authorities, for example) might still feel that these texts are open to criticism in terms of their lack of clarity, readability or the like: they would not conform to higher, "recommendable norms".

These recommendable norms will surely form part of any curriculum designed to train language experts, including translators. (If this sounds unnecessarily elitist or purist, recall that we can all breathe, but some people learn to breathe "better" than others – opera singers, for instance, or competitive swimmers – and that there are experts in breathing who give instruction in this skill.) One example of a concept worth teaching from this point of view is iconicity, the optimal structuring of form as a mirror of meaning.

6.4   Ontogenetic = phylogenetic?

One of Darwin's most provocative ideas was that the ontogenetic development of the individual parallels the phylogenetic development of the species. If we apply this metaphorically to the acquisition of translational expertise, we can ask the following question: does the ontogenetic development of an individual translator tend to follow the "phylogenetic" development of translation theory? That is, might the changing attitudes and ideas of individual translator trainees reflect the development of general translation memes through history? (A caveat: I do not wish to imply here that modern translations are somehow "better" or "more developed" than earlier ones!)

A pedagogical corollary of this question would be to wonder whether the training process could be enhanced by deliberately exploiting this similarity. Furthermore, it would provide a good (and highly motivating) reason why trainees should also be taught something of the history of translation theory: in so doing, trainees would also be acquiring the conceptual tools to observe their own progress. A degree of self-awareness would thus be built in to the training process right from the start, and trainees would see themselves quite naturally as participating in a historical process. (There are also emancipatory aspects to such an approach, which we shall return to in the following chapter.)

The idea fits well into the general Popperian view of the evolution of knowledge that I have been following. Popper applies the same heuristic schema to both phylogenetic and ontogenetic development.

Let us look at what this idea might imply in practice. Recall that, for Popper, historical development takes place via trial and error, heuristic problem-solving: proposed solutions are found wanting, they lead to new problems or reformulations of old ones, and so on. In Chapter 2, I suggested that the history of translation theory could be seen as an approximate succession of eight broad stages, each focusing on a different problem or set of problems. Suppose now that these "phylogenetic" stages represent a similar succession of "sensitive periods" in a translator's ontogenetic development. Perhaps translator training could react accordingly. Imagine, for instance, that ontogenetically each stage represents an academic term... By swinging from one viewpoint to another, in an ordered succession, trainees may even acquire a sense of the complementarity, of the coexistence of differences, which lies at the very heart of translation.

I suggested that the first stage was that of Words. Surely this is where the individual translator starts, too, e.g. deciphering an item on a menu. Or one wonders what the word for X is in language Y. Beginning translators – real novices – surely tend to translate "word for word". Indeed, teachers often complain that their students spend too much time on purely lexical problems, that they think at the word level only (cf. Séguinot 1991). A common pedagogical reaction, I think, is irritation, and an urge to get on to the next stage. But imagine possible alternatives: if it is acknowledged that this is indeed where translators start, why not exploit this tendency?

At this very first stage, trainees could be introduced to dictionaries and thesauruses, and also central theoretical concepts such as denotation and connotation, aspects of lexical semantics, componential analysis, lexicography, the translation of technical terms – in short, any significant aspects of overall translation competence that pertain specifically to lexis. At this point, too, the big debate on translatability can be opened: can words of different languages ever "mean the same"?

My second stage was the Word of God, marked by a focus on grammatical form and literal translation. In my experience, students entering university training are usually at this stage, largely because of their school experience of translation. Here again, one often hears criticism of the school tradition, but why not rather acknowledge it as one necessary stage in the overall process? This would be the point to introduce literal translation as only one variant – a perfectly valid one as such, but only one among several others. Overt attention might be given to Nida's minimal transfer (1964; Nida and Taber 1969) as compared to his literal (ungrammatical) and literary (stylistically more polished) transfers. Or one could start by introducing Newmark's distinction (1981) between semantic and communicative translation, together with a discussion on when one method might be more appropriate than the other. One focus at this stage could be on text-types that are indeed normally translated with priority given to the form of the original, such as some kinds of philosophical or legal texts. Another could be on technical translation, with its high requirement of factual accuracy.

Stage three was that of Rhetoric. This introduces criteria of stylistic naturalness and flexibility in the target language. Particularly when trainees are working out of their native language, the control of the target language needs to be broadened and deepened at this stage. This is where Jakobsen's suggestion (1994b, mentioned above) comes in: introduce more practice in original writing in the target language, including creative writing in particular. Any writing practice *not* linked to a source text would be relevant here.

One proposal that does involve source texts but still seems to fit this stage exactly is the variational method advocated by Hewson and Martin (1991). Their approach to translation is based on two sets of paraphrased variants: paraphrases are first elicited for a sentence or section of the source text, and then a second set of similar paraphrases is elicited in the target language. (The emphasis is realistically on similarity, not sameness.) Differences between the variants are analysed, for both languages. Then the optimal target version is selected from this set, in accordance with the relevant target-situation constraints and norms. This approach thus stresses the ability to produce as many variants as possible in both languages, and then to filter out the most appropriate target one – precisely corresponding to Pym's double concept of translational competence outlined above (5.1). The whole method seems an excellent way to practice proficiency-stretching, in both source and target languages.

As regards the associated theoretical concepts that seem pertinent here, obvious areas are stylistics, textlinguistics and rhetoric. Other more practical skills that relate to this stage are those of editing and proof-reading.

Stage four I called Logos, centring on language as a creative force and (hence) on literary translation. A central concept from this stage was the notion of the deliberately "hybrid" translation, where the original still shone through the translation and a foreign touch was retained. What this often meant in practice was that the translation preserved the same order of sememes as the original, the same information order (see Kelly 1979:224). One pedagogical application is thus to explore the distinction between information order (given – new) and grammatical order: with many text-types, preserving information order in translation is more important than preserving grammatical order. This distinction can then lead to an examination of the whole field of thematization, emphasis, marked vs: unmarked expression and the like.

A further application here comes from the distinction between overt and covert translation (House 1981): some source texts are so source-culture-bound that their translations must be overt translations; other kinds of translation can be submitted as being truly parallel to non-translated target-language texts. Practice work can exploit this distinction. Examples of overt translations include "hybrid-type" literary translations, political speeches, books about source-culture realia (such as the Finnish grammar mentioned above), etc. After the freer stylistic play of the Rhetoric stage which demoted the status of the source text, this Logos stage pulls trainees back to the source again, reminding them that certain kinds of texts must be translated overtly, manifesting the translator's presence quite openly. It thus underlines the importance of the text-type as a factor determining the translator's decisions. It also reminds us that the translator's task is not always to be an invisible window between source text and target reader, but a good deal more complex and varied – and this in turn emphasizes the translator's responsibility. Work might be done on the various ways in which translators do responsibly signal their presence, by footnotes, glosses, additions in brackets, deliberately marked style, or whatever.

Trainees might also find it of interest to look at deconstructionist ideas of translation at this point: see e.g. Gentzler (1993), Koskinen (1994a, b), Vieira (1994).

Stage five, Linguistic science, obviously underlines the usefulness of a basic linguistic literacy, particularly as an aid to detailed analysis of the source text: see for instance Nord (1991). The superordinate science of semiotics, too, might usefully enter the curriculum at this point, as a discipline offering a general conceptual framework in which matters translatorial can be pondered. (See for instance Gorlée 1994, and more recently Hartama-Heinonen's work, e.g. 2008.) Translators, after all, are one kind of signing animal. Both linguistics (in the broad sense, including semantics and pragmatics) and semiotics can provide conceptual tools which make it easier to assess alternative versions during the Error Elimination phase.

Contrastive analysis also becomes relevant at this stage, as a way of specifying the range of choice available in both source and target languages. It stresses the importance of being able to stand back and take an analytical view of the two *langues*. The more translators are aware of what is available, what the system offers (Catford's unconditioned equivalents), the more reliable their judgements ought to be about which variant to select (as *parole*) in any given case (Catford's conditioned equivalents).

At this stage, too, trainees could begin to explore the translation procedures discussed by Vinay and Darbelnet (1958) or the various shifts classified by Catford (1965), or the set of strategies suggested above, Chapter 4.

Stage six, emerging from the wider semiotic and pragmatic concerns of stage five, was Communication. At this stage the trainees clarify their own social images, their social roles as translators, as expert communicators. They need to take account of the overall nature of the translation commission, who requires the translation, who pays, who will publish it, who will read it, and so on. (There is an extensive discussion of such questions in Nord 1991.) After the close linguistic focus of the previous stage, the Communication stage centres not on the text but on the situation. The matters at issue here thus concern communication in general.

From the teaching point of view, several topics become particularly relevant at this stage. One would be the theory of communication itself, perhaps based on Grice's (1975) co-operative maxims of quality, quantity, relevance and manner, together with other general pragmatic principles such as those of politeness. Another, more practical topic would be readability: trainees could measure the readability of their own translations, for example, using a standard formula. A third teaching point might be a critique of the concept of equivalence, based perhaps on a reading of Gutt (1991): no communication will be interpreted by any two people in exactly the same way.

Stage seven moves out from the communicative situation to the cultural level, and in particular to the target culture. Translated texts must be embedded in the target culture, in whatever way is deemed appropriate. With this in mind, students might be introduced to the polysystem theory of culture at this stage (see 2.7). Specific attention might be paid to culture-bound terms in the source language, and to translation strategies that can be resorted to in dealing with these. (See e.g. Florin 1993, and for a later overview Leppihalme 2011.) And yet another is the translation of allusions (Leppihalme 1997, and see 7.6 below).

Such topics also illustrate that translators inevitably manipulate their texts, and manipulation is something that has ideological overtones; at this fairly advanced stage, translators would do well to be aware of this aspect of their work, and take responsibility accordingly. In order to see this, students might study the different ways in which texts are translated from dominant to peripheral cultures and vice versa. They might study how translation norms change from period to period and from culture to culture. They might be asked to specify some of the expectancy norms currently prevailing in a particular target culture. And they might even be asked to state their own beliefs about the way a translator should behave.

My final stage I called Cognition. This represented the growing interest in probing into the translator's black box, in using a variety of means to infer something about the decision-making process. Ontogenetically, too, it comes as an appropriate final stage, symbolizing a translator's self-awareness. If translators do indeed grow in expertise in something like the way I have suggested here, this self-awareness will also include an awareness of the "phylogenetic" development of the profession itself, and of ideas about it. To progress without such awareness is, I think, to progress blind, and also to translate blind. If a theory is a way of seeing, theories can indeed bring insight: hence, as I have mentioned before, the ultimate motivation for teaching translation theory alongside translation practice.

Self-awareness as a translator can also free one from inappropriate dogmas. And in so doing, it reinforces a translator's status as an emancipated subject rather than a submissive object, a subject who takes full responsibility for his or her actions.

It is instructive to compare this Translator's Progress with another account of the translator's ontological path towards emancipation. Building on Bloom's ([1975] 1980) chart of the evolution of the "strong poet", Robinson (1991: 109f.) offers a poetico-theological framework of six stages whereby the translator is gradually released from "instrumentalization" (i.e. the belief that a translator is a mere instrument, totally subservient to the source text). Robinson's stages may be paraphrased as follows:

1. Idealized instrumentality. This is said to represent the translator's infancy, which the translator must "learn to grow out of" (110). The translator is "in love" with the source text, but is entirely passive, brings no "fire" of his/her own to the relationship. In some quarters, suggests Robinson, considerable pressure is exerted upon translators to remain in this infantile state.
2. Self-conscious submission. The translator still surrenders all initiative to the source text, but does so consciously, as an act of will, and with an increasing sense of what this submission actually entails. This awareness then begins to undermine the submissiveness. The translator consciously dons a mask, and knows that it is a mask, and knows that masks can be changed.
3. Chosen instrumentality. Although the translator at this stage is no longer under the sway of the source writer's authority, "when the translator looks inside for a personal response, some unknown "force" takes over and guides him or her back to instrumentality. And it feels like his or her own desire! I *want* to

be the instrument of the SL [source-language] writer: I choose instrumentality!" (112)
4. A word of his or her own. This stage represents the beginning of the finding of one's own voice, a breaking through the "ideosomatic programming" at last, to a word of one's own. Citing Bloom, Robinson explicates this "word" as a kind of driving force, a moral act: recall my interpretation of the logos idea in Chapter 2.
5. Total interpretation. This denotes a "fullness of response" on the part of the translator. Robinson glosses this as a tolerance of contradictions and inconsistencies; I take it to represent a kind of response to the text as an organic whole.
6. Dialogical engagement. This marks "the strong translation as act, the act of translation as a dialogical engagement with both the SL writer and the TL [target-language] receptor" (115). This Bakhtinian view Robinson then develops at length in the remainder of his book. He emphasizes the translator's status as equal partner in the dialogic interaction, non-subservient, non-instrumental, able to respond flexibly in a wide variety of ways, free to edit, adapt or improve the text in any way he or she thinks fit, supremely confident in his or her own competence. For: "the dialogical richness of real life [...] allows for all kinds of relationships, including some where the SL author feels inferior to the translator and a good many where author and translator feel like equals, collaborators" (116–117).

Robinson's overall framework is very different from mine, but he too seems to see parallels between an individual translator's emancipation and the historical development of the translator's status. There is also a striking similarity in the way in which the translator's progress is seen to move from submission to emancipation, from servility to self-confidence, and from unthinkingness to self-awareness. Both outlines expand from a text-bound focus to a wider, communicative one.

Finally, I append a curious piece of anecdotal evidence in support of the ontological reality of the sort of process I have been outlining. Baker (1992: 3) cites an essay by Lanna Castellano (1988) recommending an optimum life-path for would-be translators. I will quote part of this, and add my own comments in italics. To be a translator, says Castellano, you should first ensure that you have

> grandparents of different nationalities, a good school education in which you learn to read, write, spell, construe and love your own language. [*This approximately corresponds to my stages 1 to 3: acquire a good linguistic competence in your own language and (via grandparents!) familiarity with another too.*] Then roam the world, make friends, see life. Go back to education, but to take a technical or commercial degree, not a language degree. Spend the rest of your twenties

and your early thirties in the countries whose languages you speak, working in industry or commerce but not directly in languages. Never marry into your own nationality. Have your children. [*Compare my stage 4: experience language in action.*] Then back to a postgraduate translation course. [*In other words, begin to look objectively, scientifically at language and how it is used: stage 5.*] A staff job as a translator... [*i.e. discover the communicative role a translator plays in real life, in mediation between cultures: cf. stages 6 and 7*], and then go freelance. By which time you are forty and ready to begin. [*The idea being that by this time you will have acquired the necessary expertise, a knowledge of the history and theory of translation, and also the necessary self-awareness – stage 8.*]

6.5 Bootstraps

Gary Larson has a cartoon with a man walking along thinking to himself "left foot, right foot, left foot, right foot"; a bird flies by flapping its wings carefully, thinking "up, down, up, down"; a dog looks over the fence thinking "bark, don't bark, bark, don't bark"; and down at the bottom a frog hops along thinking "hop, rest, hop, rest rest... dang!" Was the unhappy frog once a proficient translator, now transformed into lowly incompetence by a wicked theorist advocating self-awareness?

Not, I would argue, if the Dreyfuses are right about the way expertise grows. Nor if Popper is right about the way both biological and epistemological evolution has proceeded. Let me recap briefly on the bare bones of my argument here, and reduce this to five claims.

1. Memes, including translation memes (theoretical concepts, laws, norms, strategies...) exist primarily in Popper's World 3, the world of objective knowledge.
2. Popper's three worlds all affect each other. In particular, World 3 exerts a plastic control over World 2 (the world of mental states and behavioural dispositions).
3. The translator's World 2 can be influenced by his or her awareness of the translation (and other) memes in World 3.
4. The biological, phylogenetic evolution of World-1 entities can be described in terms of Popper's schema P1 → TT → EE → P2.
5. The same schema also describes an individual's ontogenetic growth, i.e. the evolution of an individual's World 2 (including expertise).

The final step in the argument is then this: Popper's schema also explains how, as he himself puts it, "we can lift ourselves by our own bootstraps" (1972: 119). Crucially, this is possible because of the role of language.

Popper's theory of language is a functional one (cf. Popper 1972: 119f.), and I outline it briefly here in order to demonstrate its relevance to this idea of evolutionary bootstraps. Partly following Bühler, Popper distinguishes a number of language functions, the most important of which are these: (a) self-expression, (b) signalling, (c) descriptive, and (d) argumentative. The first two – expression and communication – we share with the animal kingdom, and they are always present in any utterance. The descriptive function is "regulated" by ideas of truth, content and verisimilitude: in using language to describe something, we (normally) aim at a description which fits the facts (cf. Grice's maxim of quality).

It is the argumentative function that is central to Popper's theory. It presupposes not only the functions of expression and communication, but also that of description, since "arguments are, fundamentally, about descriptions: they criticize descriptions from the point of view of the regulative ideas of truth; content; and verisimilitude" (120). Further, it is precisely the development of a descriptive language that allows a linguistic World 3 to exist (and World 3 is largely linguistic); and this in turn allows the emergence of rational criticism, one of Popper's most central themes. (We have already met this as Error Elimination.)

Popper makes high claims for the development of this higher argumentative function: it is to this function, he says, "that we owe our humanity, our reason. For our powers of reasoning are nothing but powers of critical judgement" (121). This rational criticism, he argues, is the main instrument of evolutional and epistemological growth, as illustrated by his schema. The schema thus "gives a rational description of evolutionary emergence, and of our *self-transcendence by means of selection and rational criticism*" (121; emphasis original).

Hence, then, the bootstraps. World-3 entities created and given linguistic form by other people or by ourselves exert a plastic control, a feedback effect, on our brains, beliefs and actions. As this World 3 evolves, so do we, both individually and collectively: "if anybody were to start where Adam started, he would not get further than Adam did" (122). If this view is correct, by exploring the World 3 of translation memes in a systematic way we can further the evolution of our own translation expertise.

6.6 Update

This chapter focuses on the training of professional translators, and I have already commented on the fact that more translation is being done by non-professionals these days (see 3.9). However, competence is not restricted to professionals, and amateurs too may gain expertise as their experience grows. Moreover, the borderline between professional competence and expertise is a fuzzy one, drawn differently by different people. Englund Dimitrova (2005: 230) singles out some aspects of expertise that have come to the fore in her own research. One is the time aspect: professionals work faster. And another is initial planning: in her study, the professionals gave more attention to this, enabling them to work more efficiently. Professionals also worked in terms of larger text segments, they were more holistic.

In retrospect, the foregoing chapter now seems rather speculative. But since the time it was originally written both conceptual and empirical research on translation competence has flourished, and scholars are also beginning to investigate the acquisition and development of this competence in longitudinal studies, sometimes along lines that are similar to those outlined in this chapter. Current models of translation competence see it as a set of sub-competences (e.g. Risku 1998; PACTE 2005). For Göpferich (2009), for instance, these comprise bilingual language competence, domain competence, tools and research competence, competence in using translation routines (such as what I have called strategies), psychomotor competence (e.g. typing skills) and an overall strategic competence which monitors cooperation across the whole set of sub-competences.

Longitudinal studies hope to plot the sequence in which these various sub-competences are acquired. Göpferich (2013) discusses some of the first results of her longitudinal project. She found that her subjects (students at different stages) unsurprisingly showed evidence of increasing competence on various measures, such as a growing awareness of when there was a need to switch from routine behaviour to strategic behaviour. But she also found apparent evidence of "stagnation". This, she suggests, may have been because the subjects remained too equivalence-oriented, whereas the project was using more professional, functional criteria of quality. Research on competence and its development inevitably rests on assumptions about the nature of human cognition, and needs input from that field. And this is indeed the direction in which research is moving. Risku and Windhager (2013), for instance, discuss the relevance of so-called situated cognition theory, which aims to relate cognitive and sociological factors.

The non-professional development of translation skills has been given some attention in the context of the study of so-called natural translation, e.g. that done by bilingual children or other untrained people. This line of research originates with Brian Harris (1977), whose continuing blog on Unprofessional Translation is at http://unprofessionaltranslation.blogspot.fi/. See also Toury (1995: 241f. or 2012: 277f.). The third NPIT conference on Non-Professional Interpreting and Translation is scheduled for 2016. See also Antonini (in press).

Another recent development in applied research has been the attention given to the use of translation corpora of different kinds, as part of translator training. This would be relevant to my stage five, Linguistic science. Some of these corpora are contrastive (texts in matched genres in different languages), others are comparable (translations plus non-translations in the same language) or parallel (translations plus their source texts). Corpora have proved particularly useful in domains of specialized language. See e.g. Bowker and Pearson (2002), and Zanettin et al. (2003).

CHAPTER 7

On translation ethics

7.1 Background issues

Traditional discussions of translation ethics have tended to revolve round a rather limited set of recurring issues (memes, again), often focusing on one to the exclusion of others. The concept of loyalty, for instance, has been a central one: loyalty to what or to whom? What to do if loyalties clash? How to steer an ethical path between different loyalties? As we have seen earlier, different views on primary loyalty have been prevalent at different times and in different cultures, and they also vary according to text-type. Another recurring theme has been whether a translator has the right to make improvements or corrections in a text or not (see the debate in Picken 1994). Making improvements implies a higher loyalty to the reader than to the text itself; perhaps also a higher loyalty to the intention of the writer than to his actual words. This is another form of the old argument about how freely translators should translate. Here again, opinions differ on whether or when a translator should improve the original.

A related debate concerns the translator's visibility or invisibility (e.g. Venuti 1995a; Pym 1996). A translator who gives primary loyalty to ease of readability will probably opt for a fluent target style which hides the Otherness of the original; a translator who prioritizes loyalty to the original text and the original culture will choose other strategies. Berman (1984), for instance, argued that bad translation negates the strangeness of the foreign and hence makes all texts equally familiar and communicable. This choice of primary loyalty, about whether and how to acculturate, thus involves ideological choices as well. Indeed, scholars such as Cheyfitz (1991) and Venuti analyse these choices in terms of theories of imperialism, colonization, nationalism, economic issues, power struggles between cultures, and the global domination of European or Anglo-American cultural values.

The visibility issue also concerns the translator's role in society, the translator's status and power, the translator's rights. Invisible translators, who seek to efface themselves textually, also tend to get effaced socially. Hence the interest in translator's copyright, the rights of multiple authors, conditions of work and pay, the requirement that a translator's name be duly mentioned in a work's paratext, etc.; and also the interest in promoting translation studies as a discipline in its own right, with proper academic status as well.

We also find discussions of the translator's role in initiating translations, selecting source texts, acting as "patrons" themselves and thus exercising power, as well as being subject to the power of others, to the financial interests of clients, to all kinds of external constraints (Lefevere 1992). An associated question is whether translators have the right to refuse to translate texts they feel are unethical.

A comprehensive study of many aspects of translation ethics is to be found in Pym (1997, 2012; see also below, 7.5). Pym's own proposal starts with the observation that translators are typical "Blendlinge", half-castes, social actors inhabiting an intercultural space. (Compare the illuminating discussion of intermediaries in Zeldin [1994] 1995: 147f.) For Pym, a translator's primary loyalty is neither to the source culture nor the target culture, but to others inhabiting this space, i.e. to other intercultural mediators, to the translating profession as a whole: in short, the primary loyalty is to something intercultural. An ethical translator then invests a translation effort that is proportionate to the value of the resulting translation. The value of a translation (beyond its immediate financial cost) is ultimately the degree to which it contributes to intercultural relations, to mutual benefit, to co-operation leading to an increase in social wellbeing. Pym stresses the translator's responsibility for the translation, as soon as he/she has agreed to translate it, and the utilitarian importance of translations in contributing to stable and mutually beneficial intercultural relations.

These background issues give rise to three preliminary points. First, there seems to be a basic division between what we could call macro-ethical matters and micro-ethical ones. Macro-ethical matters concern broad social questions such as the role and rights of translators in society, conditions of work, financial rewards and the client's profit motive, the general aims of translation as intercultural action, power relations between translators and clients, the relation between translation and state politics: in short, the relation between the translator and the world. Micro-ethical matters, on the other hand, concern the translator's action during the translation process itself, questions dealing with specific textual matters, translation strategies and the like: in short, the relation between the translator and the words on the page. Of course, macro issues impinge on micro ones, affecting the translator's individual decisions; and micro-level decisions eventually have a wider effect on intercultural relations. But we can reasonably choose to examine translation ethics from one perspective or the other. In the discussion to follow, we shall be taking mostly the micro perspective.

Second, ideas about translation ethics seem to derive from two different kinds of ethical theory: contractual and utilitarian (see e.g. Williams [1985] 1993). Contractual theories are based on consensual agreements about what is a right or a wrong act, and thus incorporate notions of obligation, rights, duty and norms. Here, ethical considerations are "retrospective", in the sense that they concern obligations etc. that are already in existence at the time of the act in question, for instance because of the actor's status, a promise or contract made, and so on. A utilitarian theory of ethics, on the other hand, looks forward to the outcome of a given act. Here, an ethical act is one that is for the best result, e.g. in terms of maximum welfare, and the act itself is judged ethically by its consequences. In this second case, the focus is more on values than on norms. True, there already exists a *belief* in certain values at the time of a particular act, but an act is deemed to be ethical by virtue of its ability to promote or enhance these values in the future. There is obviously a good deal of overlap between the two types of theory, but the distinction does reveal a basic difference of emphasis. The discussion below draws on both contractual and utilitarian ethics, both norms and values.

Third, in the literature on translation ethics we find some scholars who take a descriptive approach and others who take a prescriptive one. Descriptive research on ethics seeks to uncover the ethical principles governing particular kinds of actions, ethical concepts that appear to be believed in by particular groups of actors. Like descriptive research on norms, descriptive research on ethics simply aims to describe what appears to be the case; no stand is taken about what the scholar thinks should be the case. For instance, we can state that when translating certain kinds of texts, translators at a particular time in a particular culture tend to behave as if they held (or were required to hold) such-and-such values; or that the role of translators in a particular situation suggests that the target or source culture entertain such-and-such values. In prescriptive ethical studies, on the other hand, the scholar makes no secret of his/her own ideological values, and seeks to establish reasons why translators should translate in certain ways rather than in other ways. For instance, I referred above to Venuti's argument that we should avoid fluent or conservative translation strategies and prefer resistant, transgressive ones, because in this way we would do more justice to the ethos of the foreign culture; by translating transgressively, using foreignizing strategies, we can best promote the true value of the foreign. Schleiermacher argued for a similar kind of translation strategy but with a very different prescriptive aim: a nationalistic one. Both Venuti and Schleiermacher want change, cultural innovation, but their ideological aims are very different: one wants more recognition of the source, the other wants to promote the target language (as noted in 2.4). For a descriptivist, it is interesting that the same kind of strategy can be advocated for such different reasons. With respect to this descriptive/prescriptive opposition, the following discussion takes a descriptive viewpoint.

7.2 Norms, actions and values

The theoretical concepts that have so far been central to my discussion of translation theory have been meme, norm and strategy. I have been developing the view that translation is a form of action, describable in terms of strategies, which are themselves governed by norms. The norms themselves, I have suggested, become crystallized from particularly favoured memes.

We are now in a position to ask a different kind of question. If the objective of strategies is to conform to norms, what then is the objective of norms? In a nutshell, I think the answer is: to promote certain values. (Favoured memes, after all, are favoured precisely because they are felt to represent or promote favoured values, to a greater degree than competing memes.)

I shall argue (cf. Chesterman 1997) in this chapter that translation ethics can be explicated in terms of four fundamental values, each relating to one of the main types of norms. (Recall that the word *ethics* goes back etymologically to the notion of a custom, customary "normal" behaviour.) My initial framework comes from deontic logic: this is the branch of philosophy that deals with normative concepts, and it makes a fundamental distinction between normative concepts and axiological (value) concepts. (See for instance von Wright 1968.) Value concepts can be seen as existing prior to normative concepts, in that norms are governed by values. A norm is a norm *because* it embodies, or tends towards, a certain value. Norms, as von Wright puts it (1968: 12), are "instrumental towards the realization of some values." Values, in other words, are examples of the regulative ideas discussed by Popper (and others). Thus, "absolute truth" and "perfect communication" are values that regulate the normative behaviour of, say, scientists and communicators.

A third group of concepts are what von Wright calls praxeological: having to do with action, with man as an agent. Praxeological concepts include those of choice, decision, desire, freedom and will. Deontic logic seeks to build normative, axiological and praxeological concepts into a general theory of action, which has already had some influence on translation theory, as we have seen. The notion of the translation skopos, for instance, is a central part of the theory of translational action (see e.g. Vermeer 1989); and recall the discussion of translation strategies, 4.1.

All actions have to do with changes in states of affairs. (I am largely following von Wright 1968 here.) If p denotes a state of affairs, and A denotes an action within or pertaining to p, then, after the occurrence of A, p changes to not-p, symbolized as -p.

On the analogy of the standard logical quantifiers of existence or universality, we can now introduce the normative operator O, for 'obligation' or 'ought'. It marks the existence of a norm.

Assume that it is *not* the case that p, i.e. that the present situation is $-p$. The formula Op then means that there is an obligation to act in such a way that the state of affairs described by p comes about. On the other hand, the formula $O-p$ means that there is an obligation to act in such a way that p does not come about, i.e. that the present situation of $-p$ continues. In other words, there is here an obligation to forbear from an action that would change $-p$ to p.

Or: assume that it *is* the case that p. The formula Op then means that there is an obligation to see to it that the present state of affairs continues, to forbear from action which would change this state. On the other hand, the formula $O-p$ then means that there is an obligation to change the current state of affairs.

I shall not go further into the formalism of deontic logic. But note that at its roots there lies the recognition that there are essentially two kinds of action: (a) action to bring about a change ("productive action"), and (b) action to prevent a change ("preventive action"). There are thus two parallel kinds of forbearance or omission: (a) non-productive: leaving something unchanged, or (b) non-preventive: letting something happen.

Action theory also needs an analysis of change itself. In general terms, von Wright (1968) bases such an analysis on three elements: (a) the initial state of affairs, which obtains before any action A; (b) the end state, or result state, obtaining after the completion of A; and (c) "the state in which the world would be had the agent not interfered with it but remained passive" (43). We could call this latter state the hypothetical state.

Together, the initial and hypothetical states constitute the "acting-situation" of the agent at a given point in time, the agent's "opportunity of action". In von Wright's words (43):

> If the world is initially in a certain state and will remain in this state, supposing that no agent interferes, then there is an opportunity for either destroying this state or letting it continue. If again the state in which the world initially is will vanish unless some agent interferes, then the situation offers an opportunity either for preventing this state from vanishing or for letting it vanish.

The three states together – initial, hypothetical and result – determine what von Wright calls the "nature" of the action. And it is this "nature" which can then be subjected to ethical analysis.

However, at any point in time an agent is not only in a particular acting-situation with respect to a particular potential action, but also in a personal life-situation comprising his or her present life-state (including state of knowledge) plus all past actions and decisions, plus foreseeable potential states and actions in the future. Decisions made about whether or not to perform a given action are not only influenced by values and norms, but also by this life-situation.

Consider now how this applies to the action of translating. First of all: when translating, a translator is in a "life-situation" whereby all previous experiences and knowledge of the world must influence translational decisions: no-one translates in a vacuum. And, because no two translators have the same life experience or world knowledge, no two translators can ever be in the same life-situation. This is obvious, but it is a relevant point in the whole argument about sameness, equivalence, and/or "perfect" translations.

The norms to which translators seek to conform (or to which they are required to conform) set them under obligations to act within a certain range of acceptable behaviour. Such action pertains to the production or prevention of change, in one way or another. It may be, for instance, that the translator will need to prevent change with respect to certain aspects of the source text, i.e. to preserve something, to leave it unchanged as far as possible. In other respects the translator needs to produce change – most obviously a change of language, for a start. Judgements about what to change and what not to change depend on the translator's assessment of the "opportunity of action" plus the desired end-state of the action.

In action-theoretical terms, therefore, what a translator has to do, at every decision-point, can be defined as follows:

a. Assess the initial state. This initial state includes the source text and its context, the translator's knowledge of the translation commission, the potential readership of the translation, its place of publication etc., and the translator's linguistic and general knowledge of the world, which itself includes knowledge of the readers' expectations.
b. Compare the hypothetical state (that would obtain were a given action *not* carried out) with the presumed end-state (that would obtain if the action *were* carried out). This comparison should (in theory) indicate which of these two states, the hypothetical one or the presumed end-state, better embodies a given value or set of values.
c. Act in accordance with the above comparison: if the hypothetical state is assessed to be "higher", do not perform act A; if the presumed end-state is assessed to be "higher", perform A.

Bearing this general framework in mind, we now turn to consider what the relevant ethical values of translation appear to be. I suggest that the four fundamental translational values are clarity, truth, trust and understanding. I do not claim that these are exclusive to translation, of course: *mutatis mutandis* they also govern other modes of communication and other forms of human behaviour. Furthermore, I do not argue prescriptively that these *should* be the values; I claim, descriptively, that these *appear to be* the values held explicitly or implicitly by most translators.

7.3 Clarity

I suggest that the value governing the *expectancy norms* is that of clarity, simply because clarity facilitates processing. Popper ([1945] 1962) takes clarity to be the most important linguistic standard of all; this is simply because language is "one of the most important institutions of social life, and its clarity is a condition of its functioning as a means of rational communication" (308). To sacrifice clarity is to weaken the possibility of rational communication, and to do that is to undermine the possibility of a human society altogether.

"Clarity" is a recurrent concept in stylistics and textlinguistics. It goes back even to Quintilian, who specified clarity to be one of the four qualities of style, together with correctness, elegance and appropriateness (see de Beaugrande and Dressler 1981: 15, for instance; and especially Rener 1989: 217f.). The value of clarity was particularly central during French classicism and the regime of the *belles infidèles*. More recent mention of the value of clarity in translation theory has usually been in relation to Grice's maxims, where it is subsumed under the maxim of manner: be perspicuous. Expanding Grice's maxim of manner somewhat, Leech (1983) proposes a Clarity Principle comprising a transparency maxim and an ambiguity-avoidance maxim. His transparency maxim runs (p. 66): "Retain a direct and transparent relationship between semantic and phonological structure (*ie* between message and text)." Perhaps under the influence of relevance theory, the value is sometimes relativized: be as perspicuous as you need to be (see e.g. Neubert and Shreve 1992: 82–83). There is one problem with this view: it ties "necessary degree of clarity", inevitably, to writers' (translators') own perception of this need; with respect to translators, this perception is partly based on their knowledge of the target-culture norms and partly on their ability to predict the particular readership within the target culture. But suppose the readership cannot be completely predicted, as is surely often the case: the relativistic view seems to exclude the need to be clear for readers outside the predicted range.

Clarity is thus primarily a linguistic value; it applies to any use of language, not just translation. (As the bumper sticker ironically puts it: ESCHEW OBFUSCATION!) However, it is a problematic concept. What is clear for me may not be clear for you; I may not even want to be clear, in some circumstances; or you may sometimes not want me to be too clear. Furthermore, the concept should not be taken to imply that the relation between language and the world can be a totally transparent one, unsullied by the discourse itself. Despite such difficulties, I think we can still claim that clarity is a universal value. True, there are exceptional cases; but the fact that they seem exceptional merely reinforces the existence of the underlying principle. And true, the language-world relation is seldom transparent. But we nevertheless continue to use language *as if* it allowed us to represent the world adequately, for our normal human purposes; we do continue to talk and write to each other. Most importantly, we continue to believe that, most of the time at least, speakers want hearers to "see what they mean". An advertiser or a comedian or a diplomat can make use of multiple meanings etc., but only because they assume that their receivers (or the relevant, intended receivers) will nevertheless "get the point". Poets may use complex imagery and ambiguous syntax, but they would surely hope that at least some readers somewhere will appreciate this, perceive their intention – even if this intention is none other than to play with language – and arrive at an interpretation. In Gricean terms: if hearers perceive a lack of clarity, if they think the clarity maxim is being broken, they will seek a reason why and interpret the message according to the perceived function of the text's apparent non-clarity.

We might therefore define linguistic clarity in terms of the hearer's perception of the speaker's intention: a message has clarity to the extent that the receiver can, within an appropriate time, perceive the speaker's intended meaning, the speaker's intention to say something about the world and/or to produce some effect in the hearer. (For further discussion of perception, meaning and intentionality, see Searle 1983.) Clarity is thus not the same as directness: in some cultures, conventions may require indirect expressions of feelings, for instance; but hearers do not perceive such expressions as being unclear, because they know the conventions and can easily perceive the intended meaning.

Recall now that we originally defined expectancy norms as linguistic norms, having to do with people's expectations about what texts of certain types ought to look like. If we postulate clarity as the value underlying these norms, we can make an important point of some comfort to those who translate into a language other than their native one. Complete mastery of a non-native language is rare, but such mastery is only a means, not an end in itself. Grammaticality, for instance, is a means to the achievement of clarity: in the last analysis, one does not write grammatically just in order to be grammatical, but to be clear, to get one's meaning across with maximum efficiency, to help understanding. It follows that translators into the non-native language could well focus primarily on clarity, not mere grammaticality as such. And this is often a more realistic aim, too. A clear, readable translation with some grammatical errors is surely often to be preferred to one that is illogical, obscure or clumsy, albeit grammatical.

The value of clarity has two general kinds of effect on the translator's action: it may prompt both preventive and productive action. Preventively, a translator normally seeks to translate in such a way as to avoid the opposite of clarity: obscurity, unintended ambiguity, illogicality, confusion etc. In most kinds of texts, these characteristics are reasons for changing and refining a tentative translation, for selecting a transediting strategy etc. They also play an obvious role in translation assessment in all its modes.

Productively, in the case of most text-types, a translator usually seeks to translate in such a way as to attain optimum clarity. One major principle here is that of iconicity: other things being equal (i.e. in non-marked environments), a version that is iconic (in which form somehow matches meaning) will be clearer that one that is not iconic. By way of brief illustration, consider the following extract from a translated text about some environmental aspects of engineering:

> TT1: Man has an inborn desire for beauty. Aesthetic properties in our environment are also tied to values which have developed in the course of history, agreement about the concept of beauty.

As it stands, the syntax of *agreement* is unclear: at first sight, it seems to be parallel to "the course of history", or perhaps to "history" alone. The intended interpretation, however, is that *agreement* should be parallel to "values", although the syntax does not help this connection. The semantic structure of the sentence is thus that the aesthetic properties are tied to (a) values... and (b) agreement... An iconic syntax would make this clear by reflecting the semantic structure, which can be done quite simply by repeating the preposition so that the parallelism is made overt:

> TT2: ... Aesthetic properties in our environment are also tied *to values* which have developed in the course of history, and *to agreement* about the concept of beauty.

The iconicity could be further strengthened by making *agreement* plural, so that we have *to values* and then *to agreements*. – Iconicity can also obtain between linguistic structure and extra-linguistic experience, as when cooking recipes or operating instructions are optimally arranged to follow the sequence of actions described.

Clarity, on this view, is a value related to expectancy norms concerning linguistic products. However, in cases of conflict I suggest that the values pertaining to process norms, to be discussed below, usually take precedence.

7.4 Truth

Of all the translation norms, it is the *relation norm* that has been most debated – understandably so, since this is the only norm that applies more specifically to translation itself: the others also apply to other kinds of communication. Recall that the relation norm was defined as follows (3.5.3): a translator should act in such a way that an appropriate relation is established and maintained between the source text and the target text. Elsewhere (1.2.2) we have argued that this relation is best not thought of in terms of sameness, but rather as a similarity or family resemblance.

Traditionally, the value governing this norm has been defined as fidelity, faithfulness to the source text. It was usually linked to the concept of equivalence, but since total equivalence is normally impossible the translator is therefore bound to be unfaithful. *Traduttore traditore,* and so on. In response to this rather unfortunate position, the concept of fidelity was then enlarged somewhat, to encompass faithfulness to the original author's intention: intentions being intrinsically somewhat more fuzzy than texts, this made it easier to relativize the notion of fidelity and thus present it as more attainable – to some extent, at least.

In my view, however, fidelity is an inappropriate conceptualization of the value governing our relation norm. As defined above, this norm is a linguistic one: it concerns the nature of the relation between two *texts,* two linguistic entities. In other words, in addition to all the other constraints bearing upon the construction of a text, a translation is also subject to the constraint that it should have a certain kind of relation to some other, already existing text. I suggest that the value governing this relation is truth.

Loosely speaking, we can say that something is true if it corresponds to reality. "Truth" (in this non-mystical sense) describes the quality of a relation between a proposition and a state of affairs. The proposition is not "the same as" the state of affairs: the statement *this is a keyboard* is not identical with the physical object upon which I am currently writing. But the one bears a recognizable relation to the other. The state of affairs to which a translation should be "true" is thus, in this sense, the source text.

But there is more than one way of being "true". British passport photos officially have to bear "a true likeness" to the person depicted. Or we talk about a report of an event being "true" or false. Or we certify that a photocopy is indeed "a true copy" of the original. These senses of truth obviously differ in the degree and kind of similarity denoted. The photo is two-dimensional, not made of flesh and blood, etc., but must still "truly represent" its bearer; many different photos may all be equally true resemblances of the same person. And many different reports of the same event may all be recognized to be true, as opposed to being false or deceptive or partial. At the other extreme, a photocopy looks very similar indeed to its original, and yet it is still not the same, however close the paper and ink quality; significantly, however good the photocopy, bureaucrats sometimes explicitly require the original document: there *is* a difference. Holmes (1988) spoke of a translation as being a map of the original: an original may have many true maps for different purposes, but it remains the case that the map is not the territory.

This range of ways in which we understand the truth of a relation is, I think, most appropriate for translation theory. Translations relate to their source texts in a wide variety of acceptable ways, depending on a whole host of intratextual and extratextual reasons. The point is that all these relations must be "true" to the original, in one way or another, as required by the situation.

Family resemblances, after all, are also of many different kinds, which was of course precisely Wittgenstein's point. Some family resemblances may even be such that we would not want to describe the resembling text as a translation at all but as something else: think for instance of the literary fashion for texts that feed cannibalistically upon other texts, thriving on intertextuality, both within and across languages (cf. fanfiction). Or of the whole business of rewriting and adapting in one way or another. When is an interlingual resemblance one of translation and when not? Here we must return to the argument introduced above in Section 3.4: definitions of what counts as a translation are culture bound, and specifically *target*-culture bound. The answer to the question thus depends simply on what people choose to call translations at a given time in a given culture. There is no universally accepted borderline.

How can we represent all this within action theory? First of all, if truth is agreed to be a regulative value, then the truth of the source-target relation is something that must be established and maintained. Minimally, in a state of affairs *p*, *something* must be preserved, change must be prevented; the state of affairs after a given action should not have *no* relation to the state of affairs before the action. Source-target relations are elastic, but the elastic must not be cut completely. After all, if we assume that a target-language text bears no relation whatsoever to a source text, we do not call this text a translation. There must, then, *be* a relation, and it must be a true one. What this true relation can be will depend on what the situational conditions deem to be relevant.

Secondly, we might stress that actions have goals, and that if an action is intended to result in a translation, one of the translating agent's goals will indeed be to act in accordance with the value of truth, in the sense just explicated. (Compare the Gricean maxim of quality, that one should not say what one believes to be false.) Such action is both productive, creating a true relation, and preventive, avoiding loss of truth. This is precisely the additional cross-language constraint which makes translational action different from other forms of communicative action.

Truth, though, is only one value for translation, and the source text is only one of several factors impinging on the translator's decision-making. It is not only the nature of the truth relation that will vary according to the nature of the overall translation task, but also the very status of the source text itself, how much priority it will be accorded. (Cf. Newmark 2004.)

7.5 Trust

George Steiner's (1975) "hermeneutic motion" starts with the translator's trust that there is "something there" in the source text, something to be understood, something worth translating. But there is more to translational trust than this. The translator also needs to trust the original writer, and also the commissioner of the translation: there must be a trust that the translation itself is worth doing. Translators must also trust that their readers will read the translation in good faith, that their readers in turn will trust that there is "something there" in the translation that makes it worth reading. It is, in fact, not only the translator who must trust, but also the other parties to the translating act: readers, plus of course the commissioner of the translation, the publisher, and also the original writer (if still alive, of course). Translational trust works both ways.

Trust, I suggest, is the value governing the accountability norm, which was formulated above (3.5.3) as stating that a translator should act in such a way that the demands of loyalty are met with regard to the various parties concerned.

"Loyalty" is the term used by Nord (1991) to denote the moral principle governing relationships between people in an act of communication. She speaks of the translator being "committed" to the target and source situations, "responsible" to ST sender and TT recipient. I have used "accountability", but all these terms imply a relation *to someone*: one is not just "accountable", but *accountable to*. The image is that of a network, with the translator-node linked accountably to a number of other nodes.

Opinions differ to some extent on what these other nodes are. The ones mentioned earlier – writer, commissioner, readership – would no doubt be agreed on, but are there others too? Pym (1992a, 1997, 2012) extends the issue beyond questions of *how* to translate to others concerning *who* has the authority to decide how to translate. In other words, who may validate translation norms? Pym suggests that one way in which translators have historically overcome the problem of where their primary loyalty lies (source or target community) is by positing a higher authority, such as a spiritual one in the case of biblical translation. More generally, however, Pym argues that translators in fact ground their accountability in *each other*; translators collectively check and assess each other's work as a community (like the global community of scientists). They derive the authority for the norms they follow from the translators' profession, collectively. As I mentioned earlier, Pym argues that translators work in an intercultural space, and so may not prioritize one culture above the other. Pym concludes: *"Translators' prime loyalty must be to their profession as an intercultural space"* (1992a: 166, emphasis original). With this in mind, we could indeed add "the translators' profession" to the list of nodes to which a translator's accountability is due. A further aspect of the reciprocal relation between the translator and the profession appears in Pym's comment that maybe we should simply translate as we would like to be translated ourselves, given similar circumstances.

But *why* should translators be loyal to their profession, why should they be accountable to these various other participants in the communication situation? My answer would be: because of the overriding value of trust. Translators, in order to survive as translators, must be trusted by all parties involved, both as a profession and individually. They must therefore work in such a way as to create and maintain this trust. The default position is perhaps that this trust is deemed to exist *unless* something happens to dispel it. Trust is typically lost rather than gained.

In terms of action theory, therefore, we could once again say that the translator should act preventively, in order to prevent a change in this situation of trust. Initially, however, entry to the profession is gained by showing that one is indeed worthy of such trust, as judged by accreditation tests etc. which are assessed by other professionals whose judgement, in turn, is trusted – by the aspiring translator, by other professionals, and by society at large. Without this trust, the profession would collapse, and so would its practice.

This notion of trust has a long pedigree, perhaps going back to the classical Greek idea of ethos in classical rhetoric: a speaker who patently lacks ethos – integrity, sincerity, authority, an acknowledged right to speak – will not be trusted; his rhetoric will be felt to be suspicious and thus prove ineffective.

Trust is also an important concept in some hermeneutic theories of language. Steiner's was mentioned above. Ebeling (1971) makes the right to speak (*Ermächtigung*) the first element of his own hermeneutic approach to a theological theory of language. On this view, the first ethical duty of a speaker is to pose the question "do I have the right to speak?" Conversely, a hearer's initial response is: does this person have the right to speak? The answer to this question will then determinine how the hearer reacts to what the speaker says. In terms of translational trust, the questions that arise are: do I, as a translator, believe that I have the right to translate this? Will my readers believe that I have this right, and hence trust me? (Presumably, the commissioner does have this trust, *de facto*.) And then, if the answers are affirmative: how do I prevent this trust from being lost?

One key way of doing this is for the translator to be visible. The translator, that is, should at the very least be mentioned; but more importantly, and especially for literary works, there may also be a translator's preface or the like, where the translator explains the main principles underlying the translation approach that has been taken. If readers' expectations are being challenged in some respect, for instance, it is the translator's responsibility to explain why. This notion of visibility is also part of Nord's concept of loyalty, mentioned above.

Ebeling's second element is responsibility (*Verantwortung*): speakers are responsible for saying the right word at the right time. They are also responsible for knowing when to keep silent. Applying this to translator-speakers, we can agree that translators are indeed accountable for what they write, and for what they decide to change, add or omit. To be seen to meet this responsibility is to maintain trust.

Pym links the question of why translators should be primarily accountable to their profession to his understanding of the aim of translation as such: "[t]ranslators should presumably be attached to the rules and procedures of their profession, justifying their actions and decisions in terms of translation's own ultimate aim" (1992a: 168). And this aim, he suggests, is *"to improve the intercultural relations with which they are concerned"* (169, emphasis original). This, then, is one answer to the question "why translate at all?" In terms of my own analysis here, improving intercultural relations is equivalent to creating more intercultural trust.

Some objections may be raised here. After all, the value of trust can also be used to define the line between those you trust and those you don't, creating a division between insiders and outsiders. In the extreme case, we end up with a closed establishment who all trust each other but no-one else, and then the existence of trust works to divide society, not unite it. Internationally, too, we have groups of trusted insiders who conclude mutual treaties of solidarity etc., such as the European Union, and these define themselves precisely in opposition to those who are not in the group, so that barriers are created between insider countries and outsider countries. However, the problem here is not so much the existence of trust in environment A but the lack of in it environment B, i.e. the difficulty of extending the trust to outsiders.

Another objection concerns potential clashes between a translator's belief in the importance of trust and the client's possible belief in the importance of other things, such as making a profit. This is a good example of the ways in which macro-ethical issues may impinge on micro-ethical ones. In such cases, the translator's own personal ethics, as distinct from his/her professional translation ethics, determine the course of action to be taken, as competing values are weighed and compared: recall the deontic model outlined in 7.2.

7.6 Understanding

The other key concepts in Ebeling's (1971) analysis are: the speaker's need to challenge the hearer to understand, to speak in a way that positively demands understanding, that requires the hearer to make the effort to understand (*Verstehenszumutung*); and finally the resulting understanding itself, as it emerges in the hearer's mind in agreement with the speaker's intention (*Verständigung*). Psycholinguistically, the initial goal of communication is understanding, and I suggest this is the value governing the communication norm. (Theologically, Ebeling ultimately interprets this as love.)

Gadamer (1960 and later) spoke of the fusion of the horizons that takes place in understanding as being the proper achievement of language. This fusion, however, is not to be taken as something absolute, because understanding always involves interpretation, and interpretation always involves difference, a subjective input; interpretation is always subject to particular conditions of time and place. We defined clarity earlier in terms of the perception of the speaker's intention, but the perception does not necessarily coincide with the intention one hundred per cent. As hearers/readers, we perceive something, and we then try to interpret this something, to understand it. But the whole process is a relative one. Perfect understanding, like perfect clarity, is only a regulative idea. Communication exists – and society exists, built upon instances of communication – because we share a belief in the *value* of understanding.

In terms of action theory, we could then say simply that the goal of translational action is to produce understanding: in other words, to produce a change of state from non-understanding to understanding. This may sound somewhat trivial when formulated thus as productive action, but the converse formulation as a kind of preventive action – preventing misunderstanding – raises a number of interesting issues.

Let us first return to Popper. The whole movement of his thought is anti-utopian: perfect, absolute, static ideals can be no more than regulative ideas. In real life, argues Popper, it makes more sense to focus on manifest examples of non-ideal states and try to do something about these. We proceed, we evolve, by trial and *error*. Science, objective knowledge, progresses via the elimination of *false* theories; society develops by gradually getting rid of obvious injustices, by "piecemeal engineering", rather than by setting up some presumed ideal system. Popper's ethics are in fact an inverse utilitarianism. He proposes ([1945] 1962: 235, 284–285) that the maxim of maximizing happiness be replaced by one of minimizing suffering. The promotion of happiness is not such an urgent moral task as the prevention of suffering: there is no moral appeal to increase the happiness of someone who is quite happy anyway, but the existence of human suffering does make a clear moral appeal for help. Instead of aiming at the greatest happiness for the greatest number, then, one should aim more modestly at the least amount of avoidable suffering. One should also demand that unavoidable suffering should be shared as fairly as possible. This view has the further advantage that suffering is much easier to recognize and define than happiness: it adds to ethical clarity, says Popper, if we thus formulate both our philosophical and ethical demands negatively.

I think there is a direct parallel between this view of ethics and the way translation can be conceived of in action theory. By the very act of translating we are of course producing change of a sort; but the traditional meme of equivalence requirement has meant that the end-result of translation has in the past tended to be seen as some kind of unattainable ideal state, a Utopia, like perfect understanding. Popperians, however, would reply that insofar as it is absolute, this view is unrealistic, unhelpful and frustrating. In its place, they would advocate a focus on the aspect of *preventive* action in translation: the minimization of *mis*understanding. Recall the slogan "Mind the gap" from Chapter 5 on assessment. Alternatively, we might speak of the avoidance of "communicative suffering".

This idea itself also seems to be acquiring the status of a meme in translation theory: several scholars have made similar points. For instance, discussing the applications of componential analysis in the translation of referential content, Nida (1969: 492) uses the image of words being like suitcases of clothes, containers for components of denotative meaning; what then matters is that the clothes should arrive at their destination "in the best possible condition, i.e. *with the least damage*" (emphasis added). In a short section on prejudice and the translator's moral responsibilities, Newmark (1988: 211) also refers to the translator's job as being "to eliminate misunderstandings".

One concrete illustration of this attitude is to be found in the notion of the culture bump. This was originally used by Archer (1986) in the context of language teaching, and has since been applied to translation studies by Leppihalme (1997). Culture bumps are features that hinder cross-cultural interaction, that prevent smooth communication. In translation studies, they are usefully defined as a source text's source-culture-bound features that, if translated "unchanged", are likely to interrupt the flow of comprehension, perhaps resulting in definite misunderstanding. Examples are culture-bound terms of all kinds, whether relating to source-culture realia (in Popper's World 1) or to the general cultural knowledge-base (in World 3) which is widely shared by source-language speakers but perhaps less well known to target-language speakers.

In translation research, the problem of what to do with culture bumps is well illustrated by the phenomenon of allusions. Allusions are often source-culture bound, referring either to World-1 entities in that culture or to World-3 entities which are familiar in it. For instance, many of the latter type are intertextual: their understanding thus requires a familiarity with the original text referred to. If it can reasonably be assumed that the target readers do not share knowledge of the original text, the translator of such allusions normally needs to remove this culture bump, or at least endeavour to flatten it a bit. Leppihalme (1997) shows that if translators choose only a strategy of minimum change, e.g. when an English detective story's allusory reference to people hurrying about with "White Rabbit expressions" is translated literally into Finnish (i.e. with my strategy Gl), Finnish readers often do not recognize the allusion and hence suffer from a culture bump: in short, they miss the point. On the other hand, translations that use some kind of explanatory strategy, such as adding a reference to Carroll's *Alice in Wonderland* or otherwise signalling that there is indeed an allusion here, smooth the reader's path to fuller comprehension.

The extent of necessary translatorial manipulation will naturally depend on the translator's assessment of the difference between the target readers' likely knowledge-base and that of the original source-language readership. (This assessment would form part of the translator's "prior theory", in Davidson's terms: see Section 3.3 above.) Similar observations apply to a wide range of intertextual features – and not only in literary texts, either – which may cause culture bumps if the translator does not do something about them.

Pym (1992a: 163) comments on the elimination of misunderstanding from a different angle, in his discussion of the need and right of translators to improve originals. In the first place, the very fact of translation itself incorporates an improvement, in that the text thereby reaches receivers "who would otherwise find that text unavailable or incomprehensible". In this sense, to "read" a text in a language one does not understand is to "misunderstand" it totally, and the translator thus diminishes this misunderstanding considerably. In so doing, the translator also extends the readership and thus diminishes the number of potential receivers who remain excluded from the communication, deprived of the chance to understand.

This interpretation of "communicative suffering" in terms of reader exclusion is also discussed interestingly by Nystrand (1992), who argues along strikingly Popperian lines that writers should focus not on reaching all potential readers, i.e. on some kind of universal, ideal understanding, but rather, more realistically, on minimizing the exclusion of particular potential readers. One relevant corollary of this argument would be that translators need to be aware of whether they are translating for native or non-native readers of the target language – especially with a language such as English, which is so widely used as a second language. Excessive complexity, obscure vocabulary or unusual idioms, for instance, may unfairly exclude non-native readers from the circle of those who may understand, the included readers. We might even go as far as to say that such excluded readers are unjustly deprived of their *right* to understand (a point that of course applies just as well to obscurely written texts in the native language, too). (See Pym 1992b, for a further distinction between excluded, observational and participative readers.)

The value of understanding, then, can be construed in two ways of relevance to the translator: (a) minimizing misunderstanding of the text among included readers, and (b) minimizing the number of potential readers who are excluded from understanding.

In the preceding sections I have done no more than sketch a descriptive outline for a translational micro-ethics, based on four values: clarity, truth, trust and understanding. Each of these values regulates one of the main kinds of translation norms: expectancy norms, the relation norm, the accountability norm and the communication norm. Clarity and truth have to do with texts and relations between them; trust and understanding have to do with relations between people.

Translators are agents who interfere with the state of the world. What right do we have to do this? What ethical values do we appeal to? The questions are at least worth asking.

7.7 The Translator's Charter

The Translator's Charter is a document (approved 1963, amended 1994) drawn up by FIT, the Fédération Internationale des Traducteurs (International Federation of Translators). (It is available at the FIT website, http://www.fit-ift.org/?p=251) It specifies the Federation's view of translators' rights and duties, and seeks to lay the basis for a "translator's code of ethics". It also incorporates recommendations concerning "lines of conduct" for translators – in other words, it explicitly sets out to formulate translation norms. It is therefore interesting to examine this document in the light of the points made so far in this chapter.

The document has five sections: (I) General obligations of the translator, (II) Rights of the translator, (III) Economic and social position of the translator, (IV) Translators' societies and unions, (V) National organizations and the International Federation of Translators. There are a total of 40 clauses, numbered consecutively through the sections. Sections (I) and (II) are of particular relevance here.

Clause 1 assumes that translation (the process) is "an intellectual activity", and clause 14 reaffirms that a translation (the product) is "a creation of the intellect". The clause defines the object of translation as "the transfer of literary, scientific and technical texts from one language into another". Why these text-types are chosen and others excluded is not stated.

Clause 2 stresses that a translation is always done "on the sole responsibility of the translator", thus appealing implicitly to the accountability norm.

Clause 3 states that the translator has an obligation (not a right, interestingly) to "refuse to give a text an interpretation of which he does not approve, or which would be contrary to the obligations of his profession". I take this as an implicit reference to the relation norm and the value of truth: a translator may not translate in such a way that the source-target relation is false. Fair enough; but the following clause (4) implies a very much narrower interpretation. It runs as follows:

> Every translation shall be faithful and render exactly the idea and form of the original – this fidelity constituting both a moral and legal obligation for the translator.

We are reminded here of the argument discussed earlier concerning what a translator does in cases where the original is plainly false, clumsy etc. The FIT formulation seems to be based on an implicit belief in the overruling priority of equivalence, formal and stylistic equivalence included ("the idea *and form* of the original"). However, the following clause (5) then counteracts this interpretation:

> A faithful translation, however, should not be confused with a literal translation, the fidelity of a translation not excluding an adaptation to make the form, the atmosphere and deeper meaning of the work felt in another language and country.

The contradiction between clauses 4 and 5 remains unresolved, so that we do not really know which has priority. A formulation in terms of the relation norm might resolve this lack of clarity.

Clauses 6 and 7 state that the translator must have adequate linguistic proficiency in both languages (but particularly the target language), general knowledge, and specific subject knowledge for the task in hand. We can add that otherwise expectancy norms will not be met.

Clause 8 refers to reasonable fees (not undercutting the profession!), and clause 9 to the general conditions of the translation task, which must not be "humiliating" either to the translator himself or to the profession as a whole. This last point thus stresses the translator's accountability to the profession, as Pym argued (see above, 7.5).

Clause 10 is about respecting professional secrets (accountability again). Clause 11 refers to the translator as a "secondary author", who must therefore accept special obligations with respect to the right of the text's original author. In particular, the translator must ensure that he has the right to translate the work in question (clause 12). This recalls the point Ebeling made about the speaker's right to speak (above, 7.5). This clause concludes the section on obligations.

Most of the clauses in this section thus have to do with the accountability norm in one way or another. Aspects of translation having to do with the relation norm remain somewhat confusingly stated. As regards the communication norm, although the document's preamble mentions "the social function of translation", there is little mention of anything related to this norm and its associated value of understanding: it can be glimpsed in clauses 5 and 6, but that's about it. Perhaps one reason is the definition of the object of translation given in clause 1: transferring *texts*. In this respect, the document seems somewhat dated: after all, texts are for people. It is surprising, too, that the translator's obligations to the original writer are mentioned, and also to the translator profession at large, but obligations to the readers of a translation are not highlighted in the same way. If the communication norm and the achievement of understanding are agreed to be central to translational action, the Charter's image of the translator's role thus seems rather one-sided.

Section II is about the translator's rights. A translator is an "intellectual worker" with the same rights as other such (clauses 13, 14); he holds the copyright to his translations (15); and can thus enjoy moral and legal rights similar to those of the original author (16). Clause 17 specifies this point in terms of translator visibility: the translator's authorship of the translation is to be recognized. This means e.g. that the translator's name must be mentioned "clearly and unambiguously" whenever the translation is used publicly, that the translation may not be subsequently altered without the translator's permission, and that the translation may not be used improperly. Clause 18 is about broadcasting rights etc., and clause 19 about fair remuneration.

It is interesting that these rights are mainly rights of ownership: they concern the translator's rights over the final product. There is no explicit mention here of any rights the translator may have which affect the translation process: the right to clarify where appropriate, the right to make changes where necessary, the right to justify his own translation decisions in terms of his own expertise, the right to make his own decisions. Perhaps these rights are not granted? Or perhaps only taken for granted?

7.8 Emancipatory translation

Work in critical linguistics has developed the idea of emancipatory discourse (e.g. Fairclough 1992). This means a discourse which liberates speakers from unnecessary constraints, which allows them to become genuinely participatory members of society, which promotes true democracy and self-fulfilment: the idea has obvious ideological and prescriptive overtones. It also has obvious pedagogical consequences for the way in which language awareness can be taught, and indeed why it should be taught. The basic pedagogical argument is that learners must be taught norms, but they must also be given the freedom to decide when they wish to break these norms, albeit in full awareness of what consequences this might have. Janks and Ivanič (1992: 317) put the point as follows:

> Learners need to understand that rules of accuracy and appropriacy are not fixed, but subject to social forces. Moving beyond passive awareness to action means learning to choose when to conform to the conventions as they are, or to challenge them, and so help to break new ground. Action involves knowing how to choose, when to choose and whether to choose. People have to choose between conventional language use on the one hand, and practising emancipatory discourse with its commitment to some sort of change on the other.

I think this argument is of some relevance also to translation theory and translator training. Recall the historical evolution of the translator's role, from humble slave to independent expert or equal partner, and the suggestion that this progress is also reflected in the individual translator's development (6.4). In an important sense, this movement is indeed one of gradual emancipation. An emancipated translator assumes the right to break norms. But not irresponsibly: from the ethical point of view, norm-breaking must be justified by an appeal to higher norms, which themselves are justified in terms of the values governing them.

Let us look at some examples. For many kinds of texts many professional translators, as a matter of course, will consider it quite normal to transedit where necessary, to clarify obscurity, improve readability etc. They will be fully aware that, as translators, they are language experts, trained to be particularly sensitive to matters linguistic and therefore naturally authorized to improve an inelegant or unclear text where necessary, whereas the original writers may have expertise in quite different fields. It is a truism to point out that not all native speakers write their own language well; not all native speakers need to, after all. Transediting might be considered as norm-breaking activity by people who interpret the relation norm to mean a maximally close similarity to the original style (as stated in the official code of conduct issued by the Finnish Association of Translators, for instance, and implied by clause 4 of the Translator's Charter). Other people might not recognize such a formulation of the relation norm, and hence would not recognize any norm-breaking here. In any case, the translator's action would be justified by appeal to the values of clarity and understanding.

Or consider Newmark's (1988: 211) advice that the translator always has the moral duty to 'desex' language, i.e. to avoid sexist formulations. Even if the original persists in using the equivalent of *he,* etc., translators should always prefer a neutral or plural form of the pronoun. Here again, translators would be breaking one version of the relation norm, but more radically this time, in that the translation would thus also present a different, less sexist image of the source writer than was really the case. More importantly, this manipulation would also break the expectancy norm to the extent that readers actually expect sexist language, as being something quite normal. In this sense, translators are being encouraged here to work towards the establishment of new expectancy norms: non-sexist ones. Newmark thinks of the underlying value as egalitarianism; we might see it as a manifestation of the trust value.

Feminist translation, which overtly seeks to "hi-jack" the original ("masculine") text, goes further. Generic masculines, for instance, will not only be removed but replaced by generic feminines ("the translator and her work..."). Other manipulations may be more radical: changing the spelling of "author" to *auther*, for instance (Lotbinière-Harwood 1991); the declared aim of such translators is thus to make the feminine as visible as possible.

Other more extreme examples are provided by Robinson (1991), who ends up taking a position that could perhaps be non-trivially summarized as: "I can translate any way I feel". I say "non-trivially" because Robinson's understanding of translational action is explicitly somatic: he stresses the importance of initial gut-reactions, of balancing rational discourse with an appreciation of the feeling of words, etc. In taking up the cudgels against traditional views of equivalence, of the translator as a mere instrument, of the metaphor ("X = Y") as the dominant trope describing translation, Robinson advocates much greater freedom, a much wider space in which translators may legitimately act as they wish. This freedom includes the right to translate "ironically" or "subversively", so that translators may even deliberately interpose themselves between original writer and target reader, manipulating the message in accordance with their own ends. Robinson quotes with evident approval, for instance (227–230), Jordan's translation of parts of the New Testament (The Cotton Patch New Testament), in which the translator overtly manipulates the Greek original in order to proclaim his own liberation theology, to the extent of setting the whole narrative in the American South and even adding references to the oppression of black people. (See https://hopefaithprayer.com/scriptures/cotton-patch-gospel-matthew-clarence-jordan/.)

Is this fair translation? One's answer will depend largely on one's own translational ideology. Insofar as Jordan replaces the original writers' messages and meanings with his own, or gives the originals interpretations which they could not have had at the time they were written, he is breaking the customary relation norm and also the expectancy norms concerning biblical translation. On the other hand, he evidently adheres to the accountability norm by making his intentions visible and explicit in the introduction; and by seeking to make the text maximally relevant to modern times he is perhaps ultimately motivated by the values of trust and understanding.

All these examples illustrate cases in which the translator assumes certain rights over the text, rights which are over and above those ascribable to the original writer. With respect to the decisions mentioned, the translator is acting in an emancipated fashion, as a responsible agent exercising freedom of choice.

However, this freedom is not absolute (although one sometimes gets the impression that Robinson feels that it is). I think that emancipatory translation seeks a balance between freedom of action on the one hand and situational constraints on the other. It is fruitless to deny that the translator is subject to constraints: who isn't? No action takes place in a vacuum, for every action has an initial state of affairs (7.2).

We seem to end up here with the knotty question of free will. Here again, one of Popper's conceptual tools seems helpful. Popper describes the mutual influence between his three Worlds as one of "plastic control" (see above, 1.3). Our actions, and our will to act, are affected by circumstances of all kinds; yet not totally, not deterministically, only plastically, as influences of varying strength. Translation norms are not iron laws; as constraints, the control they exercise is plastic. More importantly, they themselves are subject to constant revision – and this is perhaps the ultimate justification for breaking them: in order to replace them by better ones.

A strikingly similar notion to what I have called emancipatory translation is put forward in a Peircean semiotic framework by Gorlée (1994). I shall move towards my own conclusion with some comments and quotations from Gorlée which both summarize and illuminate some of my main points. Gorlée's main thesis is that translation is "contractual semiosis", a rich and complex metaphor. Let me pick up three aspects of it.

First, for Gorlée (building on Peirce), translation is "the sign- and-code-enriching confrontation between sameness and otherness" (171). This means that it is a process of genuine semiosis, as opposed to mere mimesis. As such, it is always open-ended, as signs can always be further interpreted and reinterpreted into other signs. A translation represents one hypothetical interpretation of a text, "a meaning-generating thought experiment in which a hypothesis is severally tested" (228–229). In the endless game of translation-through-time, "bad" translations "represent falsity and will be lost in the game", while "good" translations "will engender other, 'better' translations which will again engender other translations", so that eventually what emerges ideally from this flowing series of semioses is "a translation fulfilling the conditions of truth" (228). Recall the way some memes survive and spread while others fade. Further: "[k]nowledge increases because of the goodness and liveliness (in Darwinian parlance: the fitness, hence the survival) of some habits of interpretation (interpretants) and the sterility of others" (230). This reminds us of the image of translation as genetic propagation, as evolution. Gorlée stresses the idea of growth inherent in semiosis, and comments on Peirce's "post-Darwinian evolutionary optimism". "Indeed," she adds, "the image of translation that emerges from a Peircean semiotics is one of change and growth, of expansion through transformation" (231). Yet despite the ever-present opportunity for revision, there will always remain lacunae. "A translation [...] is never finished and can always, however minimally, be improved upon" (231).

The notion of memes fighting for survival comes out particularly strongly in the following quotation.

> Unless the translated sign succeeds at some point in again finding and appealing to some mind willing and able to continue the process of its translation, it becomes dormant and its meaning becomes ossified [...] [All this Universe] is perfused with translations – living agencies, that is, some of them active and full of energy, others not yet discredited, perhaps, but distinctly becoming outmoded. The translated signs populating our entire life-world, permeating it, are in different stages of either growth, vitality, and development, or of stagnancy, obsolescence, and finally death. (Gorlée 1994: 221, on Peirce's semiotics)

I have tried to illustrate in this book that the same also holds for ideas about translation theory.

Second, translation is based on a contract between two parties. Like any other contract, the translation contract too is based on a form of social organization: dialogue. The distinguishing feature of translation, however, is that the two contracting parties are within the same person: the contract is between translator-as-receiver/interpreter and translator-as-utterer. Between the two halves of this single self, there therefore must be a dialogue. This inner dialogue with the self marks translation as being akin to other forms of what Peirce called "deliberate meditation, or thinking proper". All such thought processes are neatly described by the reassuringly familiar phrase: "I says to myself, says I" (Gorlée 1994: 220, citing Peirce).

The third point to be stressed is that like any contract, the translation contract is predicated upon trust between the two parties, and upon the assumption of responsibility, of keeping to commitments and taking the consequences (cf. Gorlée, p. 220). From this point of view, "translation is a self-imposed, well-described duty for the future, a promise to perform a task, that is, to do something, and to do it 'together'" (219), i.e. with both sides of the self working in collaboration. Both sides are of course "linked by a feedback mechanism," and so "they are almost forced to continuously interact and make themselves conjointly responsible for the work done" (219).

Finally: emancipatory translation, I suggest, acknowledges three guiding principles, each of which relates to one of the professional norms.

a. *The TIANA Principle.* TIANA stands for There Is Always aN Alternative (as opposed to the TINA principle beloved of certain economists and politicians: There Is No Alternative.) TIANA denies the existence of a single perfect translation, or even of a single optimal one (with some obvious exceptions such as standard terminology: recall the discussion of equivalence in 1.2.2). It agrees with Gutt and others that no two people can interpret an utterance in precisely the same way. It stresses flexibility and openness to change, in that translation is open-ended semiosis. And it is underlined by all those who wish to stress the creativity of the translator's craft. The TIANA Principle concerns the relation norm.

b. *The Dialogic Principle.* This Bakhtinian principle (see e.g. Bakhtin 1981) states that the translator is not alone but engaged in obvious social dialogue with a number of partners: original writer, commissioner, publisher, potential readership, other members of the translating profession. Translators are equal partners in this dialogue, contributing their own particular expertise as links in the communicative chain. Furthermore, translators interact dialogically with themselves, with other facets of their own personality, as Gorlée points out. And they also engage in dialogue with the text itself, interacting intertextually with it, manipulating it, teasing another text out of it which then itself stands in a dialogic relation with the original (cf. Oittinen 1993, 1995). The Dialogic Principle therefore concerns the communication norm: language is social, translating is a social act.

c. *"Nur das Ich kann reden"* (Ebeling 1971: 103). Only the I can speak. Language is individual, translation is a personal act. I myself must take responsibility for what I say and how I say it, and to whom I choose to speak. This principle thus concerns the accountability norm. There can be no passing the buck: the translated text is mine, with my name on (cf. Mossop 1983). I am not anonymous. It is my own trustworthiness that will either be maintained, enhanced or harmed by my translation. True, not mine *alone*, in that the author and commissioner also share responsibility: ultimately we are all co-accountable for this translation. And, true, I may be working as one member of a team of translators. But I alone am responsible for my contribution, and I have a loyalty also to myself. In this sense, my words are mine.

7.9 Update

Since *Memes of Translation* was first published, the interest in translation ethics has noticeably increased. Pym has published an English version (2012) of his originally French book on ethics referred to above in several places (1997). From another point of view, Koskinen (2000) has discussed the relevance of postmodernity and deconstructionism to translation ethics. This includes an interesting analysis of the notion of translator visibility (98f.), where she distinguishes between textual visibility (as advocated e.g. by Venuti), paratextual visibility (translators' statements about their work, presence of their name etc.) and extratextual visibility (the public status of the profession). There has also been much work on the manifestation of the "translator's voice" (especially after Hermans 1996), underlining the ways in which translations are not neutral but always somehow reflect the involvement of the translator him/herself. See e.g. Taivalkoski-Shilov and Suchet (2013).

In 2001, there was a special issue of *The Translator* (vol. 7, no. 2) on ethics. In it, I had a paper (Chesterman 2001) proposing a "Hieronymic Oath" that would serve the same role for translators as the Hippocratic Oath still does for doctors. This proposal sought to take some of the ideas in the present chapter a stage further, towards practical application. My suggested oath was as follows (2001: 153). The square brackets are original, and indicate values.

1. I swear to keep this Oath to the best of my ability and judgement. [Commitment]
2. I swear to be a loyal member of the translators' profession, respecting its history. I am willing to share my expertise with colleagues and to pass it on to trainee translators. I will not work for unreasonable fees. I will always translate to the best of my ability. [Loyalty to the profession]
3. I will use my expertise to maximize communication and minimize misunderstanding across language barriers. [Understanding]
4. I swear that my translations will not represent their source texts in unfair ways. [Truth]
5. I will respect my readers by trying to make my translations as accessible as possible, according to the conditions of each translation task. [Clarity]
6. I undertake to respect the professional secrets of my clients and not to exploit clients' information for personal gain. I promise to respect deadlines and to follow clients' instructions. [Trustworthiness]
7. I will be honest about my own qualifications and limitations; I will not accept work that is outside my competence. [Truthfulness]

8. I will inform clients of unresolved problems, and agree to arbitration in cases of dispute. [Justice]
9. I will do all I can to maintain and improve my competence, including all relevant linguistic, technical and other knowledge and skills. [Striving for excellence]

A different angle has been taken by a number of scholars who have been investigating the historical role played by interpreters, professional or amateur, in wartime contexts. This work is partly historical, but it also raises important ethical issues concerning the loyalty of the interpreters themselves, the clash or overlap between professional and personal ethics, and the treatment of interpreters by their military employers during and after their assignments. This last point relates to what I called macro-ethical questions (in 7.1). See e.g. another special issue of *The Translator* (vol. 16 no. 2, 2010) on "translation and violent conflict", and Footit and M. Kelly (2012). The importance of an interpreter's personal ethical principles has been provocatively defended in Inghilleri (2012), using a Bourdieusian framework to analyse ethical relations between agents. On problematizing the notion of the interpreter's neutrality, see also Angelelli (2004), and Baraldi and Gavioli (2012).

The macro-ethical view has also influenced discussions of translation quality, as briefly noted at the end of Chapter 5. Some scholars have argued that the whole notion of translation quality should be extended to include ethical factors having to do with the status and working conditions of the translators themselves. Abdallah (2012), for instance, brings empirical evidence to show that in the translation agencies she studied there were serious problems in the way the network of various agents functioned. There were clashing concepts of quality, translators' viewpoints were often neglected, rights and responsibilities were unclear. She shows how textual quality can be dependent on macro-ethical factors, and underlines the importance of clear agreements about quality criteria in this broad sense.

And finally, a postscript on the clarity value. In 1998 a campaign was started in the EU Commission Directorate-General for Translation to improve the clarity of texts both written and translated in the EU bureaucracy. The campaign, spearheaded by Emma Wagner, was called "Fight the Fog". It drew its inspiration partly from work on simplifying legal English and the Plain Language movement (see now Cutts 2013). The Commission's booklet is available at http://www.au.af.mil/au/awc/awcgate/eu/fight_the_fog_en.pdf. There are also campaigns to promote clear writing in other languages, and an international Plain Language Association (see http://plainlanguagenetwork.org/).

Epilogue

Strand by strand, the web takes shape. When the radii are in place, the gossamer spiral is spun, outwards from the central hub to the circumference. The complete construction evolves exosomatically, from within the spider, into an independent form in the external world; and it exists there in order to fulfil a specific problem-solving function: in the short term to catch flies, and in the long term to ensure the further development – indeed, the very survival – of its creator. The web's creator remains in contact with the web, aware of it, of how it was made, of external events impinging upon it.

This is Karl Popper's metaphor, or "biological analogue", for the concept "theory" (e.g. 1972: 145). Like a spider's web, a theory is a manifestation of the way living creatures adapt to the world we live in. Theories are tools for survival. Their creation is prompted by the need to solve particular problems; once created, they may affect not only the problem in question but also the future behaviour of their creators, perhaps giving rise to new problems and new theories, and so on. Elsewhere Popper uses the metaphor of the net:

> I see our scientific theories as human inventions – nets designed by us to catch the world. To be sure, these differ from the inventions of the poets, and even from the inventions of the technicians. Theories are not the *only* instruments. What we aim at is truth: we test our theories in the hope of eliminating those which are not true. In this way we may succeed in improving our theories – even as instruments: in making nets which are better and better adapted to catch our fish, the real world.   ([1956] 1982: 42; emphasis original)

The motto Popper chose for his book *The logic of scientific discovery* (1959) was a quote from Novalis: "Theories are nets: only he who casts will catch." The task of the scientist, then, is to seek to improve the web, the net, making the mesh smaller and smaller so that more and more of the world can be conceptually caught: theories are attempts to make sense of things.

But a net can never catch everything: a net, after all, has holes.

One of the themes of this book has been to develop a Popperian theory of translation. I have tried to link some ideas from Popper's philosophy with a number of other views and analyses, in the hope of creating a coherent whole, a theory (in its original sense of 'view') of translation. The book thus represents one tentative answer to the question: how can we construct a theory of translation? The various arguments and claims are not yet specific enough to be falsifiable in Popper's sense, but I think that the general theoretical structure comprising norms, strategies and values suggests a possible research programme in which falsifiable hypotheses can be proposed and tested.

Now for the error elimination.

Appendix

These are the texts from *Sky Lines*, the Austrian Airlines magazine (no. 5, 1992), from which most of the German-English examples in Chapter 4 were taken.

Source text A

Sehr geehrte Fluggäste!

Diese Ausgabe von SKY LINES enthält ein Porträt der Hansestadt Hamburg und einen Bericht über die Dominikanische Republik. Es sind dies informativ gestaltete Hinweise auf neue Ziele von Austrian Airlines im Winterflugplan 1992/93.

Hamburg wird im Linienverkehr angeflogen. Ebenso mit Beginn des Winterflugplanes werden die Kurse nach Amman in Jordanien und Minsk in Weißrußland aufgenommen. Die Dominikanische Republik erweitert das Angebot unserer Charter-Tochter Austrian Airtransport.

Zu den Neuheiten im Produkt kommen weitere Verbesserungen unserer Dienstleistungen. Besonders erwähnenswert ist der neue Terminal 1 im Flughafen Wien. Er steht – laut Terminplanung bei Redaktionsschluß dieses Bordmagazin – ab 9. September zur Verfügung. Austrian Airlines werden dort in einem eigenen Check-in-Bereich auch die Fluggäste unserer Partner in der "European Quality Alliance", Swissair und SAS, sowie zahlreicher anderer Gesellschaften betreuen. Wir sind überzeugt, daß damit das mitteleuropäische Luftdrehkreuz Wien für Gäste aus aller Welt noch interessanter und bequemer geworden ist.

Ihr besonderes Augenmerk dürfen wir auf eine Dienstleistung lenken, die wir gemeinsam mit Swissair anbieten. Es handelt sich um das Vielflieger-Programm "Qualiflyer". Schon der Name signalisiert ein sorgfältig durchdachtes Qualitätsprogramm, mit dessen attraktiven Leistungen und dessen einfacher Abwicklung wir uns von Mitbewerbern abheben wollen.

"Qualiflyer" ist auf den kombinierten Streckennetzen von Austrian Airlines und Swissair gültig. Damit können weltweit Meilen-Guthaben gesammelt und ebenso weltweit konsumiert werden. Weitere Partner sind Austrian Air Services und Crossair sowie – im Nachbarschaftsverkehr zwischen Skandinavien und Österreich bzw. der Schweiz – Scandinavian Airlines System (SAS). Durch Einbeziehung von Mietwagenfirmen und First-class-Hotels können Qualiflyer-Mitglieder auch am Boden Dienstleistungen zu besonderen Konditionen in Anspruch nehmen und zugleich Meilen-Guthaben buchen.

Details über "Qualiflyer" finden Sie auf Seite 97 dieser SKY LINES-Ausgabe. Wenn Sie sich entschließen, die Vorteile zu nutzen, so wenden Sie sich, bitte, an unsere Mitarbeiter beim Check-in oder an unsere Flugbegleiter an Bord. Selbstverständlich können wir Ihnen die Unterlagen auch zusenden.

Wir würden uns freuen, Sie als "Qualiflyer" begrüßen zu können. Denn wir sagen unseren Fluggästen gerne "Dankeschön".

Wir wünschen Ihnen einen guten Flug mit Austrian Airlines.

D. Dr. Anton Heschgl, Vorstandsdirektor
Dr. Herbert Bammer, Vorstandsdirektor-Stv.

Target text A

Dear Passengers,

In the present issue of SKY LINES you will find a portrait of the Hansa city of Hamburg and a feature on the Dominican Republic. Both deal in a highly informative way with Austrian Airlines destinations which will be making their debut in the airline's 1992/93 winter timetable. The Vienna-Hamburg route will be one of our new scheduled services. Other innovations in the winter timetable will be scheduled flights to Amman in Jordan and to Minsk in Byelorussia. The Dominican Republic is an addition to the route network of our charter subsidiary Austrian Airtransport.

The enlargement of our destinations list is supplemented by further improvements in our range of passenger services. The most notable of these is the new Terminal 1 at Vienna International Airport. At the time of going to press, it was scheduled to be opened on September 9. Austrian Airlines will operate its own check-in area in the new terminal, for its own passengers and for those of its "European Quality Alliance" partners Swissair and SAS and of numerous other airlines. We are confident that this added degree of convenience will make Vienna even more attractive as a Central European interchange to visitors from all corners of the globe.

We should also like to draw your attention to a service which we are offering in conjunction with Swissair: the frequent-flyer program "Qualiflyer".

As its name suggests, this is a painstakingly devised quality program whose distinguishing features – attractive services and straightforward procedures – should give it a clear edge over rival programs.

"Qualiflyer" is valid on the route networks of both Austrian Airlines and Swissair. This means that passengers can clock up "Qualiflyer" mileage worldwide, and also claim the benefits worldwide. Other partners affiliated to the scheme are Austrian Air Services and Crossair and – on routes linking Scandinavia with Austria and Switzerland – Scandinavian Airlines System (SAS). Car rental companies and first-class hotels have been incorporated in the "Qualiflyer" program, so that members can take advantage of its money-saving services on the ground too – and at the same time add more miles to their total.

For details of the "Qualiflyer" program, turn to page 97 of this magazine. If you decide to become a member of the scheme, any Austrian Airlines or Swissair service office, our check-in staff or the flight attendants will be glad to be of assistance. We can, of course, also forward the documentation to you by mail.

We should be very pleased to welcome you as a "Qualiflyer" member. Because we are happy for any opportunity to say "Thank you".

We wish you a pleasant flight with Austrian Airlines.

D. Dr. Anton Heschgl, President
Dr. Herbert Bammer, Chief Executive Marketing & Sales

Source text B

Versandbedingungen

Die Produkte auf den JET SHOP Seiten sind nur eine kleine Auswahl unserer JET SHOP Produktpalette. Das gesamte Angebot finden Sie im JET SHOP Katalog, der an Bord aufliegt. JET SHOP Artikel können nur mit untenstehendem Bestellschein bezogen werden, ein Verkauf an Bord ist leider NICHT möglich.

    Unsere Flugbegleiter nehmen gerne Ihre Bestellung entgegen, die bestellten Artikel werden Ihnen mit der Post per Nachnahme zugesandt. Bitte beachten Sie, daß zu den angegebenen Preisen noch Porto und Nachnahmegebühren verrechnet werden. Bei Versand in das Ausland reduziert sich der angegebene JET SHOP Preis um 16,67% Mehrwertsteuer. Der Versand kann nur in jene Länder durchgeführt werden, mit denen ein postalisches Nachnahmeabkommen besteht. Wir möchten Sie weiters darauf aufmerksam machen, daß in einigen Ländern zusätzlich Zölle eingehoben werden und die Versandspesen dadurch relativ hoch sein können. Artikel- und Preisänderungen vorbehalten.

Target text B

The merchandise depicted on the JET SHOP pages is only a small selection of the JET SHOP articles available. The full range is detailed in the JET SHOP catalogue which can be obtained on board. JET SHOP merchandise can be purchased only by completing the order card below. We regret that these articles are NOT sold on board.

    Our flight attendants will be glad to take your orders. The articles which you order will be sent cash-on-delivery (COD) by post to your address. Kindly note that the prices quoted are exclusive of postal charges and collection fee. Deduct 16,67% [comma *sic*] VAT from the JET SHOP price quoted, when merchandise is dispatched abroad. Articles can be sent only to those countries with which a postal COD agreement exists. We should also like to remind you that some countries levy import tariffs, which makes overall dispatching costs relatively high. We reserve the right to make alterations to articles and prices.

Source and target texts C

Bestellschein / Order Card

Alle Preise inklusive MWSt., jedoch exklusive Nachnahmegebühr und Porto. Artikel- und Preisänderungen vorbehalten. / *All prices include V.A.T. (value added tax) but do not include the C.O.D. (cash on delivery) fee and mail charges. Articles and prices subject to change.*

Wir akzeptieren folgende Kreditkarten und ersuchen Sie, jene, mit der Sie Ihre Rechnung begleichen wollen, anzukreuzen. / *We accept the following credit cards. Please mark the one which you would like to have charged.*

References

Abdallah, Kristiina. 2012. *Translators in Production Networks. Reflections on agency, quality and ethics.* Joensuu: Publications of the University of Eastern Finland. Available at: http://urn.fi/URN:ISBN:978-952-61-0609-0. (Accessed 17.5.2015.)

Angelelli, Claudia V. 2004. *Revisiting the Interpreter's Role.* Amsterdam and Philadelphia: Benjamins. doi:10.1075/btl.55

Antonini, Rachele (ed.). In press. *Non-professional Interpreting and Translation: State of the Art and Future of an Emerging Field of Research.* Amsterdam and Philadelphia: Benjamins.

Archer, Carol M. 1986. "Culture bump and beyond". In J.M. Valdes (ed.) 1986, *Culture Bound. Bridging the cultural gap in language teaching.* Cambridge: Cambridge University Press, 170–178.

Arnold, Malcolm. 1924. *Essays Literary and Critical.* London and Toronto: Dent. (Extract from "On translating Homer" in Lefevere (ed.) 1992, 68–69.)

Arrojo, Rosemary. 1996. "Postmodernism and the teaching of translation". In Dollerup and Appel (eds) 1996, 97–103. doi:10.1075/btl.16.15arr

Aunger, Robert (ed.). 2000. *Darwinizing Culture. The status of memetics as a science.* Oxford: Oxford University Press.

Baker, Mona. 1992. *In Other Words. A coursebook on translation.* London: Routledge. doi:10.4324/9780203327579

Baker, Mona. 1993. "Corpus linguistics and translation studies – Implications and applications". In M. Baker, et al. (eds), *Text and Technology.* In Honour of John Sinclair. Amsterdam and Philadelphia: Benjamins, 233–250. doi:10.1075/z.64.15bak

Baker, Mona. 2006. *Translation and Conflict: A Narrative Account.* London and New York: Routledge.

Bakhtin, Mikhail M. 1981. *The Dialogic Imagination: Four Essays.* (Ed. M. Holquist, trans. C. Emerson and M. Holquist.) Austin: Texas University Press.

Ballard, Michel. 1992. *De Cicéron à Benjamin: Traducteurs, traductions, réflexions.* Lille: Presses Universitaires de Lille. doi:10.1075/target.5.2.15del

Baraldi, Claudio, and Laura Gavioli (eds). 2012. *Coordinating Participation in Dialogue Interpreting.* Amsterdam and Philadelphia: Benjamins. doi:10.1075/btl.102

Barkhudarov, Leonid. 1993. "The problem of the unit of translation". In Zlateva (ed.) 1993, 39–46.

Bartsch, Renate. 1987. *Norms of Language.* London: Longman.

Bassnett, Susan. 1991. *Translation Studies.* (Revised edition.) London: Routledge.

Bassnett, Susan, and André Lefevere (eds). 1990. *Translation, History and Culture.* London: Pinter.

Beaugrande, Robert de, and Wolfgang Dressler. 1981. *Introduction to Text Linguistics.* London: Longman.

Becher, Viktor. 2010. "Abandoning the notion of 'translation-inherent' explicitation: against a dogma of Translation Studies". *Across Languages and Cultures* 11(1): 1–28. doi: 10.1556/Acr.11.2010.1.1

Bell, Roger T. 1991. *Translation and Translating: Theory and Practice*. London: Longman.

Benjamin, Andrew. 1989. *Translation and the Nature of Philisophy: A new theory of words*. London: Routledge.

Benjamin, Walter. [1923] 1963. "Die Aufgabe des Übersetzers". In Störig (ed.) 1963, 182–195.

Berman, Antoine. 1984. *L'Épreuve de l'Étranger: Culture et traduction dans l'Allemagne romantique*. Paris: Gallimard.

Blackmore, Susan. 1999. *The Meme Machine*. Oxford: Oxford University Press.

Bloom, Harold. [1975] 1980. *A Map of Misreading*. New York: Oxford University Press.

Blum-Kulka, Shoshana. 1986. "Shifts of cohesion and coherence in translation". In House and Blum-Kulka (eds) 1986, 17–35.

Bly, Robert. 1984. "The eight stages of translation". In W. Frawley (ed.) 1984, *Translation: Literary, Linguistic and Philosophical Perspectives*. New Jersey: Associated University Press, 67–89.

Bowker, Lynne, and Jennifer Pearson. 2002. *Working with Specialized Language: A Practical Guide to Using Corpora*. London: Routledge. doi: 10.4324/9780203469255

Brainerd, Barron. 1972. "An exploratory study of pronouns and articles as indices of genre in English". *Language and Style* 5(4): 239–259.

Breedveld, Hella. 2002. "Writing and revising processes in professional translation". *Across Languages and Cultures* 3(1): 91–100. doi: 10.1556/Acr.3.2002.1.7

Broeck, Raymond van den. 1981. "The limits of translatability, exemplified by metaphor translation". *Poetics Today* 2(4): 73–87. doi: 10.2307/1772487

Brownlie, Siobhan. 2003. "Investigating explanations of translational phenomena: a case for multiple causality". *Target* 15(1): 111–152. doi: 10.1075/target.15.1.06bro

Brunette, Louse. 2000. "Towards a terminology for Quality Translation Assessment: a comparison of TQA practices". *The Translator* 6(2) [Special issue on evaluation and translation]: 169–182. doi: 10.1080/13556509.2000.10799064

Brunette, Louise, Chantal Gagnon, and Jonathan Hine (eds). 2005. "The GREVIS project: Revise or court calamity". *Across Languages and Cultures* 6(1): 29–45. doi: 10.1556/Acr.6.2005.1.3

Calzada Pérez, Maria (ed.). 2003. *Apropos of Ideology: Translation Studies on Ideology – Ideologies in Translation Studies*. Manchester: St Jerome Publishing.

Carl, Michael, Srinivas Bangalore, and Moritz Schaeffer (eds). 2016. *New Directions in Empirical Translation Process Research*. Cham: Springer. doi: 10.1007/978-3-319-20358-4

Castellano, Lanna. 1988. "Get rich – but slow". In C. Picken (ed.) 1988, *ITI Conference 2: Translators and interpreters mean business*. London: Aslib.

Catford, John C. 1965. *A Linguistic Theory of Translation*. Oxford: Oxford University Press.

Cattrysse, Patrick. 2014. *Descriptive Adaptation Studies. Epistemological and methodological issues*. Antwerp: Garant.

Cavalli-Sforza, Luca. 2005. *Évolution biologique, évolution culturelle*. Paris: Éditions Odile Jacob.

Chafe, Wallace L. 1982. "Integration and involvement in speaking, writing and oral literature". In D. Tannen (ed.) 1982, *Spoken and Written Language: Exploring orality and literacy*. Norwood, NJ: Ablex, 35–53.

Changeux, Jean-Pierre (éd.) 2003. *Gènes et cultures*. Paris: Éditions Odile Jacob.

Chesterman, Andrew (ed.). 1989. *Readings in Translation Theory*. Helsinki: Finn Lectura.

Chesterman, Andrew. 1993. "From 'is' to 'ought': translation laws, norms and strategies". *Target* 5(1): 1–20. doi: 10.1075/target.5.1.02che
Chesterman, Andrew. 1994a. "Karl Popper in the translation class". In Dollerup and Lindegaard (eds) 1994, 89–95.
Chesterman, Andrew. 1994b. "Quantitative aspects of translation quality". *Lebende Sprachen* 39(4): 153–156. doi: 10.1515/les.1994.39.4.153
Chesterman, Andrew. 1995. "The successful translator: the evolution of *homo transferens*". *Perspectives: Studies in Translatology* 2: 253–270. doi: 10.1080/0907676X.1995.9961266
Chesterman, Andrew. 1996a. "Teaching translation theory: the significance of memes". In Dollerup and Appel (eds) 1996, 63–71. doi: 10.1075/btl.16.10che
Chesterman, Andrew. 1996b. "On similarity". *Target* 8(1): 159–164. doi: 10.1075/target.8.1.10che
Chesterman, Andrew. 1997. "Ethics of translation". In M. Snell-Hornby (ed.), *Translation as Intercultural Communication*. Amsterdam and Philadelphia: Benjamins, 147–157. doi: 10.1075/btl.20.15che
Chesterman, Andrew. 1998. *Contrastive Functional Analysis*. Amsterdam and Philadelphia: Benjamins. doi: 10.1075/pbns.47
Chesterman, Andrew. 2001. "Proposal for a Hieronymic Oath". *The Translator* 7(2): 139–154. doi: 10.1080/13556509.2001.10799097
Chesterman, Andrew. 2005a. "The memetics of knowledge". In H.V. Dam, J. Engberg and H. Gerzymisch-Arbogast (eds) 2005, *Knowledge Systems and Translation*. Berlin and New York: Mouton de Gruyter, 17–30.
Chesterman, Andrew. 2005b. "Problems with strategies". In K. Károly and Á. Fóris (eds) 2005, *New Trends in Translation Studies. In Honour of Kinga Klaudy*. Budapest: Akadémiai Kiadó, 17–28.
Chesterman, Andrew. 2006. "Interpreting the meaning of translation". In M. Suominen, et al. (eds) 2005, *A Man of Measure. Festschrift in Honour of Fred Karlsson on his 60th Birthday*. Turku: Linguistic Association of Finland, 3–11.
Chesterman, Andrew. 2007. "On the idea of a theory". *Across Languages and Cultures* 8(1): 1–16. doi: 10.1556/Acr.8.2007.1.1
Chesterman, Andrew. 2008. "On explanation". In A. Pym, M. Shlesinger and D. Simeoni (eds) 2008, *Beyond Descriptive Translation Studies. Investigations in homage to Gideon Toury*. Amsterdam and Philadelphia: Benjamins, 363–379. doi: 10.1075/btl.75.27che
Chesterman, Andrew. 2009. "The Name and Nature of Translator Studies". *Hermes* 42: 13–22.
Chesterman, Andrew. 2014. "Universalism in translation studies". *Translation Studies* 7(1): 82–90. doi: 10.1080/14781700.2013.828904
Chesterman, Andrew, and Rosemary Arrojo. 2000. "Shared ground in Translation Studies". *Target* 12(1): 151–160. doi: 10.1075/target.12.1.08che
Chesterman, Andrew, and Emma Wagner. 2002. *Can Theory Help Translators? A dialogue between the ivory tower and the wordface*. Manchester: St Jerome Publishing.
Cheyfitz, Eric. 1991. *The Poetics of Imperialism. Translation and colonization from The Tempest to Tarzan*. Oxford: Oxford University Press.
Connor, Ulla. 1996. *Contrastive Rhetoric*. Cambridge: Cambridge University Press. doi: 10.1017/CBO9781139524599
Connor, Ulla, and Robert B. Kaplan (eds). 1987. *Writing Across Languages: Analysis of L2 texts*. Reading, MA: Addison-Wesley.
Copeland, Rita. 1991. *Rhetoric, Hermeneutics, and Translation in the Middle Ages*. Cambridge: Cambridge University Press. doi: 10.1017/CBO9780511597534

Coseriu, Eugenio. 1970. "System, Norm und Rede". In E. Coseriu (ed.), *Sprache, Strukturen und Funktionen*. Tübingen: Narr, 193–212.

Cowley, Abraham. [1656] 1975. Extract from "Preface to the Pindarique Odes". In T. R. Steiner 1975, *English Translation Theory 1650–1800*. Assen and Amsterdam: van Gorcum, 66–67.

Craig, George. 1993. "Fine-tuning Proust". *Times Literary Supplement*, 22 October 1993, 24.

Crystal, David, and Donald Davy. 1969. *Investigating English Style*. London: Longman.

Cutts, Martin. 2013. *Oxford Guide to Plain English*. (Fourth edition.) Oxford: Oxford University Press.

d'Alembert, Jean le R. 1784. *Morceaux choisis de Tacite*. Paris: Desaint. (Translated extracts in Lefevere (ed.) 1992, 105–116.)

D'hulst, Lieven. 1992. "Sur le rôle des métaphores en traductologie contemporaine". *Target* 4(1): 33–51. doi:10.1075/target.4.1.04dhu

Dacier, Anne. 1711. *L'Iliade d'Homère*. Paris: Rigaud. (Translated extract in Lefevere (ed.) 1992, 10–13.)

Danan, Martine. 1991. "Dubbing as an expression of nationalism". *Meta* 36(4): 606–614. doi:10.7202/002446ar

Dancette, Jeanne. 1994. "Comprehension in the translation process: an analysis of think-aloud protocols". In Dollerup and Lindegaard (eds) 1994, 113–120.

Davidson, Donald. 1986. "A nice derangement of epitaphs". In E. LePore (ed.), *Truth and Interpretation: Perspectives on the Philosophy of Donald Davidson*. Oxford: Blackwell, 433–446.

Dawkins, Richard. 1976. *The Selfish Gene*. Oxford: Oxford University Press. (New edition 1989.)

de la Motte, Antoine H. 1714. *L'Iliade, poème. Avec un discours sur Homère*. Amsterdam: Depuis. (Translated extract from the preface in Lefevere (ed.) 1992, 28–30.)

Delisle, Jean. 1988. *Translation: An Interpretative Approach*. Ottawa: University of Ottawa Press.

Delius, Juan D. 1989. "Of memes and brain bugs, a natural history of culture". In W.A. Koch (ed.) 1989, *The Nature of Culture*. Bochum: Brockmeyer, 26–79.

Dennett, Daniel C. 1991. *Consciousness Explained*. Harmondsworth: Penguin.

Dennett, Daniel C. 2004. *Freedom Evolves*. London: Penguin.

Derrida, Jacques. 1985. "Des Tours de Babel". In J.F. Graham (ed.) 1985, *Difference in Translation*. Ithaca, NY: Cornell University Press, 209–248.

Dijk, Teun van. 1988. *News as Discourse*. Hillsdale, NJ: Erlbaum.

Dolet, Etienne. 1540. *De la Manière de Bien Traduire d'une Langue en Autre*. Lyon: Presses E. Dolet. (Translated extracts in Lefevere (ed.) 1992, 27–28.)

Dollerup, Cay, and Vibeke Appel (eds). 1996. *Teaching Translation and Interpreting 3. New horizons*. Amsterdam and Philadelphia: Benjamins. doi:10.1075/btl.16

Dollerup, Cay, and Annette Lindegaard (eds). 1994. *Teaching Translating and Interpreting 2. Insights, aims, visions*. Amsterdam and Philadelphia: Benjamins. doi:10.1075/btl.5

Dreyfus, Hubert L., and Stuart E Dreyfus. 1986. *Mind Over Machine*. Oxford: Blackwell / New York: The Free Press.

Dryden, John. [1680] 1975. From "Preface" to Ovid's Epistles. In T.R. Steiner 1975, *English Translation Theory 1650–1800*. Assen and Amsterdam: Van Gorcum, 68–74. (Also in Schulte and Biguenet (eds) 1992, 17–31. Parts also in Chesterman (ed.) 1989, 7–12; and in Lefevere (ed.) 1992, 102–105.)

Ebeling, Gerhard. 1971. *Einführung in Theologische Sprachlehre*. Tübingen: Mohr.

Edelman, Gerald. 1992. *Brilliant Air, Bright Fire. On the matter of the mind*. Harmondsworth: Penguin.

Ellegård, Alvar. 1978. *The Syntactic Structure of English Texts*. (Gothenburg Studies in English 43.) Gothenburg: University of Gothenburg.
Englund Dimitrova, Birgitta. 2005. *Expertise and Explicitation in the Translation Process*. Amsterdam and Philadelphia: Benjamins. doi:10.1075/btl.64
Enkvist, Nils Erik. 1991. "Discourse type, text type, and cross-cultural rhetoric". In Tirkkonen-Condit (ed.) 1991, 5–16.
Erasmus, Desiderius. [1506] 1992. Extracts from "Letter to William Warham". In Lefevere (ed.) 1992, 60.
Even-Zohar, Itamar. 1990. *Polysystem Studies. Poetics Today* 11(1).
Faerch, Claus, and Gabriele Kasper (eds). 1983. *Strategies in Interlanguage Communication*. London: Longman.
Faerch, Claus, and Gabriele Kasper. 1987. *Introspection in Second Language Research*. Philadelphia: Multilingual Matters Ltd.
Fairclough, Norman (ed.). 1992. *Critical Language Awareness*. London: Longman.
Fawcett, Peter. 1995. "Translation and power play". *The Translator* 1(2): 177–192. doi:10.1080/13556509.1995.10798956
Ferreira, Aline, and John W. Schwieter (eds). 2015. *Psycholinguistic and Cognitive Inquiries into Translation and Interpreting*. Amsterdam and Philadelphia: Benjamins. doi:10.1075/btl.115
Florin, Sider. 1993. "Realia in translation". In Zlateva (ed.) 1993, 122–128.
Flotow, Luise von. 1991. "Feminist translation: contexts, practices and theories". *TTR* 4(2): 69–84. doi:10.7202/037094ar
Footit, Hilary, and Michael Kelly (eds). 2012. *Languages at War. Policies and practices of language contacts in conflict*. London: Palgrave Macmillan.
Foucault, Michel. 1971. *L'Ordre du discours*. Paris: Gallimard.
Francis, W. Nelson, and Henry Kučera. 1982. *Frequency Analysis of English Usage. Lexicon and grammar*. Boston: Houghton Miffin Company.
Fraser, Janet. 1993. "Public accounts: using verbal protocols to investigate community translation". *Applied Linguistics* 14(4): 325–343. doi:10.1093/applin/14.4.325
Friedrich, Hugo. 1965. "Zur Frage der Übersetzungskunst". Heidelberg: Carl Winter. (English translation in Schulte and Biguenet (eds) 1992, 11–16.)
Fuller, Steve. [2003] 2006. *Kuhn vs. Popper. The Struggle for the Soul of Science*. Cambridge: Icon Books.
Gadamer, Hans-Georg. 1960. *Wahrheit und Methode*. Tübingen: Mohr.
Gambier, Yves. 2008. "Stratégies et tactiques en traduction et interprétation". In G. Hansen, A. Chesterman, and H. Gerzymisch-Arbogast (eds) 2008, *Efforts and Models in Interpreting and Translation Research*. Amsterdam and Philadelphia: Benjamins, 63–82.
Gambier, Yves. 2012. "The position of audiovisual translation studies". In Millán and Bartrina (eds) 2012, 45–59. doi:10.1075/hts.4
Gambier, Yves, and Luc van Doorslaer (eds). 2014. *Handbook of Translation Studies*. (Four volumes.) Amsterdam and Philadelphia: Benjamins. doi:10.1075/hts.4
Gentzler, Edwin. 1993. *Contemporary Translation Theories*. London: Routledge.
Gerloff, Pamela. 1986. "Second language learners' reports on the interpretive process: talk-aloud protocols of translation". In House and Blum-Kulka (eds) 1986, 243–262.
Gile, Daniel. 1992. "Les fautes de traduction: une analyse pédagogique". *Meta* 37(2): 251–262. doi:10.7202/002907ar
Gile, Daniel. 1994. "The process-oriented approach in translation training". In Dollerup and Lindegaard (eds) 1994, 107–112.

Gile, Daniel. 1995. *Basic Concepts and Models for Interpreter and Translator Training*. Amsterdam and Philadelphia: Benjamins. doi: 10.1075/btl.8(1st)

Goethe, Johan W. von. [1819] 1963. "Noten und Abhandlungen zu bessern Verständnis des west-östlichen Divans". In Störig (ed.) 1963, 35–37.

Göpferich, Susanna. 2009. "Towards a model of translation competence and its acquisition: the longitudinal study 'TransComp'". In S. Göpferich, A.L. Jakobsen and I.M. Mees (eds) 2009, *Behind the Mind. Methods, Models and Results in Translation Process Research*. Copenhagen: Samfundslitteratur Press, 11–37. Available at: http://gams.uni-graz.at/fedora/get/o:tc-095-187/bdef:PDF/get. (Accessed 18.5.2015.)

Göpferich, Susanna. 2013. "Translation competence. Explaining development and stagnation from a dynamic systems perspective". *Target* 25(1): 61–76. doi: 10.1075/target.25.1.06goe

Gorlée, Dinda. 1994. *Semiotics and the Problem of Translation, with special reference to the semiotics of Charles S. Peirce*. Amsterdam and Atlanta, GA.: Rodopi.

Grice, Paul. 1975. "Logic and conversation". In P. Cole and J. L. Morgan (eds) 1975, *Syntax and Semantics, 3: Speech Acts*. New York: Academic Press, 41–58.

Grimes, Joseph E. 1963. "Measuring 'naturalness' in translation". *The Bible Translator* 14(2): 49–62.

Gutt, Ernst-August. 1990. "A theoretical account of translation – without a translation theory". *Target* 2(2): 135–164. doi: 10.1075/target.2.2.02gut

Gutt, Ernst-August. 1991. *Translation and Relevance. Cognition and context*. Oxford: Blackwell.

Hailman, Jack P. 1982. "Evolution and behavior: an iconoclastic view". In H. C. Plotkin (ed.) 1982, *Learning, Development and Culture*. Chichester: Wiley, 205–254.

Haiman, John (ed.). 1985. *Iconicity in Syntax*. Amsterdam and Philadelphia: Benjamins. doi: 10.1075/tsl.6

Halverson, Sandra. 1999. "Conceptual work and the 'translation' concept". *Target* 11(1): 1–31. doi: 10.1075/target.11.1.02hal

Harris, Brian. 1977. "The importance of natural translation". *Working Papers on Bilingualism* 12: 96–114.

Harris, Brian. 1990. "Norms in interpretation". *Target* 2(1): 115–119. doi: 10.1075/target.2.1.08har

Hartama-Heinonen, Ritva. 2008. *Abductive translation studies: the art of marshalling signs*. Imatra: International Semiotics Institute.

Hartmann, Reinhard R. K. 1980. *Contrastive Textology. Comparative discourse analysis in applied linguistics*. (Studies in Descriptive Linguistics 5.) Heidelberg: Groos.

Hartmann, Reinhard R. K. 1981. "Contrastive textology and translation". In W. Kühlwein, G. Thome, and W. Wilss (eds) 1981, *Kontrastive Linguistik und Übersetzungswissenschaft*. München: Fink, 200–208.

Harvey, Keith. 1995. "A descriptive framework for compensation". *The Translator* 1(1): 65–86. doi: 10.1080/13556509.1995.10798950

Hatim, Basil, and Ian Mason. 1990. *Discourse and the Translator*. London: Longman.

Heidegger, Martin. [1957] 1963. *Der Satz vom Grund*. Pfullingen: Günther Neske. Excerpt in Störig 1963, 369–383.

Hermans, Theo (ed.). 1985. *The Manipulation of Literature. Studies in literary translation*. London: Croom Helm.

Hermans, Theo. 1991. "Translation norms and correct translations". In Leuven-Zwart and Naaijkens (eds) 1991, 155–169.

Hermans, Theo. 1996. "The translator's voice in translated narrative". *Target* 8(1): 23–48. doi: 10.1075/target.8.1.03her
Herodotus. 1920. *Histories* Volume 1. Translated by A. D. Godley. London: Heinemann.
Hervey, Sándor, and Ian Higgins. 1992. *Thinking Translation. A course in translation method: French-English*. London: Routledge.
Hewson, Lance, and Jacky Martin. 1991. *Redefining Translation. The variational approach*. London: Routledge.
Heylen, Romy. 1993. *Translation, Poetics and the Stage. Six French Hamlets*. London: Routledge.
Hinds, John. 1987. "Reader versus writer responsibility. A new typology". In Connor and Kaplan (eds) 1987, 141–152.
Hochel, Braňo. 1991. "The cross-temporal and cross-spatial factors and the translation of literary language". In Leuven-Zwart and Naaijkens (eds) 1991, 41–48.
Holmes, James S. 1978. "Translation theory, translation theories, translation studies, and the translator". In P.A. Horguelin (ed.) 1978, *La Traduction, une Profession / Translating, a Profession*. Montréal: Conseil des traducteurs et interprètes du Canada, 55–61. (Also in Holmes 1988, 93–98.)
Holmes, James S. 1988. *Translated! Papers on literary translation and translation studies*. Amsterdam: Rodopi.
Holmes, James S., José Lambert, and Raymond van den Broeck (eds). 1978. *Literature and Translation: New perspectives in literary studies with a basic bibliography of books on translation studies*. Leuven: Acco.
Holz-Mänttäri, Justa. 1984. *Translatorisches Handeln*. Helsinki: Suomalainen Tiedeakatemia.
Hönig, Hans G., and Paul Kußmaul. 1982. *Strategie der Übersetzung. Ein Lehr- und Arbeitsbuch*. Tübingen: Narr.
Horguelin, Paul A., and Louise Brunette. 1998. *Pratique de la révision*. Brossard, Québec: Linguatech.
House, Juliane. 1977. "A model for assessing translation quality". *Meta* 22(2): 103–109. doi: 10.7202/003140ar
House, Juliane. 1981. *A Model for Translation Quality Assessment*. (2nd edition.) Tübingen: Narr.
House, Juliane. 1988. "Talking to onself or thinking with others? On using different thinking aloud methods in translation". *Fremdsprachen lehren und lernen* 17: 84–98.
House, Juliane, and Shoshana Blum-Kulka (eds). 1986. *Interlingual and Intercultural Communication: Discourse and cognition in translation and second language acquisition studies*. Tübingen: Narr.
Hu, Gengshen. 2003. "Translation as adaptation and selection". *Perspectives: Studies in Translatology* 11(4): 283–291. doi: 10.1080/0907676X.2003.9961481
Huetius, Petrus D. 1683. *De Interpretatione Libri Duo*. The Hague: Apud Arnoldum Leers. (Translated extracts in Lefevere (ed.) 1992, 86–102.)
Hull, D.L. 1982. "The naked meme". In Plotkin, H.C. (ed.) 1982, *Learning, Development and Culture*. Chichester: Wiley, 273–327.
Huss, Roger. 1993. "Flaubert in English". *Times Literary Supplement*, 22 October 1993, 24.
Inghilleri, Moira. 2012. *Interpreting Justice. Ethics, politics and language*. London: Routledge.
Inoue, Kyoko. 1991. *MacArthur's Japanese Constitution. A linguistic and cultural study of its making*. Chicago: University of Chicago Press.
Itkonen, Esa. 1983. *Causality in Linguistic Theory*. London: Croom Helm.

Jääskeläinen, Riitta. 1989. "The role of reference material in professional vs non-professional translation: a think-aloud protocol study". In S. Tirkkonen-Condit and S. Condit (eds) 1989, *Empirical Studies in Translation and Linguistics*. Joensuu: University of Joensuu, Faculty of Arts, 175–200.

Jääskeläinen, Riitta. 1993. "Investigating translation strategies". In S. Tirkkonen-Condit and J. Laffling (eds) 1993, *Recent Trends in Empirical Translation Research*. Joensuu: University of Joensuu, Faculty of Arts, 99–119.

Jakobsen, Arnt Lykke. 1994a. "Translation – a productive skill". In H. Bergenholtz, et al. (eds) 1994, *OFT Symposium. Translating LSP texts*. Copenhagen: Copenhagen Business School, 41–70.

Jakobsen, Arnt Lykke. 1994b. "Starting from the (other) end: integrating translation and text production". In Dollerup and Lindegaard (eds) 1994, 143–150.

Jakobsen, Arnt Lykke. 2011. "Tracking translators' keystrokes and eye movements with Translog". In C. Alvstad, A. Hild, and E. Tiselius (eds) 2011, *Methods and Strategies of Process Research*. Amsterdam and Philadelphia: Benjamins, 37–55. doi: 10.1075/btl.94.06jak

Jakobson, Roman. 1959. "On linguistic aspects of translation". In R. A. Brower (ed.), *On Translation*. Cambridge, MA: Harvard University Press, 232–239. (Also in Chesterman (ed.) 1989, 53–60.)

Janks, Hilary, and Roz Ivanič. 1992. "CLA [Critical language awareness] and emancipatory discourse". In Fairclough (ed.) 1992, 305–331.

Jodl, Friedrich. 1918. *Allgemeine Ethik*. Stuttgart and Berlin: J. G. Cotta'sche Buchhandlung Nachfolger.

Johansson, Stig. 1978a. *Some Aspects of the Vocabulary of Learned and Scientific English*. (Gothenburg Studies in English 42.) Gothenburg: University of Gothenburg.

Johansson, Stig. 1978b. *Studies of Error Gravity*. (Gothenburg Studies in English 44.) Gothenburg: University of Gothenburg.

Johansson, Stig, and Knut Hoflund. 1989. *Frequency Analysis of English Vocabulary and Grammar*. Oxford: Clarendon Press.

Jones, Francis R. 1989. "On aboriginal sufferance: a process model of poetic translating". *Target* 1(2): 183–199. doi: 10.1075/target.1.2.04jon

Jumpelt, Rudolf W. 1961. *Die Übersetzung Naturwissenschaftlicher und Technischer Literatur*. Berlin: Langenscheidt.

Karlsson, Fred. 1983. *Finnish Grammar*. (Translated by Andrew Chesterman.) Helsinki: Werner Söderström.

Katz, Jerrold. 1978. "Effability and translation". In F. Guenthner and M. Guenthner-Reutter (eds) 1978, *Meaning and Translation*. London: Duckworth, 191–234.

Keenan, Edward. 1978. "Some logical problems in translation". In F. Guenthner and M. Guenthner-Reutter (eds) 1978, *Meaning and Translation*. London: Duckworth, 157–189.

Kelly, Louis G. 1979. *The True Interpreter*. Oxford: Blackwell.

Kemmis, Stephen, and Robin McTaggart. 1988. *The Action Research Planner*. Deakin: Deakin University Press.

Kiraly, Donald C. 1995. *Pathways to Translation. Pegagogy and process*. Kent, OH: Kent State University Press.

Klaudy, Kinga. 1996. "Back-translation as a tool for detecting explicitation strategies in translation". In K. Klaudy, J. Lambert, and A. Sohár (eds) 1996, *Translation Studies in Hungary*. Budapest: Scholastica, 99–114.
Kolb, David A. 1984. *Experiential Learning. Experience as the source of learning and development*. Englewood Cliffs, NJ: Prentice Hall.
Koller, Werner. 1972. *Grundprobleme der Übersetzungstheorie*. Bern: Francke.
Koller, Werner. 1979. *Einführung in die Übersetzungswissenschaft*. Heidelberg: Quelle und Meyer. (4th revised edition 1992.)
Komissarov, Vilen. 1993. "Norms in translation". In Zlateva (ed.) 1993, 63–75.
Königs, Frank G. 1990. "'Die Seefahrt an der Nagel hängen'? Metaphern beim Übersetzen und in der Übersetzungswissenschaft". *Target* 2(1): 97–113. doi:10.1075/target.2.1.06kon
Korpel, Luc. 1993. "Rhetoric and Dutch translation theory (1750–1820)". *Target* 5(1): 55–69. doi:10.1075/target.5.1.05kor
Koskinen, Kaisa. 1994a. *The Invisible Hand: The literary translator's role*. Unpublished Licentiate thesis, University of Tampere, Finland.
Koskinen, Kaisa. 1994b. "(Mis)translating the untranslatable – the impact of deconstruction and post-structuralism on translation theory". *Meta* 39(3): 446–452. doi:10.7202/003344ar
Koskinen, Kaisa. 2000. *Beyond Ambivalence. Postmodernity and the ethics of translation*. Tampere: University of Tampere.
Kovala, Urpo. 1996. "Translations, paratextual mediation and ideological closure". *Target* 8(1): 119–147. doi:10.1075/target.8.1.07kov
Krings, Hans P. 1986. *Was in den Köpfen von Übersetzern vorgeht: eine empirische Untersuchung zur Struktur des Übersetzungsprozesses an fortgeschrittenen Französischlernern*. Tübingen: Narr.
Krings, Hans P. 2001. *Repairing texts. Empirical investigations of machine translation post-editing processes*. Kent, OH: Kent State University Press.
Kučera, Henry, and W. Nelson Francis. 1967. *Computational Analysis of Present-day American English*. Providence, Rhode Island: Brown University Press.
Kuhn, Thomas. 1970. *The Structure of Scientific Revolutions*. Chicago: University of Chicago Press. (Second edition.)
Kundera, Milan. 1993. *Les Testaments Trahis: Essai*. Paris: Gallimard.
Künzli, Alexander. 2007. "Translation revision – A study of the performance of ten professional translators revising a legal text". In Y. Gambier, M. Shlesinger, and R. Stolze (eds) 2007, *Doubts and directions in Translation Studies*. Amsterdam and Philadelphia: Benjamins, 115–126. doi:10.1075/btl.72.14kun
Kußmaul, Paul. 1991. "Creativity in the translation process". In Leuven-Zwart and Naaijkens (eds) 1991, 91–101.
Kußmaul, Paul. 1995. *Training the Translator*. Amsterdam and Philadelphia: Benjamins. doi:10.1075/btl.10
Ladmiral, Jean-René. 1994. *Traduire: Théorèmes pour la traduction*. Paris: Gallimard.
Lanstyák, István, and Pál Heltai. 2012. "Universals in language contact and translation". *Across Languages and Cultures* 13(1): 99–121. doi:10.1556/Acr.13.2012.1.6
Leech, Geoffrey N. 1983. *Principles of Pragmatics*. London: Longman.
Lefevere, André (ed.). 1992. *Translation / History / Culture. A sourcebook*. London: Routledge.
Lefevere, André. 1992. *Translation, Rewriting and the Manipulation of Literary Fame*. London: Routledge.

Leppihalme, Ritva. 1997. *Culture Bumps. An Empirical Approach to the Translation of Allusions*. Clevedon: Multilingual Matters.
Leppihalme, Ritva. 2011. "Realia". In Y. Gambier and L. van Doorslaer (eds) 2011, *Handbook of Translation Studies*. Amsterdam and Philadelphia: Benjamins, 126–130. doi:10.1075/hts.2.rea1
Leuven-Zwart, Kitty M. van. 1989/1990. "Translation and original. Similarities and dissimilarities", I and II. *Target* 1(2): 151–181 and 2(1): 69–95. doi:10.1075/target.1.2.03leu
Leuven-Zwart, Kitty M. van, and Ton Naaijkens (eds). 1991. *Translation Studies: The state of the art. Proceedings of the First James S. Holmes Symposium on Translation Studies*. Amsterdam and Atlanta: Rodopi.
Levý, Jiří. 1967. "Translation as a decision process". In *To Honor Roman Jakobson*, vol. II. The Hague: Mouton, 1171–1182. (Also in Chesterman (ed.) 1989, 37–52.)
Levý, Jiří. 1969. *Die Literarische Übersetzung*. Frankfurt: Athenäum.
Lewis, David K. 1969. *Convention: A philosophical study*. Cambridge, MA: Harvard University Press.
Lewis, Philip E. 1985. "The measure of translation effects". In J. Graham (ed.) 1985, *Difference in Translation*. Ithaca, NY: Cornell University Press, 31–62.
Liddell, Henry G., and Robert Scott. 1940. *A Greek-English Lexicon*. (9th edition.) Oxford: Clarendon Press.
Linnarud, Moira. 1988. *Lexis in Composition: A performance analysis of Swedish learners' written English*. Lund: Gleerup.
Lörscher, Wolfgang. 1989. "Models of the translation process: claim and reality". *Target* 1(1): 43–68. doi:10.1075/target.1.1.05lor
Lörscher, Wolfgang. 1991. *Translation Performance, Translation Process and Translation Strategies: A psycholinguistic investigation*. Tübingen: Narr.
Lotbinière-Harwood, Susanne de. 1991. *Re-belle et Infidèle. La traduction comme pratique de réécriture au feminin / The Body Bilingual. Translation as a rewriting in the feminine*. Montréal/Toronto: Les éditions du remue-ménage / Women's Press.
Malmkjær, Kirsten. 1993. "Underpinning translation theory". *Target* 5(2): 133–148. doi:10.1075/target.5.2.02mal
Malmkjær, Kirsten. 2004. "Censorship or Error: Mary Howitt and a Problem in Descriptive TS". In D. Gile, G. Hansen, and K. Malmkjær (eds) 2004, *Claims, Changes and Challenges in Translation Studies: Selected Contributions from the EST Congress, Copenhagen 2001*. Amsterdam and Philadelphia: Benjamins, 141–155. doi:10.1075/btl.50.12mal
Malone, Joseph L. 1988. *The Science of Linguistics in the Art of Translation*. Albany: State University of New York Press.
Mauranen, Anna. 1993. *Cultural Differences in Academic Rhetoric: A textlinguistic study*. Frankfurt am Main: Lang.
Mauranen, Anna, and Pekka Kujamäki (eds). 2004. *Translation Universals. Do they exist?* Amsterdam and Philadelphia: Benjamins. doi:10.1075/btl.48
May, Rachel. 1994. *The Translator in the Text. On reading Russian literature in English*. Evanston, Ill.: Norhwestern University Press.
Millán, Carmen, and Francesca Bartrina (eds). 2012. *The Routledge Handbook of Translation Studies*. London: Routledge.
Molina, Lucia, and Amparo Hurtado Albir. 2002. "Translation techniques revisited: A dynamic and functionalist approach". *Meta* 47(4): 498–512. doi:10.7202/008033ar
Morgenstern, Christian. 1969. *Galgenlieder*. Memmingen: Maximilian Dietrich Verlag.

Mossop, Brian. 1983. "The translator as rapporteur: a concept for training and self-improvement". *Meta* 28(3): 244–278. doi:10.7202/003674ar
Mossop, Brian. 2007a. *Revising and editing for translators.* (Second edition.) Manchester: St. Jerome Publishing.
Mossop, Brian. 2007b. "Empirical studies of revision: what we know and need to know". *The Journal of Specialised Translation* [on-line series], 8. Available at http://www.jostrans.org/issue08/art_mossop.php. (Accessed 15.5.2015.)
Mounin, Georges. 1963. *Les Problèmes théoriques de la traduction.* Paris: Gallimard.
Munday, Jeremy. 2012. *Introducing Translation Studies. Theories and applications.* (Third edition.) London: Routledge.
Nabokov, Vladimir. [1955] 1992. "Problems of translation: Onegin in English". In Schulte and Biguenet (eds) 1992, 127–143.
Neubert, Albrecht. 1981. "Translation, interpreting and text linguistics". In B. Sigurd and J. Svartvik (eds) 1981, *AILA 82 Proceedings: Lectures,* 130–145. (Studia Linguistica 35.) (Also in Chesterman (ed.) 1989, 141–156.)
Neubert, Albrecht, and Gregory M. Shreve. 1992. *Translation as Text.* Kent, OH: Kent State University Press.
Newmark, Peter. 1981. *Approaches to Translation.* Oxford: Pergamon Press.
Newmark, Peter. 1988. *A Textbook of Translation.* Hemel Hempstead: Prentice Hall International.
Newmark, Peter. 2004. "Non-literary in the light of literary translation". *The Journal of Specialised Translation* 1: 8–13.
Nida, Eugene A. 1964. *Toward a Science of Translating.* Leiden: Brill.
Nida, Eugene A. 1969. "Science of translation". *Language* 45(3): 483–498. doi:10.2307/411434
Nida, Eugene A., and Charles R. Taber. 1969. *The Theory and Practice of Translation.* Leiden: Brill.
Niiniluoto, Ilkka. 1978. "Notes on Popper as follower of Whewell and Peirce". *Ajatus* 37: 272–327.
Niranjana, Tejaswini. 1992. *Siting Translation Theory. History, post-structuralism and the colonial context.* Berkeley and Los Angeles: University of California Press.
Nord, Christiane. 1991. *Text Analysis in Translation.* Amsterdam and Atlanta: Rodopi.
Nouss, Alexis. 1994. "Translation and the two models of interpretation". In Dollerup and Lindegaard (eds) 1994, 157–163.
Nylander-Tuominen, Sirkka-Liisa. 1992. "La Kanteletar and I will sing what I know: semiotic features in two translations of Kanteletar". In E. Tarasti (ed.) 1992, *Center and Periphery in Representations and Institutions.* Imatra: International Semiotics Institute, 333–345.
Nystrand, Martin. 1992. "Social interactionism versus social constructionism: Bakhtin, Rommetveit and the semiotics of written text". In A.H. Wold (ed.) 1992, *The Dialogical Alternative. Towards a theory of language and mind.* Oslo: Scandinavian University Press, 157–173.
O'Brien, Sharon, and Michel Simard (eds). 2014. *Machine Translation,* 28. (Special Issue on Post-Editing.) doi:10.1007/s10590-014-9166-8
O'Malley, J. Michael, and Anne Uhl Chamot. 1990. *Learning Strategies in Second Language Acquisition.* Cambridge: Cambridge University Press. doi:10.1017/CBO9781139524490
Oittinen, Riitta. 1993. *I am Me – I am Other: On the dialogics of translating for children.* (Acta Universitatis Tamperensis, ser. A vol. 386.) Tampere: University of Tampere.
Oittinen, Riitta. 1995. *Kääntäjän Karnevaali.* Tampere: Tampere University Press.

Ortega y Gasset, José. 1937. "La miseria y el esplendor de la traducción". *La Nación* (Buenos Aires), May-June. (Reprinted in J. Ortega y Gasset, Obras Completas: Tomo V (1933– 1941). Madrid: Revista de Occidente, 429–448. Translated extract in Schulte and Biguenet (eds) 1992, 93–112.)

PACTE. 2005. "Investigating translation competence: conceptual and methodological issues". *Meta* 50(2): 609–619. doi:10.7202/011004ar

Paepcke, Fritz. 1986. "Textverstehen – Textübersetzen – Übersetzungskritik". In M. Snell-Hornby (ed.) 1986, *Übersetzungswissenschaft: eine Neuorientierung. Zur Integrierung von Theorie und Praxis*. Tübingen: Francke, 106–132.

Paz, Octavio. 1971. *Traducción: Literatura y Literalidad*. Barcelona: Tusquets. (Translated extract in Schulte and Biguenet (eds) 1992, 152–162.)

Pesonen, Pekka. 1993. "Venäläiskertojat löysivät uuden sävellajin". *Helsingin Sanomat*, 30 October 1993, C2.

Picken, Catriona (ed.). 1994. *Quality – Assurance, Management and Control*. (Proceedings, ITI Conference 7.) London: Institute of Translation and Interpreting.

Plotkin, Henry C. 1993. "Hunting memes". *Behavioral and Brain Sciences* 16(4): 768–9. doi:10.1017/S0140525X00032891

Pöchhacker, Franz. 2004. *Introducing Interpreting Studies*. London: Routledge.

Pokorn, Nike K. 2005. *Challenging the Traditional Axioms. Translation into a non-mother tongue*. Amsterdam and Philadelphia: Benjamins. doi:10.1075/btl.62

Popper, Karl R. [1945] 1962. *The Open Society and its Enemies*. (4th edition.) London: Routledge and Kegan Paul.

Popper, Karl R. [1956] 1982. *The Open Universe*. Totowa, NJ: Rowman and Littlefield.

Popper, Karl R. 1959. *The Logic of Scientific Discovery*. London: Hutchinson.

Popper, Karl R. 1972. *Objective Knowledge. An evolutionary approach*. Oxford: Clarendon Press.

Popper, Karl R. 1992. *Unended Quest*. London: Routledge.

Purves, Alan C. (ed.). 1988. *Writing Across Languages and Cultures. Issues in contrastive rhetoric*. Newbury Park: Sage Publications.

Puurtinen, Tiina H. 1995. *Linguistic Acceptability in Translated Children's Literature*. (University of Joensuu Publications in the Humanities 15.) Joensuu: University of Joensuu.

Pym, Anthony. 1992a. *Translation and Text Transfer*. Frankfurt am Main: Lang.

Pym, Anthony. 1992b. "The relation between translation and material text transfer". *Target* 4(2): 171–189. doi:10.1075/target.4.2.03pym

Pym, Anthony. 1994. "Twelfth-century Toledo and strategies of the literalist Trojan horse". *Target* 6(1): 43–66. doi:10.1075/target.6.1.04pym

Pym, Anthony. 1995. "European Translation Studies, une science qui dérange, and Why Equivalence Needn't Be a Dirty Word". *TTR* 8(1): 153–176. doi:10.7202/037200ar

Pym, Anthony. 1996. "Venuti's visibility". *Target* 8(1): 165–177. doi:10.1075/target.8.1.12pym

Pym, Anthony. 1997. *Pour une Éthique du Traducteur*. Arras: Artois Presses Université; Ottawa: Presses de l'Université d'Ottawa.

Pym, Anthony. 1998. *Method in Translation History*. Manchester: St. Jerome Publishing.

Pym, Anthony. 2007. "Natural and directional equivalence in theories of translation". *Target* 19(2): 271–294. doi:10.1075/target.19.2.07pym

Pym, Anthony. 2010. *Exploring Translation Theories*. London and New York: Routledge.

Pym, Anthony. 2011. "Translation theory as historical problem-solving". *Intercultural Communication Review* 9:49–61. Available via http://usuaris.tinet.cat/apym/publications/publications.html. (Accessed 6.5.2015.)

Pym, Anthony. 2012. *On Translator Ethics. Principles for mediation between cultures.* Amsterdam and Philadelphia: Benjamins. doi:10.1075/btl.104

Pym, Anthony. 2016. *Translation Solutions for Many Languages – Histories of a Flawed Dream.* London: Bloomsbury Publishing.

Pym, Anthony, Miriam Shlesinger, and Zuzana Jettmarová (eds). 2006. *Sociocultural Aspects of Translating and Interpreting.* Amsterdam and Philadelphia: Benjamins. doi:10.1075/btl.67

Pym, Anthony, Miriam Shlesinger, and Daniel Simeoni (eds). 2008. *Beyond Descriptive Translation Studies. Investigations in homage to Gideon Toury.* Amsterdam and Philadelphia: Benjamins. doi:10.1075/btl.75

Quine, Willard van O. 1960. *Word and Object.* Cambridge, MA: MIT Press.

Quirk, Randolph, Sidney Greenbaum, Geoffrey N. Leech, and Jan Svartvik. 1985. *A Comprehensive Grammar of the English Language.* London: Longman.

Randell, Elina. 1986. "William Faulknerin teosten suomennoksista". In U. Kovala (ed.), *Maailmankirjallisuuden ja sen Klassikoiden Suomentamisesta, Osa III.* (Monisteita 32.) Jyväskylä: Jyväskylän yliopiston kirjallisuuden laitos, 17–30.

Rawson, Claude. 1993. Review of Fima by Amos Oz. *Times Literary Supplement*, 8 October 1993, 28.

Reiß, Katharina, and Hans J. Vermeer. 1984. *Grundlegung einer Allgemeinen Translationstheorie.* Tübingen: Niemeyer. doi:10.1515/9783111351919

Rener, Frederick M. 1989. *Interpretatio: Language and Translation from Cicero to Tytler.* Amsterdam and Atlanta: Rodopi.

Retsker, Jakob. 1993. "The theory and practice of translation". In Zlateva (ed.) 1993, 18–31.

Richards, Ivor A. 1936. *The Philosophy of Rhetoric.* New York: Oxford University Press.

Riley, Philip. 1979. "Towards a contrastive pragmalinguistics". *Papers and Studies in Contrastive Linguistics* 10: 90–115.

Ringbom, Håkan (ed.). 1993. *Near-native Proficiency in English.* (English Department Publications 2.) Åbo: Åbo Akademi University.

Risku, Hanna. 1998. *Translatorische Kompetenz.* Tübingen: Stauffenburg.

Risku, Hanna, and Florian Windhager. 2013. "Extended translation. A sociocognitive research agenda". *Target* 25(1): 33–45. doi:10.1075/target.25.1.04ris

Rissanen, Matti. 1971. *Problems in the Translation of Shakespeare's Imagery into Finnish.* Helsinki: Société Néophilologique.

Robert, Isabelle, and Luuk Van Waes. 2014. "Selecting a translation revision procedure: do common sense and statistics agree?" *Perspectives: Studies on Translatology* 22(3): 304–320. doi:10.1080/0907676X.2013.871047

Robinson, Douglas. 1987. "Koskenko yli saareen? Pentti Saarikoski kääntäjänä ja käännösteoreetikkona". In A. Ollikainen and M. Pulakka (eds) 1987, *Kääntäjät Kulttuurivaikuttajina.* (Monisteita 35.) Jyväskylä: Jyväskylän yliopiston kirjallisuuden laitos, 143–165.

Robinson, Douglas. 1991. *The Translator's Turn.* Baltimore: Johns Hopkins University Press.

Robyns, Clem. 1994. "Translation and discursive identity". *Poetics Today* 15(3): 405–428. doi:10.2307/1773316

Rooten, Luis van. 1967. *Mots d'heures: gousses, rames.* London: Angus and Robertson.

Roscommon, Earl of. [1685] 1975. "An essay on translated verse". In T.R. Steiner 1975, *English Translation Theory 1650–1800.* Assen and Amsterdam: Van Gorcum, 75–85. (Also in Lefevere (ed.) 1992, 43–45.)

Rose, Hilary, and Steven Rose. 2001. *Alas, Poor Darwin.* London: Vintage.

Rosenberg, Tina. 1993. "Playwright on the stage of history". *Guardian Weekly*, 24 October 1993.

Rydning, Antin F. 1991. *Qu'est-ce qu'une traduction acceptable en B? Les conditions d'acceptabilité de la traduction fonctionnelle réalisée dans la langue seconde du traducteur*. Oslo: University of Oslo.
Sager, Juan C. 1994. *Language Engineering and Translation – Consequences of automation*. Amsterdam and Philadelphia: Benjamins. doi:10.1075/btl.1
Schiavi, Giuliana. 1996. "There is always a teller in a tale". *Target* 8(1): 1–21. doi:10.1075/target.8.1.02sch
Schleiermacher, Friedrich. [1813] 1963. "Ueber die verschiedenen Methoden des Uebersezens". In Störig (ed.) 1963, 38–70.
Schreiber, Michael. 1998. "Übersetzungstypen und Übersetzungsverfahren". In M. Snell-Hornby et al. (eds) 1998, *Handbuch Translation*. Tübingen: Stauffenburg, 151–154.
Schulte, Rainer, and John Biguenet (eds). 1992. *Theories of Translation. An anthology of essays from Dryden to Derrida*. Chicago: University of Chicago Press.
Schultze, Brigitte. (ed.). 1987. *Die Literarische Übersetzung: Fallstudien zu ihrer Kulturgeschichte*. (Göttinger Beiträge zur Internationalen Übersetzungsforschung, vol. 1.) Berlin: Erich Schmidt Verlag.
Schwarzwald-Rodrigue, Ora. 1993. "Mixed translation patterns: the Ladino translation of Biblical and Mishnaic Hebrew verbs". *Target* 5(1): 71–88. doi:10.1075/target.5.1.06sch
Searle, John. 1983. *Intentionality*. Cambridge: Cambridge University Press. doi:10.1017/CBO9781139173452
Séguinot, Candace. 1982. "The editing function of translation". *Bulletin of the Canadian Association of Applied Linguistics* 4(1): 151–161.
Séguinot, Candace. 1988. "Pragmatics and the explicitation hypothesis". *TTR* 1(2): 106–113. doi:10.7202/037024ar
Séguinot, Candace. 1989. "The translation process: an experimental study". In C. Séguinot (ed.) 1989, *The Translation Process*. School of Translation, York University: H.G. Publications, 21–53.
Séguinot, Candace. 1991. "A study of student translation strategies". In Tirkkonen-Condit (ed.)1991, 79–88.
Sell, Roger. 1990. *Literary Pragmatics*. London: Routledge.
Shlesinger, Miriam. 1992. "Lexicalization in translation: an experimental study of students' progress". In C. Dollerup and A. Loddegaard (eds) 1992, *Teaching Translation and Interpreting 1: Training, talent and experience*. Amsterdam and Philadelphia: Benjamins, 123–127. doi:10.1075/z.56.20shl
Shveitser, Alexander. 1993. "Equivalence and adequacy". In Zlateva (ed.) 1993, 47–56.
Snell-Hornby, Mary, H.G. Hönig, P. Kußmaul, and P.A. Schmitt (eds). 2004. *Handbuch Translation*. (Second edition.) Tübingen: Stauffenburg.
Snell-Hornby, Mary. 1988. *Translation Studies. An integrated approach*. Amsterdam and Philadelphia: Benjamins. doi:10.1075/z.38
Snell-Hornby, Mary. 2006. *The Turns of Translation Studies*. Amsterdam and Philadelphia: Benjamins. doi:10.1075/btl.66
Snell, Bruno. 1975. *Die Entdeckung des Geistes*. (4th edition.) Göttingen: Vandenhoeck & Ruprecht.
Steiner, Erich. 1988. "Describing language as activity: an application to child language". In R.P. Fawcett and D.J. Young (eds) 1988, *New Developments in Systemic Linguistics, Vol. 2. Theory and applications*. London: Pinter, 144–173.

Steiner, George. 1975. *After Babel*. London: Oxford University Press.
Stetting, Karen. 1989. "Transediting – a new term for coping with a grey area between editing and translating". In G. Caie, et al. (eds) 1989, *Proceedings from the Fourth Nordic Conference for English Studies*. Copenhagen: Department of English, University of Copenhagen, 371–382.
Störig, Hans J. (ed.). 1963. *Das Problem des Übersetzens*. Darmstadt: Wissenschaftliche Buchgesellschaft.
Suojanen, Tytti, Kaisa Koskinen and Tiina Tuominen. 2015. *User-Centred Translation*. Abingdon: Routledge.
Swales, John. 1991. *Genre Analysis*. Cambridge: Cambridge University Press.
Tabakowska, Elzbieta. 1993. *Cognitive Linguistics and Poetics of Translation*. Tübingen: Narr.
Taivalkoski-Shilov, Kristiina, and Myriam Suchet (eds). 2013. *La traduction des voix intratextuelles / Intratextual Voices in Translation*. Montréal: Éditions québecoises de l'œuvre.
Tannen, Deborah, and Muriel Saville-Troike (eds). 1985. *Perspectives on Silence*. Norwood, NJ: Ablex.
Tirkkonen-Condit, Sonja. 1990. "Professional vs. non-professional translation: a think-aloud protocol study". In M.A.K. Halliday, J. Gibbons, and H. Nicholas (eds) 1990, *Learning, Keeping and Using Language. Selected papers from the Eighth World Congress of Applied Linguistics*. Amsterdam and Philadelphia: Benjamins, 381–394.
Tirkkonen-Condit, Sonja (ed.). 1991. *Empirical Research in Translation and Intercultural Studies. Selected papers of the TRANSIF Seminar, Savonlinna 1988*. Tübingen: Narr.
Tirkkonen-Condit, Sonja. 2004. "Unique items – over- or under-represented in translated language?" In A. Mauranen and P. Kujamäki (eds) 2004, *Translation Universals. Do they Exist?* Amsterdam and Philadelphia: Benjamins, 177–184. doi:10.1075/btl.48.14tir
Toma, Peter. [1976] 1989. "An operational machine translation system". In Chesterman (ed.) 1989, 162–172. (Originally published in R.W. Brislin (ed.) 1976, Translation. Applications and Research. New York: Gardner Press Inc., 249–260.)
Tommola, Jorma. 1986. "Translation as a language process: an empirical approach". In Y.M. Gambier (ed.) 1986, *TRANS*. Turku: School of Translation Sudies, University of Turku, 118–140.
Toury, Gideon. 1980. *In Search of a Theory of Translation*. Tel Aviv: Porter Institute.
Toury, Gideon. 1985. "A rationale for descriptive translation studies". In Hermans (ed.) 1985, 16–41.
Toury, Gideon. 1991. "What are descriptive studies into translation likely to yield apart from isolated descriptions?" In Leuven-Zwart and Naaijkens (eds) 1991, 179–192.
Toury, Gideon. 1995. *Descriptive Translation Studies and Beyond*. Amsterdam and Philadelphia: Benjamins. doi:10.1075/btl.4
Toury, Gideon. 2012. *Descriptive Translation Studies – and Beyond*. (Revised edition.) Amsterdam and Philadelphia: Benjamins. doi:10.1075/btl.100
Tymoczko, Maria. 2006. "Reconceptualizing Western translation theory: Integrating non-Western thought about translation". In T. Hermans (ed.), 2006, *Translating Others* (vol. 1). Manchester: St. Jerome Publishing, 13–32.
Tytler, Alexander F. [1790] 1978. *Essay on the Principles of Translation*. (Amsterdam Classics in Linguistics 13.) Amsterdam: Benjamins. doi:10.1075/acil.13
Ullmann-Margalit, Edna. 1977. *The Emergence of Norms*. Oxford: Oxford University Press.

Ulrych, Margherita. 2009. "Translating and editing as mediated discourse: focus on the recipient". In R. Dimitriu and M. Shlesinger (eds) 2009, *Translators and Their Readers. In Homage to Eugene A. Nida*. Brussels: Editions du Hasard, 219–234.
Vehmas-Lehto, Inkeri. 1989. *Quasi-correctness. A critical study of Finnish translations of Russian journalistic texts*. Helsinki: Neuvostoliittoinstituutti. Available at https://helda.helsinki.fi/bitstream/handle/10138/154308/quasicor.pdf?sequence=1.
Venuti, Lawrence. 1992. "Introduction". In L. Venuti (ed.) 1992, *Rethinking Translation*. London: Routledge, 1–17.
Venuti, Lawrence. 1995a. *The Translator's Invisibility: A history of translation*. London: Routledge. doi:10.4324/9780203360064
Venuti, Lawrence. 1995b. "Translation, authorship, copyright". *The Translator* 1(1): 1–24. doi:10.1080/13556509.1995.10798947
Vermeer, Hans J. 1989. "Skopos and commission in translational action". In Chesterman (ed.) 1989, 173–187.
Vermeer, Hans J. 1992. *Skizzen zu einer Geschichte der Translation*. Vols 1 and 2. Frankfurt am Main: Verlag fur Interkulturelle Kommunikation.
Vermeer, Hans J. 1997. "Translation and the 'meme'". *Target* 9(1): 155–166. doi:10.1075/target.9.1.10ver
Vermeer, Hans J. 1998. "Starting to unask what translatology is all about". *Target* 10(1): 41–68. doi:10.1075/target.10.1.03ver
Vieira, Else R.P. 1994. "A postmodern translational aesthetics in Brazil". In M. Snell-Hornby, F. Pöchhacker, and K. Kaindl (eds) 1994, *Translation Studies: An interdiscipline*. Amsterdam and Philadelphia: Benjamins, 65–72. doi:10.1075/btl.2.09rib
Vinay, Jean-Paul, and Jean Darbelnet. [1958] 1969. *Stylistique Comparée du français et de l'anglais*. Paris: Didier.
Vuorinen, Erkka. 1994. "Kääntäjän 'tarkkuudesta' ja 'vapaudesta' sekä hyvästä kääntämistavasta". *Kääntäjä* 2: 1–3.
Weaver, Warren. 1955. "Translation". In W.N. Locke and A.D. Booth (eds) 1955, *Machine Translation of Languages*. New York: Wiley, 15–23.
Wierzbicka, Anna. 1991. *Cross-cultural Pragmatics. The semantics of human interaction*. Berlin: Mouton de Gruyter.
Will, Frederic. 1973. *The Knife in the Stone*. The Hague: Mouton. doi:10.1515/9783111342412
Willamowitz-Moellendorff, Ulrich von. [1925] 1963. "Was ist Übersetzen?" In Störig (ed.) 1963, 139–169.
Willems, Dominique, and Bart Defrancq (eds). 2004. *Contrastive Analysis in Language: Identifying Linguistic Units of Comparison*. London: Palgrave Macmillan.
Williams, Bernard. [1985] 1993. *Ethics and the Limits of Philosophy*. London: Fontana.
Wilss, Wolfram. 1977. *Übersetzungswissenschaft*. Stuttgart: Klett.
Wilss, Wolfram. 1982. *The Science of Translation. Problems and methods*. Tübingen: Narr.
Wilss, Wolfram. 1988. *Kognition und Übersetzen. Zu Theorie und Praxis der menschlichen und der maschinellen Übersetzung*. Tübingen: Niemeyer.
Wittgenstein, Ludwig. 1953. *Philosophical Investigations*. (Parallel English translation by G.E.M. Anscombe.) Oxford: Blackwell.
Wolf, Michaela, and Alexandra Fukari (eds). 2007. *Constructing a Sociology of Translation*. Amsterdam and Philadelphia: Benjamins. doi:10.1075/btl.74
Wright, Georg H. von. 1968. *An Essay in Deontic Logic and the General Theory of Action*. (Acta Philosophica Fennica 21.) Amsterdam: North-Holland.

Xiao, Richard (ed.). 2010. *Proceedings of The International Symposium on Using Corpora in Contrastive and Translation Studies (UCCTS 2008)*. Newcastle: Cambridge Scholar Publishing.

Zabalbeascoa, Patrick. 2000. "From techniques of translation to types of solutions". In A. Beeby, D. Endinger, and M. Presas (eds) 2000, *Investigating Translation*. Amsterdam and Philadelphia: Benjamins, 117–127. doi:10.1075/btl.32.15zab

Zalán, P. 1990. "Zur Problematik von Normen und Übersetzen". In R. Arntz and G. Thome (eds) 1990, *Übersetzungswissenschaft. Ergebnisse und Perspektiven*. Tübingen: Narr, 55–58.

Zanettin, Federico, Silvia Bernardini, and Dominic Stewart (eds). 2003. *Corpora in Translator Education*. Manchester: St. Jerome Publishing.

Zeldin, Theodor. [1994] 1995. *An Intimate History of Humanity*. London: Minerva (Mandarin Paperbacks).

Zlateva, Palma (ed.). 1993. *Translation as Social Action*. London: Routledge.

Author index

A
Abdallah 143, 193
Angelelli 193
Antonini 165
Archer 182
Aristotle 18
Arnold 28
Arrojo 27, 44
Aunger 14

B
Baker 37, 46, 162
Bakhtin 191
Ballard 17
Baraldi 193
Barkhudarov 8
Bartsch 52–53, 55–56, 61
Bassnett 17, 38
Beaugrande 80, 173
Becher 69
Bell 41, 43, 50, 70
Benjamin, A. 27
Benjamin, W. 7, 9, 25
Berman 17, 26, 167
Biguenet 7, 28
Blackmore 14
Bloom 162
Blum-Kulka 69
Bly 116, 142
Bowker 166
Brainerd 132
Breedveld 142
Broeck, van den 103
Brownlie 82
Brunette 142

C
Calzada Pérez 37
Carl 47
Castellano 162
Catford 29, 90, 93, 160
Cattrysse 15

Cavalli-Sforza 14
Chafe 81
Chamot 85
Changeux 14
Chatterton 57
Chesterman 3, 5, 13–14, 17, 29, 41, 44, 46–47, 53, 57, 60, 66, 72, 75, 78, 97, 131, 148, 170, 192
Cheyfitz 36, 167
Cicero 23, 41
Connor 81
Copeland 17, 23–24
Coseriu 56
Cowley 23
Craig 115
Crystal 122
Cutts 193

D
Dacier 22
d'Alembert 22
Danan 36
Dancette 68
Darbelnet 21, 29, 90, 92–93, 113–114, 160
Darwin 1, 156
Davidson 55
Davy 122
Dawkins 1–3
Defrancq 82
de la Motte 23
Delisle 116
Delius 11
Dennett 12, 38
Derrida 6, 9, 26–27
D'hulst 18
Dijk, van 81
Dolet 19, 22, 49
Dressler 80, 173
Dreyfus 145–151, 154, 163
Dryden 8, 23–24, 112

E
Ebeling 179, 181, 185, 191
Edelman 11
Ellegård 80, 131–132
Englund Dimitrova 165
Enkvist 79
Erasmus 20
Even-Zohar 8, 34–35

F
Faerch 40, 85
Fairclough 186
Fawcett 36
Ferreira 47
Fitzgerald 23
Florin 105, 160
Flotow, von 37
Footit 193
Foucault 27
Francis 80, 131
Fraser 40
Friedrich 6
Fuller 45

G
Gadamer 181
Gambier 45, 47, 112–113
Gavioli 193
Gentzler 9, 25–26, 34, 40, 159
Gerloff 40
Gile 89, 118, 150, 153
Goethe 25, 97, 116, 123
Göpferich 165
Gorlée 159, 189–191
Grice 55
Grimes 131
Gutt 33, 41, 43–44, 129, 160, 191

H
Hailman 3
Haiman 79
Halverson 83

Harris 66, 165
Hartama-Heinonen 159
Hartmann 29
Harvey 112
Hatim 33
Heidegger 27
Heisenberg 3
Heltai 84
Hermans 36, 61–62, 108, 192
Hermes 60
Herodotus ix
Hervey 5, 39, 141
Hewson 158
Heylen 36
Higgins 5, 39, 141
Hinds 80
Hochel 88
Hölderlin 26
Holmes 5, 34, 41, 43, 176
Holz-Mänttäri 31–32
Hönig 33, 87
Horguelin 142
House 5, 63, 98, 104, 122, 129, 134, 159
Hu 14
Huetius 20
Hull 2
Hurtado Albir 112
Huss 122–123, 126

I
Inghilleri 193
Inoue 37
Itkonen 52, 55
Ivanič 187

J
Jääskeläinen 40, 70, 85, 87–89, 134
Jakobsen 5, 47, 87, 153
Jakobson 6, 9
Jandl 58, 108
Janks 187
Jerome 20–21
Jodl 53
Johansson 80, 131–132, 137
Jones 104
Jordan 188
Jumpelt 39

K
Kant 138
Kaplan 81
Karlsson 155
Kasper 40, 85
Katz 7
Keenan 7, 32
Kelly, L. G. 17–18, 24, 41, 43, 159
Kelly, M. 193
Kemmis 150
Kiraly 39–40, 87, 149
Klaudy 69
Kolb 150
Koller 5, 42
Komissarov 50
Königs 103
Korpel 23
Koskinen 27, 159, 192
Kovala 38
Krings 39, 134, 143
Kučera 80, 131
Kuhn 13, 45
Kundera 121
Künzli 142
Kußmaul 5, 33, 40, 87, 137, 150

L
Ladmiral 6
Lanstyák 84
Larson 163
Leech 173
Lefevere 22, 34, 37–39, 70, 76, 109, 168
Leppihalme 160, 182–183
Leuven-Zwart 29, 34, 90
Levý 33, 39
Lewis, D. 53
Lewis, P. 26
Linnarud 80
Lörscher 40, 85, 87, 89, 134
Lotbinière-Harwood 188
Luther 23

M
Macpherson 57
Mallinen 108
Malmkjær 32, 143
Malone 29, 90, 111
Martin 158

Mason 19, 33
Mauranen 46, 81
May 26
McTaggart 150
Molina 112
Morgenstern 58
Mossop 142, 191
Mounin 6

N
Naaijkens 34
Nabokov 21
Neubert 29, 130, 173
Newmark 5, 21, 41, 43, 91–92, 103, 112, 178, 182, 188
Nida 5, 30–31, 90, 125–126, 128, 158, 182
Niiniluoto 13
Niranjana 36
Nord 5, 32, 66, 119, 142, 159–160, 178
Nouss 60
Novalis 195
Nylander-Tuominen 123
Nystrand 183

O
O'Brien 143
Oittinen 27, 191
Ollinen 59
O'Malley 85
Ortega y Gasset 6

P
PACTE 165
Paepcke 9
Paz 9
Pearson 166
Peirce 13, 189–190
Pesonen 108
Picken 167
Plato 18–19
Plotkin 2
Pöchhacker 14
Pope 23
Popov 108
Popper 10–13, 45, 117, 138, 157, 163–164, 170, 173, 181–182, 189, 195
Pound 25

Purves 81
Puurtinen 129–130
Pym 3, 15, 20, 24, 32, 41, 43, 45, 47, 54, 57, 73, 92, 113–114, 117–118, 167–168, 178–180, 183–185, 192

Q
Quine 32, 41, 43
Quintilian 22, 173
Quirk 79

R
Randell 110
Raudseps 124
Rawson 131
Reiß 31
Rener 17–18, 22, 173
Retsker 5
Richards 102
Riley 81
Ringbom 78
Risku 165
Robert 142
Robinson 8, 18, 41, 43, 110, 161–162, 188–189
Robyns 37
Rooten, van 58
Roscommon 39
Rose, H. and S. 14
Rosenberg 123
Rubelis 124
Rydning 79

S
Saarikoski 110
Sager 118
Saville-Troike 110

Schiavi 108
Schleiermacher 9, 24, 26, 28, 169
Schreiber 113
Schulte 7, 28
Schultze 38
Schwarzwald-Rodrigue 21
Schwieter 47
Searle 174
Séguinot 69, 88, 111, 152, 157
Sell 38, 100
Shlesinger 150
Shreve 29, 173
Shveitser 30
Simard 143
Snell ix
Snell-Hornby 6, 14, 32, 35, 41, 43, 45, 56
Spears 124
Steegmuller 122–123, 126
Steiner, E. 9, 86–88, 149
Steiner, G. 9, 178–179
Stetting 108
Suojanen 142
Swales 81

T
Tabakowska 5
Taber 31, 125, 128, 158
Tannen 110
Tirkkonen-Condit 40, 46, 134
Toma 29
Tommola 40, 87, 134
Toury 5–6, 8, 34–38, 47, 57–58, 60–62, 68–70, 83, 103, 115, 142, 165
Tymoczko 83
Tytler 24

U
Ullmann-Margalit 61
Ulrych 84

V
Vehmas-Lehto 69, 79, 111, 128, 132–133, 136
Venuti 17, 23, 26, 37, 74, 105, 108, 117, 167, 169, 192
Vermeer 13–14, 17, 31, 170
Vieira 23, 159
Vinay 21, 29, 90–91, 93, 98, 113–114, 160
Vuorinen 155

W
Waes, Van 142
Wall 122–123, 126
Weaver 28
Wierzbicka 55
Will 26
Willamowitz-Moellendorff 28
Willems 82
Williams 168
Wilss 31, 39, 133, 135–136
Windhager 165
Wittgenstein 5, 68, 83, 133, 177
Wright, von 170–171

X
Xiao 82

Z
Zabalbeascoa 113
Zalan 49
Zeldin ix, 168
Zlateva 33
Zukovsky 58

Subject index

A
abstraction change   98, 100
abusive fidelity   26
accountability norm   66–67, 74, 76–78, 109, 135–137, 141, 152, 178, 184–186, 188, 191
action theory   86, 171, 177, 179, 181–182
adaptation   8, 15, 22–23, 27, 31–32, 68, 90, 104, 112–113, 123, 185
addition   106, 111, 113–114
adequacy   30, 58, 121
antonymy   99
articles (English)   131–132
assessment   115–143, 175
   see also descriptive, evaluative, introspective, lateral, pedagogical, prospective, retrospective, revision, translation reviews
attention units   87
awareness   60, 65, 74, 148–152, 154, 157, 161, 163, 165, 187
   see also consciousness

B
belles infidèles   23, 173
Bible   6, 19, 20, 23, 30, 35, 126, 131, 178

C
calque   90–92
causality   73
clarity   23, 26, 64, 74, 80, 111, 154, 156, 172–175, 181–182, 184, 187, 192–193
clause structure change   94
cognition   38, 47, 161, 165
coherence change   107
cohesion   80–81, 95–96, 107, 151

collocation   82, 98
communication   31–33, 44, 46, 84, 85, 160, 164, 173, 181–184
   see also communication norm, communicative suffering
communication norm   55, 67, 74, 77, 109, 111, 126, 130, 136–137, 141, 153, 181, 184, 186, 191
communicative suffering   182–183
compensation   112, 114
consciousness   10, 12, 38, 40, 52–53, 88, 146, 148, 150
   see also awareness
constraints   37, 54, 75–77, 83, 110, 168, 186, 189
contrastive analysis   29, 77, 159
contrastive rhetoric   81
contrastive stylistics   29
conventions   2, 53, 56, 68, 174, 187
convergent creativity   118
converses   100, 151
covert error   131
covert translation   63, 69, 159
criticism   12–13, 40–41, 45, 52–53, 64, 68, 71, 83, 117–119, 122, 129, 141, 164
   see also assessment, translation reviews
cultural filtering   104, 123
culture-bound terms   71, 160, 182
culture bump   182–183

D
daina (Latvian)   124
deconstructionism   192
deliberative rationality   147–149, 151

deontic logic   170–171
descriptive assessment   121, 127, 134
descriptive vs. prescriptive   xi, 34, 50–52, 56, 66, 72, 117, 143, 169, 172
direct/indirect speech   26, 107, 110
discovery procedure   35, 60
distribution change   100
divergent creativity   117
domesticating   37, 123
double presentation   92
dubbing   36, 68

E
eco-translatology   14
Effability Principle   7, 32
effect   24, 33, 111, 116, 119–120, 125–130, 137
emancipatory translation   186–191
emotiveness   106, 111
emphasis change   101
end focus   79
end weight   79
equivalence   4–9, 14–15, 19–21, 24, 27–36, 58, 60, 67–68, 116, 121–122, 125–126, 137, 154, 160, 172, 176, 182, 185
equivalence probabilities   29
Error Elimination   12–13, 43, 115–143, 164, 181
error gravity   136–137
errors   *see* Error Elimination, error gravity, covert error, overt error
ethics   76, 167–193
evaluation   *see* assessment, translation reviews
evaluative assessment   117, 121, 134

exercises for teaching 151–156
expectancy norms 62–66, 68, 74, 76, 78–80, 82, 109–110, 130–133, 135–136, 139, 156, 161, 173–175, 184–185, 188
explanation 51, 72–75, 83, 109, 138
explicitation 69, 84, 105, 112–114, 123, 132, 140
explicitness change 105

F
falsifiability 13, 43, 69, 196
family resemblance 5, 68, 83, 130, 133, 176–177
feminism 37, 188
fidelity 26, 36, 118, 176, 185
fluency 23, 26, 117, 119
foreignizing 26, 104, 169
formality 81, 106
functions of language 164

G
game theory 39
gaps 138–141
global strategies 88
goals of translation theory 38, 45

H
hermeneutics 9, 24, 31, 40, 44, 178–179
homogeneous readership fallacy 33
hyponymy 99, 123

I
iconicity 79, 97, 156, 175
ideology 13, 36–38, 44–45, 64, 76–77, 92, 105, 109, 120, 141, 160, 167–169, 186, 188
illocutionary change 107
implicitation 105–106, 109, 114
indeterminacy 32, 41
indirect translation 37, 61
information change 106, 109, 123
initial norm 61–62
interference 22, 33, 46, 69–70, 75, 78, 82, 92, 120, 150, 153

interpersonal change 106
introspective assessment 133–135

J
Japanese constitution 37

L
lateral assessment 130–131
level shift 91, 96
lexical density 80
lexical variety 80
linguistics 4, 29–32, 38, 45–46, 55, 85, 159, 186
literal translation 8–9, 20–21, 91–92, 109, 121, 123, 142, 158, 185
loan 91–92, 102–103
local strategies 88
logos 24–28, 30, 40, 158–159, 162
loyalty 31, 64, 66–67, 167–168, 178–180, 191–193

M
machine translation 28–30, 83, 143
manipulation 36, 77, 160, 183, 188
meaning 7, 9–10, 18–20, 25–27, 30, 37, 67, 98, 110–111, 122–123, 156, 174–175, 182, 189–190
meme pool 1, 3, 18, 25, 40–41, 49, 85
memes 1–4, 10–14, 17–18, 40, 45, 49, 85, 89, 148–150, 170, 189–190
metaphors of translation x, 4, 19, 21–22, 25, 28, 31, 36–38, 41, 188–189
metatext 81
minimal transfer 21, 158
minimizing suffering 181–182
modulation 90, 98
motivation 20, 109–112, 114

N
naturalistic fallacy 72
naturalization 104, 125
natural translation 165

normalization 70, 122, 131
normative 49–51, 54–55, 68, 71–75, 83, 138, 170
normative laws 68, 71–75
norm-breaking 64–65, 110, 135, 138–139, 187
norms 49–83
   see also accountability, communication, expectancy, initial, normative, norm-breaking, operational, preliminary, process, product, professional, recommendable, relation
norm theory 36, 42–54
   see also norms

O
omission 68, 90, 106, 113–114
ontogenetic development 156–157
operational norms 61
Otherness 26–27, 37, 120, 167, 189
overt error 131
overt translation 122

P
parallel texts 62, 130–131, 133, 153, 156
paraphrase 24, 28, 85, 99, 101, 112, 158
paratexts 37
partial translation 108
patronage 37, 76
pedagogical assessment 135–138
phonetic translation 139
phrase structure change 93
plastic control 11–12, 75, 163–164, 189
poetics 36–37, 76–77, 110
polysystem 35–36, 61, 63, 75, 123, 160
postmodernism 9, 23, 108, 192
preliminary norms 61, 76
prescriptive *see* descriptive vs. prescriptive
process norms 53, 55, 61–62, 65–66, 175

Subject index

product norms   53, 55, 61–62
professional norms   65–68, 71, 191
prospective assessment   125–128
protocol studies   39, 87, 134
pseudo-translations   37

Q

quality   *see* assessment, revision, standard

R

readability   23, 30, 64, 74, 80, 111, 128–130, 136, 154, 156, 160, 167, 187
recommendable norms   79, 136, 156
regime   54, 173
regulative ideas   43, 138, 150, 164, 170, 181
relation norm   67–68, 75–78, 109, 121, 126, 135, 137, 141, 154, 175–176, 184–188, 191
relevance   33, 39, 43, 55, 74, 160, 173
retrospective assessment   121–125
revision   47, 116, 118, 141–143, 153, 189–190
rhetoric   21–24, 27, 30, 34–35, 70, 81, 97–98, 101–103, 107, 111, 123, 158–159

S

sameness   *see* equivalence
scheme change   97–98, 125
semantic translation   21
semiotics   7, 32, 123, 159, 189–190
sentence structure change   95, 125
significance threshold   110–111
silence threshold   110

similarity   1, 5, 15, 32, 60, 67, 147, 157–158, 176, 187
skopos   14, 31, 45, 73, 87, 126–127, 129, 139, 153, 155, 170
speech act   107, 125
standard (CEN, ISO)   142
standardization   46, 70, 75, 82
strategies   85–114, 121, 123, 151–152, 160, 167–170
   see also global, local
subtitling   36
supermemes   3–10, 14–15, 30, 150
synonymy   99

T

target-language enrichment   22, 35,
Tentative Theory   12–13, 17, 42–43, 115–119, 141, 147, 149, 174,
text-type   5, 9, 19, 21, 30, 32, 62, 65, 67, 70–71, 76, 79–81, 83, 130, 137, 139, 153, 155, 158–159, 167, 175, 184
thematic focus   101
theory
   etymology   ix–x
   attitudes to   x–xi, 40–45
   translation as   115–119
   of expertise   145–148
   of ethics   168–169
   as a net   195
   see also action theory, eco-translatology, memes, norm theory, polysystem, Popper, relevance, skopos
transediting   108, 114, 139, 153, 175, 187
translation   *see* covert, overt, emancipatory, indirect, literal, machine, metaphors, partial, phonetic, pseudo-, semantic

translational competence   71, 115, 117–118, 145, 148, 158
translation copyright   37
translation ethics   167–193
translation from LI   78–79
translation laws   38, 68–75, 82, 149–150
translation reviews   122–123, 126–127, 131
translation status   56–61
Translator's Charter   184, 187
translator training   44–45, 50, 78, 83, 89, 118, 135, 137, 150–162, 165–166, 187
Translog   47
transposition   90, 93, 151
trope change   101–103
trust   57, 114, 172, 178–180, 184, 188–190
truth   ix, 10, 13, 20–21, 115–116, 138, 164, 170, 175–177, 184–185, 189, 192, 195

U

understanding   42, 55, 146–148, 181–184, 186–187, 189, 192
unit of translation   8
unit shift   93
universals   45–46, 55, 69, 82, 84
untranslatability   6–7, 10, 41–42

V

validation of norms   54, 64, 156
values   3, 12, 37, 76, 111, 116–117, 119, 130, 138, 141, 167, 169–172, 184, 187, 189, 192
visibility   108, 167, 180, 186, 192

W

Worlds (Popper)   10–11, 163, 189